THE INTERNET LEFT

Ideology in the Age of Social Media

Graham Harrison

I0135766

BRISTOL
UNIVERSITY
PRESS

First published in Great Britain in 2024 by

Bristol University Press
University of Bristol
1-9 Old Park Hill
Bristol
BS2 8BB
UK
t: +44 (0)117 374 6645
e: bup-info@bristol.ac.uk

Details of international sales and distribution partners are available at bristoluniversitypress.co.uk

© Bristol University Press 2024

British Library Cataloguing in Publication Data
A catalogue record for this book is available from the British Library

ISBN 978-1-5292-3256-1 hardcover
ISBN 978-1-5292-3257-8 paperback
ISBN 978-1-5292-3258-5 ePub
ISBN 978-1-5292-3259-2 ePdf

Cover design: Blu Inc
Front cover image: Leudej Rodjanapaitoon / Alamy Stock Photo

For Jane, Jack, and Lydia

Contents

Part I

1

Introduction

> [Marxism] is an almost subterranean tradition which cannot
> be defined institutionally and finds organised expression only
> fleetingly in periods of special stress.[1]

The choreography of Twitter

I joined Twitter in order to get a stream of tweets letting me know about
new research activity and press on various East African countries. I followed
individual researchers and research centres in Europe and East Africa and was
daily reminded that there was a fantastic amount of activity which I needed
to keep up with.

One of my countries of interest was Rwanda. As I checked my stream,
I followed more people, especially Rwandans that I was interested in
interviewing. And then, gradually, things began to change. Anyone who has
researched Rwanda will be familiar with the fact that commentary on the
country's prospects is extremely contentious and that a lot of this contention is
hosted within Twitter and other social media. Some of the people I followed
were constantly attacking critical commentators, often in ways that were
hyperbolic and rather nasty. It came to seem, at times, choreographed.
A certain well-known professor (Rwanda specialists will know who this is
if they have Twitter accounts) would post a critique of some aspect of the
government's human rights record and immediately elicit a thread of hostile
responses in which he would be accused of being imperialist, a genocide
apologist, or senile. I could read this professor's posts and pretty much guess
the content of the responses. Furthermore, the endless repetition of this call
and response made me realise that it served no purpose at all. Neither side
changed their views.

I remained on Twitter and, as my research interests changed, I started to
follow a clutch of socialist commentators who were active on the platform
providing commentary on contemporary affairs, largely in the UK. These

accounts connected to a set of associated news sites, blogs, podcasts, YouTube accounts, and research papers. They allowed me to connect to lively and seemingly diverse socialist positions during a time (around the time Corbyn was elected leader of the Labour Party) when it was possible to hold on to some slender hope that some move away from the political and economic stagnation of neoliberalism was possible.

And then the same thing happened again. Through my own choices, the logic of the algorithm, and the repertoires of those who tweet, a certain kind of choreography developed in which certain people would say certain things and elicit certain responses. Over and over. The serial contentions that this produced helped me think through certain political issues, for a while. And then, checking in on Twitter became a noisy experience in which I started to feel frustrated and disoriented. This was in part because the language was sometimes angry or petulant. I was not so much learning about politics but rather learning about social media and how it works.

I would be lying if I claimed that I didn't enjoy the sound and fury. There was jouissance in checking threads. The ad hominens, j'accuses, and satirisations were fun. They generated discussions, some of which were insightful and some of which seemed pleasingly erratic and idiographic. Often, they made a refreshing change from academic writing. I came to consider this a mode of political discourse that had its own procedures. And, political discussion in the public sphere has always been commonly polemic, theatrical, based in conviction, rude. While much of the research and journalism I read on social media claimed that it was degrading politics, it seemed to me that some of it at least was in fact *productive*. It was using new technologies of communication to achieve something that open and public politics has always done: generate political argument as if politics mattered to people.

Approaching the politics of social media

This book is my attempt to say something about the productivity of social media in this respect. It is not a book about digital democracy. That term, and the research connected to it, tends to see social media in civic and deliberative terms: a means to generate new decision-making communities or to disseminate the requisite information to informed and rational citizen voters.[2] My interest is in something more chaotic and vigorous, something more radical, something more attuned to the mood of socialist ambition rather than deliberative policy steering.

Relocating social media

But, the chaotic and vigorous nature of what I am calling the internet left is not immediately amenable to academic analysis. There is an immediate challenge of transposition: of taking something of the content of social media and locating it within an analytical framework that follows well-understood analytical procedures. This innately requires some loss. The verve of social media cannot remain intact if one wishes to analyse it as a social scientist. This is very apparent in the academic analysis of social media which tends to base itself on textual analysis: the frequency and placing of certain words or terms.[3] Social media is rendered as grammar. One loses the aesthetic or affective sense that open public-political discussion has its own pleasures, strategies, and spontaneities. I did not want to lose this because it seemed to me that these things were fundamentally the point of it all.

In using my own mode of transposition, I had to consider the fact that I am writing from within the matrix. I have never been an avid tweeter or blogger but I have engaged in these practices. I have my own positions vis-à-vis the ideas presented in some detail throughout the book. I disagree with quite a lot of the content of what I call political social media (PSM) and some tweeters occasionally annoy me. I have sought to set out an analytical framework that does not eviscerate the discourse of social media of its intrinsic political qualities while also decontaminating it to some extent of its endless desire to provoke agreement (or disagreement) from the reader.

Political social media (PSM)

This book relies on some conceptual coinages. The internet left simply refers to the fact that a great deal of Left-leaning political discourse has energetically moved into cyberspace. It has done so, characteristically, in an undisciplined way, just as other traditions of political thought have done. There are Left- and Right-leaning conspiracy theories, niche debates, and overheated responses to the events of the day. At a general level, social media is overwhelmingly expansive and extremely difficult to make sense of. It needs some initial categorisation if we are to get anywhere.

Political social media (PSM) refers to a province within social media more generally. It is defined by a set of procedures that underpin content provision. These procedures can be characterised as hybrid: a combination of the generic trait of social media to intensify its messages by making arguments brief, provocative, extreme, and rhetorically flourished and an acceptance that those ideas will not only provoke reactions but also be tested. The testing of content involves discussions of accuracy, coherence, and integrity in ways that resemble what most would recognise as the epistemic foundations of the social sciences. PSM is, then, a cluster of discourses that want to be right but also want to be noticed and liked. It is a matter of balance how these two imperatives play out in text. There is no formula here but rather a twofold and closely interwoven intention. The best tweet is one that both feels right and is right.

PSM resists the closure of a full definition. Its boundaries are porous and its internal content volatile. But it is not internally lacking in form. The PSM this book is interested in is that oriented towards innovation in socialist thinking. Herein, there are some salient patterns that will be developed throughout the book. In the first place, there is a lot of material not considered here. Saying something about what is left out will give us a useful way to identify our own lines of inquiry and especially the internal contours of socialist PSM.

It is obviously the case that socialist discourses are endlessly diverse and scattered. That is in the nature of the internet. Some will cluster around specific political movements. These are not necessarily substantive enough to resemble consistent projects of ideational construction, which is what drives our interest. Much of the diverse and scattered socialist discourse specialises in specific things, or it does not work hard to achieve the hybridity that PSM demands. I had a draft chapter on 'campaign socialism' in the early stages of writing this book but had to abandon it when it became clear that social media posts about protests, rallies, and meetings were largely direct transcripts of text one would ordinarily and previously see on a flyer or in a socialist newspaper. There was a lack of *creative* entry into the realm of social media: to make the headlines of outrage and information about activism resonate with intensifications of irony, satire, and rhetoric.

The most salient controls of PSM coalesce around two palpably dynamic traditions: *Democratic Marxist Nationalism* (DMN) and *Identitarian Socialism*. The book treats these as case studies. DMN is a tradition based in a Marxist rather than socialist theoretical origin, and it seeks to assert consistently the value of democracy and the nation-state as the shells within which a historic working-class politics might emerge. Identitarian Socialism is more ecumenical, drawing on Marxism but also a broader socialist tradition. It aims to demonstrate the contemporary and diverse politics of socialist movements, realised through diverse community-based struggles not only against capitalism but also in favour of rights and recognitions for oppressed and marginalised minorities.

Clearly, both of these 'feel' socialist, but they are in many ways distinct and antagonistic. We will discover how this is so in the body of the book. What matters more immediately here is the question of category construction. Both DMN and Identitarian Socialism are my categorisations; neither of these traditions self-identifies as such, even if they might have an affinity to the nomenclature. The categories have been constructed through a careful but ultimately heuristic process. The categorisations need to stand up beyond the singular impression of one writer, but they are not discrete and stable enough to be treated as external political phenomena that are sufficiently self-evident not to require some interpretive underlabour. This might seem ambiguous to some, but it is arguably the most apt way to proceed when seeking to understand a subject matter that is sui generis unstable, partially bounded, and diverse. The setting of strong and externalising boundaries might enhance the scientific status of a piece of research but it would lose something of the nature of the observed in the process.

Nevertheless, we should set out some of the methodological procedures that have guided the categorisations and their construction. Although not named in list fashion here, the source material in the endnotes avers to two separate communities. There are individuals – some with virtual status that is itself avatar-like – that strongly represent the two traditions. These individuals are themselves producing content across sites in some form of collaboration or coordination with others within the tradition. All of the writers allocated into the two traditions have some cross-cutting activity with others in the group: writing with others, producing blogs for others who host or edit that site, hosting each other in podcasts, referencing each other's work in ways that generate the sinews of connectivity between different writers. Thusly, although each writer does not identify as a Democratic Marxist Nationalist or Identitarian Socialist, they would acknowledge interconnections between themselves and others who are identified as contributing to the traditions set out here. Furthermore, each tradition has its own venues: online news commentary, podcasts and webcasts, and publishers. And these venues are seen adversarially by the other tradition, reaffirming the sense of categorical difference.

Not all venues are entirely based in one camp or the other. Some writers place material on websites that are not 'of the Left'. Some writers have engaged positively in venues associated with the other traditions.[4] Some writers are relatively distant, but none are disconnected. Of course, all contributors disagree or have different core interests. One may think that I have missed some people or that some should not have been included. This is intrinsic to the analytical matter at hand, as I've said. Neither of these traditions is a 'canonical' project because they have emerged in a medium that is not interested in this kind of construction and, in a sense, if a tradition of thought was ossified into a programme with a name, manifesto, constitution, and leadership, it would no longer be a project of ideological construction *via* social media. Ultimately, the proof of concept lies in whether the reader can trace the weblinks in the endnotes and get a convincing sense of a shared political vision contrasting with the other. I am confident that they will.

The book offers two case study chapters and a subsequent discussion of how each relates to the other. In these case studies, the analysis is evidenced by links to webpages and tweets, all of which were accessed between 2020 and 2023. This material was the product of an exhaustive review of tweets and blogposts. The material generated was dealt with heuristically; no keyword-frequency analysis was used. The use of specific phrases is not in itself the point of interest. Rather, it became evident that it was the valency of the phrases that mattered. The intentionality and force of rhetoric. Indeed, because both traditions are socialist, they shared a good deal of the same political lexicon.

Ideology

If this is the body of evidence before us, then how do we set about analysing it? There are two considerations here. In the first place, we need to make some distinctions as to what we mean by 'Left', socialist, and Marxist. These are not only formal distinctions; they colour the differences between the two traditions. DMN has a fundamental grounding in Marx and if often disparaging of the Left in general, especially the 'liberal Left', it does not use the term socialism a great deal either. Identitarian Socialism uses the term socialism because it seeks a more encompassing and malleable Left orientation than its rival-other. It draws on socialism's particular history as an ideological marker not only of class struggle but also rights and recognition to make a case for a broad and diverse movement.

We will detail these distinctions, and some of their repercussions for ideological construction, in Chapter 3. The second consideration concerns what we previously described as transposition: how to relocate PSM into a reasonably academic analytical framing. This is done in two steps. Firstly, we adopt a modified morphological approach. That is, we take Michael Freeden's morphological studies of political ideology and add in some changes of emphasis. The morphological approach (as we shall see in Chapter 4) is particularly amenable to categorical construction. Political ideologies are seen pragmatically as prioritised assemblages of interconnected concepts. One can see an ideology's shape: its centre, the ways in which concepts allow an ideology to convince, the ways in which an ideology establishes its own boundaries.

Because we are dealing with PSM, not dedicated academic journals or political parties, we need to recognise that we should not expect purposeful and linear ideological construction. Rather, we can use a morphological approach to discern concepts in construction. And, we can readily recognise that this process of construction is in part based in a logic of thought and also a logic of combat. If a set of concepts is to gain ideological terrain, it must be able to assert itself – not only in relation to established canons of socialist theory but also in the rougher and more changeable terrain of virtuality.

So, we offer a definition of proto-ideologies: ideologies in construction in which construction is itself a project of engaging in social media, not only generating clear and coherent concepts. In the two case study chapters, we set out the conceptual morphologies of each proto-ideology. This is in part descriptive: simply to establish that there is something here to analyse. It is also analytical in that we will seek to establish the prioritisations and relations between concepts in each case. We will pay special attention to the ambition and combativeness of each proto-ideology, born as they both are in PSM. We will then go on to analyse how the two compare and contest around the two most provocative issues in PSM: Brexit and the COVID-19 pandemic.

Argument

The argument of the book is principally that the dour prognoses that characterise our time are not entirely convincing (a mood we review in the next chapter). Social media is not, tout court, dysfunctional. Ideological innovation and political hope are not expunged. New ideas continue to emerge. Socialism – as a tradition of political thinking in relation to real politics – is most assuredly not dead. It remains as the best subterranean tradition, to recall the quotation at the start of the chapter. But, what we find in the case study treatment and reflections is that, if we see two socialist proto-ideologies emerging in PSM, we need to acknowledge that, although each feeds of a sense of adversariality in order to remain present and relevant in cyberspace, this comes at the cost of either addressing their own shortcomings or seeking out a broader synthesis of ideas and practices. Obviously, nothing can remain 'proto' forever.

2

Chaos, Crisis, Decline, Contention

Our times of re/insurgent politics

How recent, how long ago

We live in a time when the deadening aesthetics of the end of history seem very remote. This was a period, not so long ago, in which politicians, public intellectuals, and academics set the mood of the times as one characterised by a dissipation in political energies. This was the political tone of the 1990s in much of the West.

Francis Fukuyama – often caricatured and perhaps less often read – saw politics as historically transformed by the ascendance of liberal democracy and capitalism.[1] For Fukuyama, liberal democracy and capitalism are not the coordinates of a geographically and historically sited political settlement; rather, they are the historical resolution of universal and transhistorical dialectics. These dialectics are in part material – what Fukuyama calls The Mechanism[2] – and cultural – what he calls *thymos*, or, the struggle for recognition.[3] The broad blush of history that Fukuyama rushes through moves towards a clear telos: that Historic[4] contestations between ideologies are almost entirely ended.[5]

Once peoples and societies identified with the market, individual rights, and the vote as ways to channel their desires, politics does not disappear but rather no longer generates the tectonic battles of major rivalrous ideological systems. The ideological global contest of liberalism against communism ended with the latter's collapse, ushering in a politics of individual choice and minimal liberal rights written into constitutions. This is how Fukuyama identifies a Hegelian-styled end of history: as the passing of major ideological contention and some form of unification that spelt the end of major political contention. It is not that the world becomes liberal democratic, it is that this is the only progressive future they might advance towards. It is not that violence and social instability absent themselves from the world, it is that the order of these disturbances does not offer up any Historical possibility. There is an impression of bathos in Fukuyama, who sees a kind of world-historical victory ushering in a form of political quiescence and perhaps banality, a banality that leads him to conclude his book with the image of a settler community looking around and wondering what's next.[6] Fukuyama's claim on history has been commonly refuted and revised, not least by the author himself. But, others have also characterised the sweep of history as the sweeping away of ideological combat in that period and afterwards.

The 1990s also saw a shift in intellectual mood towards post-structuralism within which Foucault was the main source for the writing up of a new terminology concerning politics and possibility. Ideas drawn from Foucault collectively served to portray politics as a totalising system of power. Marxist and some liberal notions of the state as a focus of struggle, contestation, and debate were replaced by the notion of sovereignty as an absolute power. Power (a term Foucault commonly uses as if it was its own agency) flows through states and individuals. It is inescapable. It makes docile subjects, a (biopolitical) sovereignty in which the human body is regulated by states, and a market society which serves as a universal form of domination. And, ideology is presented as a relic or a ruse in what is in reality a tight combination of truth and power; indeed, it is not uncommon for those writing in the Foucauldian tradition to see these two as indistinct: truth/power. If one supposes that truth can only be understood within a governing regime's totalising sovereignty, no space is left for ideological contestation.

There are other visions of the political which aim to erase the idea that politics is an ideological contestation of import. One of these was the 'third way' and 'stakeholder society' image of politics championed by the Blair government and intellectuals around it.[7] In this writing (most prominent in the UK), politics is identified as having escaped the Left versus Right struggle of post-Second World War boom/bust and growth/redistribution. The apogee of this understanding of politics is the claim that lower turnout in the polling booths was a result not of a political failure but rather success: people were just too content to go out and vote. Here, the sense of ideological weakening derived from a portrayal of politics as having solved core conflicts of political economy concerning the state and market, growth and redistribution, and government and civil society.

New institutionalism drew attention towards the ways in which the right combination of rules and norms might generate regime-like systems of political economy. Emerging from an economists' concern that societies were not governed by price systems, new institutional economics sought to identify the social norms and rules across the public, private, and civil spheres that would create the right incentive structures to solve political problems in market-approximating ways. Politics was set within sets of practices, incentives, and rules that generated conformity, path dependency, self-adjustment, and dynamic equilibria. Moments of rupture were exceptional, brief, and the product of a poorly aligned regime rather than any sense of major political and ideological contestation. For economists, some of whom came to advise government or run powerful agencies, this was the period in which the modelling of stable, homeostatic political economies led to a shared sense of consensus[8] and 'great moderation'. Political problems could be solved by expert manipulation of incentive structures, information flows, and managerial technique. And, without the agonies of Left versus Right, boom versus bust, or communism versus capitalism, there was no need to evoke grand ideals or worry much about which party was elected to power. Set within a hegemonic neoliberalism, the framing of politics as institutional efficiency erased the political role of ideology, leaving in its wake a substantial depoliticisation in all matters of governance.

An interregnum

Although each of these currents in political thought emerged with different normative content, they shared an affinity with Alexander Pope's aphorism: for forms of government let fools contest; whatever is best administered is best. Fukuyama's median consumerism, Foucault's administration of things, the third way's centrism, and new institutionalism's incentive adjustment and path dependency all evacuated politics of its ideological charge. It was in the midst of these images that the possibility of ideological contestation almost disappeared. Politics came to be represented as managerialist and technicist governance, wielded over a content, docile, consumerist, or depoliticised population, set within a sensibility that ideology was no longer a driver of history. The historiography that underpinned most of these narratives was homeostatic: it expected that the becalming of politics was not contingent but rather epochal. It inaugurated an enduring shift in the nature of politics, a shift that was explained as a completion or resolution of those phenomena that had made politics so turbulent in previous periods.

What is striking about the political mood of the 1990s in the West is that it did not entirely dissipate in 2001. Rather, the War on Terror militarised it. Ideologically, a form of imperial liberalism dominated, albeit one that drew on a neoconservative tradition that articulated core liberal ideals to a more worldly understanding of power and a focus on culture.[9] Al-Qaeda and its offshoots did not pose even minimally credible political opposition. Rather, it posed a kind of apocalyptic eschatology that found barely any resonance in Western societies, although resonance there was, especially among some groups of young men.[10] Anxieties and contentions concerning Islam more generally certainly intensified after 2001 in Europe, but these anxieties did not generate major new ideological contours in which political contestation was revived. Rather, they were canalised into pre-existing and increasingly prominent matters concerning political identity.[11]

In the West, the first decade of the new millennium was defined by what seems in retrospect as a rather odd state of affairs. A series of terrorist attacks by a global network of apocalyptic Islamic groups generated a major militarisation and securitisation in Western societies that was accompanied by a sense that the quietude of the 1990s had been destroyed. But, amid the political heat generated by fear, insecurity, heavy-handed state action, and considerable debate about culture and identity, no discernible *ideological* contestation emerged. From 2001 to 2007, the vast majority of political discourse remained wedded to the creed of liberalism, electoral democracy, capitalism, individual citizenship, and a view of the world that even in those most unstable of places, nothing threatened the regnant ideas of the homeland.

Anatomies of change

It was not 2001 but rather 2008 that generated a recrudescence in political contention. Indeed, it was after the attacks of 9/11 that sub-prime mortgage loans started to balloon consistently up until 2006.[12] The global economic crisis (GEC) was very much the outcome of Western patterns of financial activity – both in America and the European Union.[13] The immediate causes and effects of economic crisis – unlike the War on Terror – could not be articulated as external threats to an established ideological hegemony. Public intellectuals could not meditate on the economic crisis as a challenge to the West, a measure of what it means to be a liberal, or a stress test for the world's dominant ideology. The economic crisis was inescapably an *immanent* one and its social effects were immediate and severe. The effects of crisis generated a series of vigorous political responses, all of which openly raised the possibility that profound and systemic political change was necessary.

The field of financial trading had both expanded and been subjected to more permissive regulatory control from the 1990s and had, in fact, been causing all manner of economic instability and recession throughout the world since 1994. In a sense, the sub-prime loans crisis which triggered the recession was not so much an unprecedented event as an exceptionally intense iteration of a global trend, one that manifested at the heart of the West and with exceptionally widespread effects. Currency speculation, illegal or 'exuberant' gambling practices, the financialisation of natural resources and debt, and the complex repackaging of these as assets, bubbles in urban property rents, and prices had all generated a massive increase in the amount of value manipulated by financial speculation agencies. It also enabled a bewildering set of innovations in financial practice and the packaging up of financial assets which aimed both to generate greater trading values (through leverage and multi-layered reselling of the same assets) and to evade regulatory discipline.

From the early 2000s, investment banks had been purchasing mortgages held by those with low-paid precarious or even no jobs. These mortgages were aggressively sold by mortgage companies (including the US government-backed Freddie Mac and Fannie Mae) on the basis of minimal diligence. They did this on the expectation that as long as house prices rose, mortgage companies could repossess houses and sell at a profit. The investment banks that purchased these sub-prime mortgages integrated them into multiple layered (tranche) investments that included more secure assets. By bundling the sub-prime mortgages with other assets and by maintaining their status as 'collateralised' (secured by property), these packages came to be traded in derivative markets. Some banks borrowed to purchase these collateralised debt obligations (CDOs) as a way to get in on the trade or to hold income-generating assets, exposing themselves heavily to this market. When house prices started to flatten, the core trend that had underpinned the sub-prime bubble weakened. Defaults on mortgage payments rose and, predictably, traders began to sell structured mortgage assets. The price of the CDOs fell rapidly and banks struggled to repay debts. Some banks went bankrupt, others stopped trading, and credit markets generally weakened. Credit generally plummeted and, as a result, investment also fell. Unemployment rose and sub-prime mortgage holders lost their homes.

The extremities of the global financial crisis are now well recognised. The common refrain is that the world had not experienced recession like it since the early 1930s. It is also well understood that The Crash came in a period when growth, productivity, and investment were flattening in what appeared to be a secular fashion.[14] In other words, a global recession had hit a generally stagnating global economy in which the world's largest national economies were posting low rates of growth and struggling to sustain healthy growth in any of the core macroeconomic diagnostics such as income growth, productive (direct) investment levels, or economic diversification and dynamism. Between late 2007 and 2010, a sustained and severe global recession had significantly changed the terrain upon which political discourse and action were taking place.

The GEC has generated a set of profound political shifts. Firstly, Western states have transferred massive amounts of money into the financial sector, generating huge public debts and also a return to fiat money, that is, the creation of money by the state. This quantitative easing has allowed governments to transfer money into stressed finance banks in the hope that this will allow investment lending to revive. As a result, throughout the Western world, public debt has emerged as a major-order political issue. This has led to a variety of strategic government responses in which generalised public provision has been severely cut back (over the short or medium terms).[15] Public service payrolls, the transfer of money to regional and urban government, and spending on benefits have all been hit. A political narrative (which is economically illiterate) of 'belt tightening' and 'only spending what you earn' has emerged.[16] The collective noun for this politics is austerity.

Secondly, there has been a substantial decline in the legitimacy of neoliberal nostrums of governance. It was the broad ideological orientation of neoliberalism that advocated the liberalisation of finance in the name of market efficiency through more intelligent and rapid price signalling and the supposed increasing access to finance that it would allow. More generally, neoliberalism advocated deregulation and was indifferent to rising inequality, political orientations that did not weather the crisis well. Public intellectuals and institutions that might broadly be seen as neoliberal both confessed to their own cognitive failings or opened up to 'unorthodox' policy measures that led some to wonder if neoliberalism was now in decline.

Thirdly, in relation to national societies and globally, the GEC has witnessed a recrudescence of inequality, this coming after a period from the mid-1990s to the mid-2000s in which economists started to believe that liberal globalisation was addressing global poverty and inequality, most particularly, the fact that some individuals and companies had concentrated massive amounts of wealth and assets before and during the GEC rose in public prominence.

Fourthly, and as the core strength of the liberal consensus has weakened, there has emerged a raft of political oppositions that have manifested ideological ambitions to remake politics in potentially profound ways. In other words: to bring ideology back as a *via media* through which contrasting visions of the future can be articulated. There is no space to explore these here, but we can register the core vectors of political opposition. Most directly, there is the anti-finance capitalism social movements of Occupy, which combine a series of social movement agendas that pre-existed the GEC with a renewed energy and focus on finance banking. There is also what loosely gets called populism and is associated with a revived anti-liberal Right. This politics is based in a hostility towards the elite or the establishment (however portrayed) that effectively poses politics as a struggle against an entire political elite involved in national government. The *gilets jaunes* is sometimes referred to as 'populist' but it is, in fact, based in a series of policy issues and has combined a remarkable range of social groups. It has also sustained a rolling protest which demonstrates that it is not driven by the populist demagoguery of following a single maverick leader, a property commonly noted in studies of populism. In the UK, there has been a resurgence of socialist ideas and movements of which Momentum was for a time the most prominent example.

In short: we are in a political economy of crisis. If one takes the last 15 years in the political economy of the G20 member states (the G20 arguably being the most important intergovernmental organisation of leading global economies), at least 12[17] can easily be described as having moved into a state of political rupture, uncertainty, and adversity that seems distinct and very prominent in the present day. One might add Spain, Egypt, Tunisia, Turkey,

Greece, and Ireland to this list. Although not a state – but a member of the G20 – one could most certainly add the European Union.

Founded on a weak and unstable set of national economies, matters of politics have quickly and in some cases drastically lost their 'end of history' or Great Moderation properties. These have been replaced by new discourses, policy unorthodoxies, ruptures, rebellion and protest, and major-order mooting of the legitimacy of governing regimes.

The desert of the real: three popular statements

The changing times have, naturally, fed into a diverse set of academic and journalistic reflections. Within this diversity, there is a shared sense of change towards heightened uncertainty and crisis. There has been an uptick in research on 'radical' political parties and movements, often accompanied by a sense of normative vexation in which a concern is expressed that the good things – which is to say the relatively moderate or stable things – in politics are being eroded irrevocably. They reflect and amplify a broader sense that a besieged ideological and political stability is facing existential crisis.

There is a clutch of books concerning the end or secular decline of liberal democracy. These books often make arguments about increasingly tense and disparate social divisions within previously more convivial civil societies. Another genre treats politics as shifting towards a 'post-truth' mode of address in which policy, evidence, and deliberation have been replaced by forcefulness, charisma, positionality, and what one might call strategic falsehood. 'Bullshit', 'truthiness', and 'fake news' are now part of our political lexicon. Some books make the argument that politics is in some form of epochal or existential crisis or failure.

There is neither the space nor the need to map out the constellation of 'new and uncertain times' political literature. We can get a good sense of the shifted mood by identifying three key contributions that make broad commentary on political change in the spirit set out earlier. Furthermore, each of these books has been – by the standards of a book on politics – bestsellers, reaching out to a broader readership than most academic books, winning awards, and in some degree being written by public intellectuals as well as researchers. Reviewing these contributions allows us to set an intellectual context within which prevailing understandings of politics see the form and direction of change in the generation of political ideas. Consequently, we can move into our own interest in the social media and the politics of the Left.

The end of the nation?

David Goodhart's book *The Road to Somewhere*[18] is the most popular encapsulation of a fairly generalised sensibility in political commentary. This is that British society has become increasingly divided between a university-educated, mobile, urban, and liberal-cosmopolitan group and a school-educated, community-based, small-town, and liberal-nationalist group. Goodhart calls these two groups 'anywheres' and 'somewheres'. He bases his distinction on education and mobility. Anywheres are spatially shallow-rooted and possess higher education that gives them 'broad horizons: portable achieved identities'.[19] Somewheres are deeply rooted in a community and possess school education that may or may not have fed into a school-leaving job: 'rooted and ... ascribed identities'.[20]

Goodhart generates an image of British politics as caught in the thralls of a mutual stand-off or tension between these two groups: a 'potential long-term divergence problem'.[21] The stand-off is no more apparent in Goodhart's analysis than in relation to Brexit, which is seen as the shock event that revealed how a commonly assumed aspect of British society – the north–south, middle class–working class, young–old, multicultural–'indigenous' cultural distinctions that are easily identified across post-war British public culture[22] – had hardened into something of a schism that had changed the terrain upon which party politics is practised.

Goodhart's analysis suggests that, since the turn of the century, governments have become dominated by 'anywhere' agendas: labour mobility, human rights legislation, university expansion, European integration, and liberal global economics. This social shift was most strongly present in the long government of New Labour.[23] This has created a major social faultline which Goodhart is bold enough to call tribalism: 'separate and barely comprehending cultural blocs'.[24] This tribalism has generated an unprecedented political challenge to government's legitimacy or ability to encompass and articulate a national politics. As with a lot of commentary concerning Brexit and the 'two tribes' image of British politics, there is an interest in populism which has become a leitmotif of British political crisis and instability. Somewheres are more likely to be populists, and this means putting democracy before liberalism, meaning that 'rights and reason' are understood as secondary values.[25]

Goodhart and others[26] have identified the contours of the crisis generated by this widening social schism. Populism and a hardening of socio-cultural divisions between those 'left behind' and 'metropolitan middle classes' have (in this account) bequeathed a form of political crisis, manifest in a protracted Brexit process, an irredeemably contentious public discussion about immigration, a destabilisation of established political constituencies (notably, the notion of a collapsed 'red wall'), and a political culture of cynicism and mistrust.

Goodhart's nowheres and somewheres are constructed to pose an argument about an imminent crisis of democracy. The suggestion is that the identitarian bifurcation in civil society has undermined a well-functioning democracy which, after all, is at its heart a political system that is supposed to manage the socio-political differences of a population in a cohesive and consensual fashion. But, although Goodhart offers an augury of crisis, the book does not wish to pursue its own line of analysis too far. Goodhart states that both sides do share a kind of liberalism and some sense of nationalism.[27] He also says that both sides are in flux. The divide is, we discover, less tribal and more dispersed through a wide range of socio-economic factors. Concerns about immigration, ethnicity, culture, authority, community, and so on are in fact distributed in more complex ways than the 'tribal' idiom suggests. The suggestions he makes and the identity traits he sets out are most readily understood as intensifications of quite familiar British socio-political anxieties, set in a fluid political context.

If there is a major political impasse as Goodhart suggests, it would seem that the socio-cultural distinction between nowheres and somewheres is not the entirety of the problem. Residing in a less well-figured form is something of an awareness that the institutions and procedures of democracy are themselves inadequate and failing. After all, to the degree that the nowhere and somewhere categories are mutable, there is opportunity to reconcile and mollify their differences. In other words, if there is a systemic shift in politics into a period of uncertainty and/or crisis, one requires a more concerted focus on the nature of democracy and governance than Goodhart offers.

The end of democracy?

David Runciman[28] argues that (traditional) democracy[29] is in such a condition that it is no longer fit for purpose. It continues – in his phrasing in a kind of late middle age – through a form of path dependency and in a condition of complacency, facing a lack of clear alternatives. Runciman is too nuanced (or perhaps evasive) to set up some epochal historiography in which all is ended and all will be changed.[30] But, he does assemble a wide-ranging set of considerations to suggest that democracy is not so much in transition but rather failing in a systemic fashion and that, as a result, it might not have much life left in it. So, the implication that drives the book is that democracy is in a state of senescence and is likely coming to an end.[31]

There are three main challenges that seem to overwhelm democratic states: coup, catastrophe, and technological takeover. In each of these considerations, Runciman considers democracies as unable to generate the political purpose required effectively to tackle them. The reasons for this vary between challenges.

Runciman states that traditional democracies are both robust and inflexible because of their entrenchment and this leaves them struggling effectively to respond to novel challenges. The coups that Runciman talks of are incremental and technocratic, not the military storming of presidential palaces. Democracy is 'hollowed out' through a kind of techno-elite capture. He speaks of a 'zombie' quality in democracy as the energies it released in its early years dissipate. In relation to catastrophe, democratic states do not have the wherewithal to deal purposefully with existential threats from climate change or autonomous machines. In relation to the rise of large tech companies, Runciman speaks of the rise of concentrated corporate 'Leviathans' that control social media which, although unarmed, push the locus of political interest away from government while also exercising considerable influence over it. In summary, democracy has become 'tired, vindictive, paranoid, self-deceiving, clumsy, and frequently ineffectual'.[32]

Democracies require a certain kind of public that, arguably, is in decline. The citizen-voter, connected to government through broad and inclusive political parties, is now one political identity among others rather than a principal or essential one. The suggestion is that this civic identity is in decline in relation to other features of (anti-)political identity. Throughout the book, Runciman suggests that ordinary people channel their political sociability in directions that do not support democratic politics. People seek their recognition and meaning not in democracy but in disparate virtual spaces in which a generalised 'mindlessness', indifference, and welter of conspiracies overwhelms accountable and deliberative governance.[33] People might see the government as an increasingly irrelevant or archaic institution in an age when social media campaign politics and vision making are so much more prominent and nimble. Democracy is slow and tedious. People might despair of government as it plods through reformist policy making. And, people might find themselves caught up in the sound and fury of debate on Twitter rather than consider debates around policy.[34]

In regards to the latter, Runciman follows a common argument: that social media has generated a new kind of political tone in which the vernacular is the language of hate. This is often seen as socially destructive, not only virtual: creating online campaigns of hatred that can also manifest in real life. Read in conjunction with Goodhart, one gets a sense that increasingly undemocratic or anti-democratic societies are governed by increasingly ill-equipped democratic states. In the midst of this double movement of decline resides a burgeoning social media which amplifies and confuses political discourse. This brings us to the third thread in our framing of political crisis and uncertainty: the rise of falsehood in politics.

The end of truth?

Peter Oborne[35] claims that politics in the UK and America has declined into a post-truth era. He is insistent that what was once a constant but deviant aspect of politics – lying – is now hardwired into government. Lying is habitual, automatic.[36] He makes this claim by arguing that political success has become increasingly based in the ability of certain individuals to 'lie upwards'. That is, lying and even being caught lying does not necessarily mean trouble if the individual can simply keep moving: finding new forms of employment, making use of social networks, and carrying on with denials and dissimulations. Lies upon lies. This is a political practice that Oborne sees as a 'new normal'. He associates it also with a mediatisation of politics and a degeneration of standards in the media. The major newspaper companies have become increasingly supine to Cabinet and the Press Office, 'part of the official apparatus of deceit',[37] taking the increasingly mendacious messaging of the core of the ruling party as trustworthy and in the process enabling or colluding with the obscurantism of governance. There is a mutual capture here: politicians are now products of a media that is no longer concerned with investigative journalism, balance, and fact checking.

In all, Oborne presents an image of a British politics in which the formal procedures of good governance are a sham and his image of the political future is dystopian, something akin to Orwell's *Nineteen Eighty-Four*. As with all allusions to *Nineteen Eighty-Four*, there is an ingredient of apocalypse in Oborne's vision: a 'moral emergency', an end to 'the idea of truth that has lain at the heart of public discourse … for the last 250 years'.[38]

Oborne's book has made an impression and it has resonated with a more pervasive public mood. There is a general sense – at least within the intelligentsia – that politics has been corrupted by a combination of venality and dissembling. As a result, the general population – on whom the edifice of democracy rests – no longer engages with politics or is in some fashion or another duped by the elites.

This is, for our purposes, the mainweakness in Oborne's analysis: its elitism. The assault on truth that Oborne identifies is only sustainable on its own terms because of his 'great leader' framing of politics, his focus on the apex of power in the media and government, and his neglect of other political dynamics. He understands Johnson and Trump as 'gifted popular entertainers' and offers highly reduced biographies of their eccentric ascendance to power based in their privilege and personal resources. The elite-biographical style also leads Oborne to contrast his two villains with an odd hagiographical style in his account of Angela Merkel.[39] Systemic lying is an elite-personal condition that, it is assumed, generates a cynical or duped public. 'The British people no longer care about the difference between fact and fiction'; the public let Boris Johnson 'get away with anything … it feels [like] innocent fun'.[40]

If there has been a depletion of truthfulness at the apex of power, it does not follow that more general and popular political cultures have also depleted. In an age of bullshit, democratic failure, and intensified social divisions, it is important to recognise how *energised* popular politics has become. A prominent example is one Oborne pays particular attention to: Brexit.

Like many others, Oborne sets out how Johnson and Gove knowingly, recklessly, and repeatedly deployed falsehoods in the Leave campaign. This is all accounted for as a low point in the decline of politics. But, Brexit was also the largest expression of singular political preference in British history. During campaigning, national identity, democracy, the structures of the EU, various renditions of historical tradition, moral economies of inequality and injustice, and some aspiration for a changed political future were all vibrantly present in the public sphere. *Pace* Oborne, the referendum on whether to remain in the European Union was, if anything, a moment of political *excess* that had at its heart the meta-norm that the people should have a final say on the constitution of their government.

Political debate and contention have always been rude, partially true, outrageous, and divisive. Arguably, the political cultures of democratisation are always like this. And these characteristics pertain to both elite and popular politics. Controversies concerning the 'Brexit bus' claim that £350 million a week could be recouped from EU payments for the NHS, and speculative predictions of economic damage as a result of leaving are not so much signifiers of an end to truth in politics but rather a distinctly energised instance of campaign and contestation. The assumption that 'fake news' corrodes the polity relies on an elitism and patronising attitude towards society more generally. There is no logical or empirical connection between falsehoods and exaggerations disseminated and their effects on people's politics. Oborne claims that there is a 'moral emergency' in British politics, that it has changed the nature of truthfulness which has held for the previous 200 years, and that, as a result, politics has changed.[41] It might be more accurate to say that politics has become more unruly and that, in these conditions, some political leaders have developed a kind of dynamic unprincipled entrepreneurialism in order to maintain themselves in power.

This section has briefly reviewed well-read overviews of the direction of flow of British politics to illustrate a new and powerful political attitude. As economic crisis, failing governance, and Brexit have torn apart the certainties of the End of History, there has emerged not a revival in the meaningful contestation of ideas but rather a kind of decrepitude and dysfunction – more decay and reinvigoration. As a result, the opportunity to explore new politics of possibility has been largely avoided.

Prospectives

Framing the near future I: Techno anxieties

Goodhart, Runciman, and Oborne – and one could select others[42] – collectively give a good sense of the mood that sets the context for this book: that we are entering into, or are on the precipice of, a changed politics. Change not in the sense of the ordinary cycles of plus ça change but rather something more systemic and declinist. The books share a historiography in which a largely stable political state of affairs has entered into collapse and that, as a result, we need to pay attention to the morbid symptoms of systemic decline. Comforting premises concerning virtue, citizenship, and democracy are denied; the future might well be more chaotic than we have witnessed in modern politics since the first half of the 20th century.

In the process of decline, new forms of politics appear. These new forms of politics – insurgently problematic, unstable, and eschatological – bring with them new ideas about political subjectivity and authority. These ideas are not meliorist or reformist but are rather challenges or alternatives to the prevailing ideas that dominate politics: electoral democracy, liberalism, and a market society. Accordingly, one can read each and all of these texts as situated in a particular kind of transition: a rising and profound ideological uncertainty in the midst of epochal decline. And each book maintains a portentous mood within this setting. None are sunny in their prospective.

These books position social media as pivotal to the morbid symptoms of political decay. For Oborne, social media is a pernicious device used strategically to broadcast lies.[43] For Goodhart, it is an echo chamber for the nowheres to generate political values outwith the rest of the population.[44] For Runciman, it is mainly a way of hollowing out democracy, replacing it with the impotent venting of frustrations.[45] Many books share the same sensibility with a stronger focus on social media in politics.[46]

It is fair to say that, perhaps more than any other recent and dynamic trend of change, politics in social media has articulated the strongest anxieties concerning the prospects for 'normal' politics. We will not deny that any of these concerns are to some degree well founded. Rather, in the next section, we will make a case that there is a distinction to be made between politics in social media and PSM. We will argue throughout the book that PSM is a politically productive 'habitus'. And, we will aim to convince readers that the prevailing and underlying misanthropy that accompanies so much critique and content of social media misses an important facet of its growth and social broadening: that it has become the seedbed for new ideological components of socialism to emerge, test themselves, and seek to convince others. Among the intrinsic analytical failings of misanthropy, there resides a more specific failure: an inability to identify discrete and significantly social practices within virtual information-sharing technologies. But, before we come to these arguments more squarely, we should offer a note of caution in relation to the historiography of decline.

Framing the near future II: The political economy of a collision of disorders

The phrase 'collision of disorders' comes from Anwar Shaik.[47] All histories tell stories. These stories rely on an imagery of periodic successions, and peaks and troughs. Periods of history that were contemporaneously seen as rather ordinary can become halcyon and prelapsarian when located before a fall of some kind or other. Times that seemed genuinely uncertain for those who lived through them can be characterised as interregna that moved a political situation from one state to another. And, times of trepidation can be written as the dawning of a new era in hindsight. To set any sequence into political history is to storify it through retrospection.

This truism applies to writings on the decline of politics in which previously stable times have ended and the future looks ominous. The historical sense is enthralled by an uncertain present, and this affects how one sees the relevant past and the near future. Writing in the midst of crisis and uncertainty opens up the risk of favourably glossing the properties of the past and furrowing one's brow to imagine the near future.

Detailed contextualisations and some revisionist political history in the UK has shown that one of the mainstays of present-day crisis narrative – the idea of a post-Second World War stability and prosperity – is in good part a retroactive construction rather than a true rendition of the historical experience of the baby boomer generation. The 'embedded liberalism' of the 1960s and early 1970s was replete with instability in the supposedly Lockean heartlands.[48] The British political economy recovered slowly from the Second World War, endured a crisis in the late 1940s, lost its empire,[49] moved into a structural trade deficit, and lost (further) relative economic power vis-à-vis other European economies.[50] It also had to manage the loss of its energy security, which had major geopolitical repercussions.[51] It faced its own share of serious political strife, especially into the early 1970s, and most especially in relation to Commonwealth immigration and racism and Northern Ireland which led the British state to reintroduce troops into the province.[52]

There is a lot one might unpack in the previous paragraph, but it does serve to demonstrate how predominantly retrospective presentations of a *trentes glorieuses* are. At the time – as an African-American, a Northern Irish Catholic, a colonised African fighting for independence, a woman worker re-domesticated into the household, or a recently immigrated Commonwealth citizen – politics was not a historically stable regime. And political elites saw crises in relation to Suez, the Soviet Union's invasion of Czechoslovakia and Hungary, the 'red menace' in post-colonial liberation struggles, race and ethnic rebellion, and even the threat of a 'permissive society' which might seem quaint now but arguably shared both an intensity and 'othering' with the present day's 'culture wars'.

Any arguments that things are falling apart need to recognise that things were never that together beforehand. This is not simply a plea for nuance and a recognition of complexity as much as it is for calibration. If we are in unprecedentedly or exceptionally unstable times, some acknowledgement that this historical sensibility is not that uncommon is required and very likely instructive.

And, that calibration is most pivotally embedded in the nature of the continuing, unstable, and contested reproduction of capitalism. Most familiarly, the continued dominance of capitalism is manifested in the social practices of trade, investment, finance, and labour; but it is also extant within a persistent set of political-strategic orientations within government which largely concern economic growth, the disciplining of labour, and the sustenance of profitability. However, we see the nature of politics changing in epochal ways, capitalism (in all its dynamism and institutional variation) is going nowhere soon. One does not need to be a determinist or a structuralist to recognise that its *persistence* can hardly be analytically separated from any account of political *rupture*.

Shaik's presentation of capitalism as a historically dynamic system has at its core historic tendency a tense cohabitation of chaos and structure.[53] He represents capitalism's frequent crises as both systemic and 'granular', that is, based in the agencies of individuals, groups, and states. These properties underdetermine the dynamics of politics: the nature of governance, the quality of democracy, and the ideological currents within publics. Underdetermination does not connote some kind of formula of causation, much less an Althusserian base/superstructure approach. Rather, it is that political change occurs within the 'bandwidth' of capitalism's social relations of property and relentless drive for profit. This historic orientation cautions against the now fashionable (and arguably cliché) 'the old is dying and the new is yet to be born' understanding of profound change. It suggests that major political transformations *within* capitalism are set within certain continuities.

In times of major change, we should, then, seek out the specific causes of change and consider them as novel, disruptive, and possibly powerful influences on the broader patterning of politics with a political economy of capitalism. It is within this framing that we consider one of the most unequivocally novel and transformative aspects of political discourse and practice in the crisis years within which we are living through: the rise of PSM. The 'capitalist' framing sketched here is not merely a pedantic scholarly point. It is central to our line of inquiry because it allows us not only to avoid apocalyptic narratives of political futurology.[54] It also secures us the context within which to expect that ideologies of socialism and Marxism maintain a historic pertinence, even in an age when some commentators imagine the end of the world more than the end of capitalism.[55]

Political social media (PSM)

Troubled virtual politics

All of the authors discussed earlier recognise that the political shifts they identify and consider have been realised through or intensified within social media. Centred around Twitter, social media is a remarkable cacophony of political energies. Virtual political discourse has drawn in large numbers of people, generating a massive amount of content and organising complex networks of peer groups. It is at the heart of any analysis of the politics of uncertainty, crisis, and change. It is the focus of our argument that this political discourse is not exclusively worrisome – defined by conspiracy, hatred, and falsehood – but also *productive*.

Our argument requires some categorical distinction in order to proceed. We shall identify a realm of online discourse called *political social media* (PSM) that, in a sense, decontaminates itself from some of the sound and fury of social media more broadly. But before we move on to this, we should acknowledge the nature of concern in relation to social media more broadly.

Research and commentary on social media's role in politics is a litany of anxieties. Social media generates echo chambers of consensus, hostile to other views and therefore undermining the underlying principles of open deliberation.[56] Often relying on idioms concerning the 'dark web', some commentators have identified within PSM a seedbed for new extreme political movements.[57] There is a concern about the nature or tone of conversation: the 'increasingly bitter and polarized nature of political discourse',[58] a combination of virtuality and isolation that facilitates extreme responses, insults, and bullying.[59] Relatedly, there is an anxiety about the degree to which social media hosts and moderators should censor and moderate political discourses that veer close to the limits of what is acceptable speech.[60] The intensified hostilities of social media have sometimes bled into the real world, making social media the conduit through which attacks and even murders have been plotted.[61] Social media has been a hotbed for conspiracy theory, racism, sexism, and all manner of hatred. The limitless capacity of social media sites to accommodate text means that there has been an explosion of truth claims and data, none of which are verified, curated, or subjected to any clear authoritative oversight. This is why social media has been a common point of reference in discussion of 'post-truth', fake news, and so on, especially in relation to digital campaigning.[62] The use of banks of censors that remove flagged material, the tweaking of algorithms, the mining of data, and the loss of privacy embedded in what are, after all, corporate platforms have raised concerns about the extent to which freedom of information and a right to privacy have been profoundly undermined.[63] And, this troubling 'infosphere' is delivered to increasingly 'zombified' individuals, addicted to device checking and increasingly alienated from the material circumstances of life and society.[64] The principal way in which discourse is assessed is not accuracy or pertinence but rather 'rating and trolling', forms of validation based in rapid emotive senses of outrage and personal validation.[65]

Salvaging the political value of the virtual

There is a distinction to be made between the very wide terrain of political discourse on social media and a more specific collection of hubs within which political discourse follows more exacting and delineated rules of procedure. This is a distinction between social media and PSM. PSM can be defined as follows:

- Content is identified with or attached to discrete projects which are at least partially dedicated to an openly defined public political purpose.
- Content is produced with an implicit acknowledgement that evidence and falsifiability matter.
- Content is produced in a manner that endeavours to develop a set of concepts which, in their advocacy, are seen as the means of persuasion or debate.
- Content is subjected to some form of mediation and quality control.

These characteristics do not mean that PSM is simply ordinary political discussion transposed into tweets and blogs. PSM does take on some of the accoutrements of social media more generally. It has its memes, hot takes, high sarcasm and irony, and sharp-eyed attacks. Additionally, it often reiterates and intensifies points of difference rather than move deliberatively towards some form of reasoned (in the Habermasian sense) consensus. But, unlike the more diffuse, unmediated, and sometimes unpleasant sway of social media more generally, it does so within recognisable rules of political discourse.

In the midst of the cut and thrust of serial contention, PSM works towards the systematisation of ideas, displays an awareness of established canons of political thought, has some respect for the boundaries between different traditions of politics, and deploys some conceptual language. These properties allow us to extrapolate PSM from the irresolvable noisiness and low-grade politics of social media as a whole. The mode of extrapolation that this book offers is to treat PSM as the host for a set of *proto-ideologies*, that is, a collocation of conceptual terms within social media traffic in ways that reveal an aspiration to dominate a political field. We will return to ideologies and proto-ideologies in the next chapter.

So, within social media, we define PSM as a discourse set within Twitter, Facebook, Substack, and public-facing (that is, not exclusively academic or policy-focused) blogs and podcasts. The content provided in PSM is curated and edited in some fashion and comments and debates are moderated. There are often thematic drop-down menus. There is an open attempt to engage broader publics, even within often acerbic or contrarian attitudes. In a nutshell, there has emerged within the turbulence, uncertainty, and crisis of the present a robust political discourse within social media that offers very rich raw material to explore new or revived ideological currents set within the public sphere.

PSM is a social realm within which relatively popular political discourses have emerged in a historically unprecedented fashion. It is important to identify and value this phenomenon in an age where moral anxiety (social media is dangerous), a certain kind of misanthropy (people are nasty), and a political fatalism (this is the end of politics) tend to characterise social media as a morbid symptom of systemic collapse. The point is that not all social media is a manifestation of the end of democracy, truth, or political community.

Mapping PSM

PSM cannot be mapped definitively. It is a network of networks, different identifications, multi-sited and clustering around certain personalities and issues. It is fluid. It is not possible to identify a definitive host, hub, or hard set of categorical criteria without losing something of the essence of what PSM is. Nevertheless, we can set some coordinates.

There is, of course, Twitter. Herein, 'academic Twitter', generated by academics in the social sciences, is key. Not all of this content is 'political' in the sense we are interested in. A lot of academic Twitter is either self-promotion, lifestyle confessional, or research dissemination. But, it is also the case that many academics have come to use Twitter for political debate and engagement. This might involve commentary on current events, responses to others' commentary, threads, or even academic attempts at satire and lampoonery.

Connectedly, Twitter hosts content that spins off from the promotional activities of other political agents. Journalists from the legacy media, impact-seeking writers, think tanks, political party members, social movement activists, politically engaged artists and celebrities who consider themselves public intellectuals, and campaign and advocacy movements fill Twitter with PSM content. Furthermore, all of these organisations have their own social media web presence. Blogsites with comment sections and rejoinders are common currency for any political organisation's public face. University departments and political research institutes host blogsites which aim to provide short and contemporary commentary pieces on spiking media issues. PSM has spurned a wealth of what one might describe as hybrid online journalism: opinion, reporting, and debate combined into a scroll of content presented in the format of fresh news.[66] Independent political organisations or academics and commentators might set up a blog or podcast which again follows social media rules of regular provision and *en courant* topics, commonly with a roster of invited guests. Think tanks, social justice movements, and campaign/advocacy groups do the same in relation to specific topics such as human rights, poverty, social policy, and health.

Online-only 'alt-media' organisations generate content often free of charge, often culling and redacting material from elsewhere and adding opinion to it. There are also academic/media hybrid sites such as Open Democracy and The Conversation which effectively use a franchise to receive content from academics free of charge in return for the publicity their research receives.

Universities, campaign groups, groups of political commentators, think tanks, and media outlets all generate their own social media content and link/promote this via the 'meta-medium' of Twitter. In doing so, they co-construct a dense set of associations between content, curated by (hash)tags and site-specific search engines, shaped by cross-posting and embedded HTMLs, and all motivated to seek out and discuss what is considered the 'upworthy' topic of the time. One can readily see how PSM is structured through this *nébuleuse* and how it shares an implicit protocol of behaviour. Posts and comments are edited, moderated, and curated. There is some institutional accountability, even if it is distributed throughout the different content editors and moderators. There are named people who take responsibility for the general nature of content. Noms de plume are rare.

The ferment of PSM

We have defined PSM as a component of a wider traffic of political ideas and imagery. It is defined by a set of protocols that represent a hybrid of generally accepted and broadly deliberative academic standards and an aesthetic turn towards what makes social media content valuable: short, impressive, playful. It is also hosted within a network that revolves around Twitter as a kind of clearing house for generator hubs located within think tanks, universities, political journalism and commentary, and a set of more artisanal blog and podcast projects.

PSM is not institutionally bound. It does not require membership of a university, a certain prerequisite qualification, or professional standing. Participants might be understood as public intellectuals in a way that perhaps resembled public political discourse in Western societies before the rise of modern universities and the professionalisation of politics as public service. There are independent writers, politicians, journalists, researchers and advocates based in think tanks and campaign organisations, and academics. The individual social histories of participants in PSM vary from long-established professors and politicians to entrepreneurial non-institutionalised individuals who set up podcasts or write commentaries that capture broader attention.

As with social media more broadly, within PSM, hierarchies of authority are flatter and less stable than one would expect within the hierarchies of academe or government. Senior academics have to put up with a lack of deference or even rude commentary. Different individuals make claims to authority or special knowledge based not only on their research or experience but on all manner of personal experiences and declarations of identity. Some are more skilled than others in the art of social media phrasing so that an astute comment can garner preference over a more accurate or sophisticated comment phrased in wooden language. The validity claims within PSM are, then, ambivalent: defined by quality of content and the affect of prose. One posts and then sees what happens: endorsement, disagreement, lampoonery, ad hominem, or nothing at all. This is very different to previously established procedures of political discourse in which institutions provide the scaffolding within which one will be listened and responded to and it has manifold effects on the nature of content.

There is a general rule within PSM that if you cannot say it in 1,500 words or less, you will have lost your audience. PSM has to fit within the general social media aesthetic of the scrolling attention span. Above 1,500 words, text often gets the advisory 'long read', or caveat that an article will take eight or ten or 12 minutes to get through. Thus, the demands of brevity weigh heavily on all content providers who are more or less well equipped to be concise. Many academics will recall – either in themselves or in conversations with colleagues – the vexations of trying to show how things are 'complicated' within the brevities of PSM. Others might be more skilled or relaxed at writing punchy commentary or argument, possibly because they don't think things are that complicated.

Brevity has effects on PSM beyond the culling back of complexity. Content is not read in order to add to existing knowledge, to use an aphorism from academe. It is read within a veritable slew of other texts and it is likely forgotten, even after an hour or two. The most one can hope for is that there is a 'tail' of references to your text through (re)tweets and other endorsements, but this will only extend the lifespan of the content by a day or so.

Disposability means that the aspiration is to burn brightly but briefly. This has further effects on content. There is a structural entreaty to say what one wishes to say in as strong terms as possible. In the attention economy of PSM, the first few words matter vitally. Authors strive to impact immediately upon the consumer's passing gaze. The terminology that brands a post commonly contains phases such as 'the end of', 'what's wrong with', 'the new', or 'why I'm no longer'. Or, titles might identify a politician or political personality in crisis, a specific scandal or outrage, or make a claim to exposé.

Another strategy pursued in order to achieve some posterity is to construct opinion silos. These are clusters of arguments, connected to specific individuals and then endowed with a handle. Colloquially, one might call them 'camps'. Of course, politics has always been debated through ideological flagging. The naming of factions is in itself a core political activity. What social media does is intensify these distinctions. There may be more categories; they may be constructed rapidly and defined roughly with a 'you-know-who-I-mean' sensibility; they might project a strong sense of their own distinctiveness. They are 'opinionated' in that they are defined not by their subject matter or the sociological origins of key members but by their 'take' on politics or a specific political issue. They are inescapably and explicitly normative. The affect contained within opinion silos moves towards controversy and combativeness.

Brevity, simplicity, and disposability all offer opportunities to make political communication with many people more readily than through a manifesto, policy brief, or newspaper article, and most certainly in comparison with a peer-reviewed article. But, in order to maximise these opportunities, content needs to be as striking as possible. This has repercussions. Points of view and arguments which might have been made in some moderation and perhaps with caveats are pushed to a more stark posture. If there are many things someone agrees with someone else about, these are likely to be jettisoned to make space for as dense a disagreement on the matter at hand as possible. Commentators will filter the subjects they write about so that interesting nuanced differences of opinion on matters where the main positions are already established and understood are neglected in favour of controversies, spiked media attention, and very recent events.

This mode of address favours some topics more than others. Naturally, much of this might be fitted under the rubric of 'scandal': corruption, hypocrisy, and deception. Political matters of major and immediate import are also favoured: the terrorist bombing, a new war, a pandemic, a police shooting. Crisis and conspiracy are preferable to unintended consequence. Also, if one can frame a text as importantly and profoundly connected to the fundamentals of rights, legitimacy, democracy, and culture, then this will likely muster more attention. If one's own interests are not 'interesting', couch them in a context in which human rights, cultural identity, or the decline of democracy are at issue, even if the actual matter at hand is a new policy initiative or a specific historical revision.

And, because the academic prerequisites for commentary are lowered and/or calibrated by a commentary's ability to generate attention, regular contributors to PSM speak not only about those things they have researched or have embedded knowledge. They might also engage in matters to which they are as much a novice as anyone else. The spoof Twitter account 'Professor BritPol' regularly declared: 'today, I am an expert on ...' before noting a peaking political issue and following it with mimetic hashtags.

To summarise, although we have defined PSM as a niche in social media that is relatively clearly defined by academic procedures, it is also the case that PSM necessarily has to adhere to the aesthetics of social media: fast, attention-grabbing, extremely concise, and controversy-savvy. Taken together, these two patterns are not so much paradoxical or contradictory as in fact the productive essence of PSM. As such, one should be aware that claims that social media is destroying proper political discourse should be taken with a good pinch of salt. Rather, PSM has become host to a healthy profusion of political discourse that is more accessible, less cognisant of hierarchy, and generally eager to focus on contemporary matters of import. It is one of the mainstays of this book that the rise of social media has not simply corroded political discourse into a trigger-happy miasma of post-truth echo chambers but also – and arguably more importantly – served as a forum for political debate which is in many ways quite familiar and, normatively, seems pretty healthy.

3

'A Largeness of Vision and Imagination': Marxism and Socialism

Introduction

In the previous chapter, we argued that narratives of epochal political crisis are misleading in one particular sense: these narratives tend to portray the rise of social media as another (perhaps the key) morbid symptom of a public political discourse that is in collapse. This declinism does not care so much to identify how much energy, normativity, and discussion has emerged through social media and, inasmuch as they do, they do not treat it as analytically interesting. We identified a virtuality that we defined as PSM, in which a kind of hybridity between established protocols of political discussion (broadly deliberative) and the flat, fast, and 'hot' grammar of social media cohabit to generate considerable and considerably engaged political discussion. PSM enjoys the energy of social media as a technology but also broadly cleaves to a set of rules concerning political discourse that are well established and lead to the exercise of curatorial discipline.

Over the next two chapters, we will set out an agenda and analytical framework to explore PSM in detail. This requires two things in preparation. In this chapter, we will discuss the political tradition of Marxism/socialism. We will identify its properties, boundaries, and contours and offer some commentary on what makes this tradition of political thought unique and in some ways distinctively amenable to PSM. In the following chapter, we will offer an analytical framework within which one might begin to assess the nature of Marxism/socialism in PSM as a political force. We will do this by coining the notion of a proto-ideology, a concept that aims to 'decontaminate' the texts of social media from the noise of endless and often angry social media intercourse.

Some coordinates

Why socialism?

We have not yet made an account for our selection of a political tradition. The main reason is the author's own political sympathies and to some degree academic specialism. The websites used as raw material in this book are those I frequently click to access news, commentary, and analysis. Although not without its faults, Marxist/socialist approaches to politics seem to me to combine a deep realism that derives from their foundations in political economy and an ambitiously radical political prospective. With the passing of decades, I expected that I would relinquish Marxism (as quite a few do) as a result of repeated political disappointment and the institutional pressures towards liberal 'problem-solving' approaches,[1] especially as the latter are so heavily incentivised by academic funding bodies and enjoy the support of university management.[2] But, contrarily, I have been struck at how tenaciously insightful Marxism continues to be.

Secondly, Marxism/socialism[3] possesses properties that make it strongly amenable to PSM because of its continued pertinence. Goran Therborn characterises liberalism and Marxism as rival siblings of modernity.[4] Socialism – and most certainly much of Marx's more normative writing – is motivated by a desire to surpass the limitations that capitalism imposes on the achievement of a thriving modernity. At its best, socialism offers a distinct 'largeness of vision and imagination'[5] that is based in social and technological creative dynamism, an end to hardship and poverty,[6] and a full flourishing of all individuals.[7] But, its orientation towards Enlightenment modernity and a 'progressivist' understanding of history is accompanied by an equally distinct adversarialism in which it critiques bourgeois society for its elitism, its irrationalities, its oppression of labour, its exploitation, and the limits of its ambition. Indeed, 'socialism' as a general signifier tends to evoke images of a radical, insurgent rival to predominant liberal discourses.

As a result, there is a specific agonism within socialism which gives it considerable energy: a conditional positivity towards (bourgeois or liberal) modernisation, a critique of the very same, an impatience with the depth and pace of progress, and a radical positioning that moves it away from reform and towards revolutionary change. In short, most socialist traditions[8] of political thinking are focused on matters of modernisation, progress, and change that are mainstays of dominant (usually liberal) ideological traditions. But they are also intensely oppositional, and socialists commonly 'identify' as radical, marginalised, and insurgent. In relation to the contours of PSM, this gives socialist discourse a uniquely engaged but also highly critical property that is, as the last chapter suggested, very fitting for the voicing of PSM. There is no political matter that predominant political ideologies can disseminate that will not provoke an engaged and critical socialist response.

Thirdly, the socialist tradition has generated a remarkable archive of political analysis and theory. Indeed, mapping socialist genealogies and historiographies is a substantial sub-discipline in itself. Only liberalism has offered up as weighty an archive. As a result, in any consideration of ideological ferment on PSM, one would expect that socialist approaches would come armed with a substantial repertoire of terms, normative and aesthetic modes of analysis, references to historical events, and so on. There is a scope and depth of interest within the socialist tradition that outweighs all but the dominant tradition, which is liberalism.

Fourthly, socialism endures and even flourishes. Although the historical record of socialist politics is far from encouraging, the optimism and anger of socialist discourse has not been successfully expunged and, indeed, has periodically experienced summers of revival and innovation. In my own career, I can recall how the collapse of the Soviet Union, the rise of academic preferences for postmodern approaches to politics, and the rise of neoliberalism all seemed to spell the substantial decline of socialist thinking. Nevertheless, a consistent stream of major reflections and rethinking of Marx's work and legacy continued.[9] New journals, research projects, and conferences sustained socialist and Marxist inquiry within academe throughout the 1990s and 2000s. The rise of global social justice movements in the late 1990s carried with them fragments of socialist thinking.[10] Marx and Engels' *The Communist Manifesto* continues to attract the attention of an 'educated' reading public and sustain historical pertinence.[11] This is not an argument that socialism will always enjoy its prominent 'rival sibling' status, insist on telling truth to power, or possess some kind of kernel of truth that will disallow it from going into terminal historical decline. All we are saying here is that, in spite of the persistently hostile environment it has faced over its 200 years or so, it continues to innovate, renew, and speak to major political matters even as its own prospective vision seems remote, unrealistic, or arguably utopian.

Finally, this rich and persistent rival modernity, angrily over-optimistic and constitutively radical and oppositional, is made for social media. For example, it is fascinating to read Marx's correspondence – newspaper articles and unpublished letters – and note how the narrative style seems to presentiment the traffic of Twitter: personalised attacks, righteous outrage, exaggeration and ad absurdum rhetorical devices, and some ad hominem flows of thought.[12] Until recently, liberalism has struggled to generate the same amount of normative energy, perhaps because of its more comfortable incumbency.[13] And, other righteous furies display none of the intellectual richness and scope of socialism. Socialism's opposition and anger engages with all aspects of public life, and it deploys concepts and terms which are the equal of its opposing dominant ideology. As such, and as we shall see in the next two chapters, socialist thinking has flourished through PSM.

Defining socialism and Marxism

> Great disunity has prevailed even in the 'socialist' camp as to what
> constitutes the essence of Marxism, and which theses it is 'permissible'
> to criticise and even reject without forfeiting the right to the title of
> 'Marxist'.[14]

> The term 'Marxism' conceals an immense conflict going on between
> different claimants to the Marxist tradition … If we move from
> intellectual to political and social movements, the conflict is even
> more obvious.[15]

What's in a name?

These observations, made by Georg Lukács and E.P. Thompson, who
themselves encapsulate opposing theoretical traditions, seem permanently
timely. In Lukács' time of writing (1910s),[16] the changing nature of Marxism
was largely a matter of Marx's own work and its revisions. It was defined
by exegetical and strategic concerns about Marx's writing. From the early
20th century, when academic and archival projects to retrieve and compose
Marx and Engels' writings took off, Marxism most centrally subsisted on a
diet of textual editing, curation, translation, and subsequent internal debates
about Marx's work: early and late phases, the relation between one text and
another, and the division of labour between him and Engels. There were
discussions of the lack of theory of state or global society and how one
might draw implications from Marx's more scattered considerations on these
matters. There were technical complexities concerning the labour theory of
value or the transformation problem. There were debates about the historical
and intellectual milieux within which Marx wrote and how his ideas fared
subsequently. And there has been a profusion of cliques and movements that
have declared themselves to represent the authentic Marxist tradition of political
thinking and action: vanguard parties, intellectual sects, mass movements,
organised labour, militias, guerrilla movements, and political parties.

In the early decades of the 20th century, being a Marxist meant holding
a conviction that one had the correct view on Marx and Marx's view was
correct. This intellectual configuration has given Marxism a reputation
as exceptionally doctrinaire. This is surely to some degree a result of its
eponymous nature: *Marx*ism is about fealty to the thinking of Marx (and
Engels); those who follow claim to be carrying the true faith in their own
writings and political actions. There is some truth in this, although the
intensity of Marxists' monadic tendency has certainly waned as time has passed.

From the early 1900s, Marxism was sustained not only by a fealty to Marx's
own work but also a kind of passing of the baton in which specific individuals

became the bearers of orthodoxy. These individuals were sometimes political leaders, sometimes intellectuals, and sometimes both.[17] Vladimir Lenin, Leon Trotsky, Eduard Bernstein, Karl Kautsky, and Rosa Luxemburg would all be on the shortlist of this tradition of orthodox Marxist paradigm maintenance. Each made claim to be interpreting Marx properly and each also brought to Marxism new ideas, including concepts that have endured into the present. Lenin brought vanguardism, democratic centralism, and a theory of imperialism. Trotsky brought the notion of a permanent revolution and a theory of uneven and combined development. Bernstein brought a non-(violent) revolutionary politics to socialism. Kautsky (in conversation with Lenin) brought a conceptualisation of the 'agrarian question': how peasant agriculture was impacted by the rise of capitalism. Rosa Luxemburg brought political arguments concerning syndicalism and the mass strike as well as her own rather complex theory of imperialism.

There is a great deal to unpack here. We only need acknowledge the historical patterning at work: the inheritance of a Marxist canon by leaders of political struggles and/or intellectual movements in which theoretical correctness generated orthodoxy. There is a particular intellectual sociology at work here in which Marxism was sustained as a project to identify the correct political programme during a period in Europe's history in which socialism seemed possible and even for some inevitable.[18]

Marx's own work was not doctrinaire. It changed over time; it dealt with a great many things at different 'levels' and with different tones of voice. He was certainly a democrat[19] and, although relentlessly critical, also happy to keep open the political possibilities that the overthrow of capitalism might lead to.[20] If *Capital* displayed theoretical complexity and abstraction, *The Eighteenth Brumaire of Louis Bonaparte* showed an attentiveness to concrete political situations and the agonies of judgement. Biographies of Marx commonly recognise that he was often unsatisfied with his work, distracted by specific literatures or issues that were not clearly relevant to the project at hand, and left manuscripts unfinished or hurriedly completed. He had a constant desire to revise what he had written. As a result, the notion of a Marxist 'line' is as much a product of a bounded intellectual sociology of the early 20th century as it is Marx's own intellectual predisposition or writing.

Marxism and socialism

Apocryphally, and in response to the use of the term 'Marxist' by a group of French socialists, Marx asserted (according to Engels) 'if they are Marxists then I myself am not a Marxist'.[21] With some interpretive licence, one might read this statement as an expression of Marx's own uncertainty as to how his own writing related to the epithet of socialism. In his remarkably detailed magnum opus, Kolakowski sets out how Marx's writing was deeply invested in the intellectual currents that flowed around him, not least the socialist writers that had emerged from the 1830s.[22] It is evident that Marx was as cynical – or even hostile – to some currents to socialist thought as he was supportive of them.

There is too much equivocation, complexity, and tension between Marxism and socialism simply to assume that Marxism is some kind of parsimonious subset in a larger socialist circle of a Venn diagram. We need to explore in a little detail how these two major traditions of left-wing political thought relate to each other in order that we can proceed with sufficient clarity to classify and analyse the content of different Marxist and socialist discourses.

Studies of political ideologies tend to take socialism over Marxism as their focus. There are two principal reasons for this. Firstly, 'socialism' sets out a broader field of ideas. Although Marx's writings might be seen as primus inter pares within socialist thought, they do not constitute the exclusive source code for all socialisms. Secondly – and we shall return to this in the next chapter – socialism serves as a more apposite term to frame a political ideology. Marxism seems more a *theory*[23] and socialism an *ideology*. The former has premises, axioms, logics, and analytical terminology. Socialism is more normative, codified into policy, strategically focused, disciplinary and mobilisational in relation to its followers.[24] In short, socialism looks more like a political ideology because it is more openly political: concerned with authoritative power, legitimacy, contestation, and justice.

If Marxism largely operates within a broader socialist ideology, we should recognise the main currents in the latter in order to achieve some clarity as to how these two master terms of left-wing political thought relate to each other. Socialism was a term coined in the 1830s, before Marx was writing. It developed as a result of two cardinal political forces: the French Revolution of 1789 and capitalist industrialisation.[25]

The French Revolution (and its consequent instability, further insurrections, and changing forms of government until the Second Republic) posed to socialists (as well as some liberals) the possibility of a certain kind of modern politics, previously largely unknown. That possibility was based in the notion that radical political rupture could create a systemic transformation in a country's political economy. Incumbent forms of inherited power, land ownership, religious belief, and 'tradition' might be eradicated through condensed moments of purposeful and violent rebellion. The political phenomenon that would come to be labelled modernity might be achieved through a combination of correct vision and force of will. In this scenario, a revived sense of political agency was identified: the masses, *le peuple*. There is a great deal to unpack in the French Revolution and its impact on political ideology. Proto-socialisms[26] emerged within the National Assembly and political groupings, and they were most prominently manifested in the

Paris Commune at the end of the Second Empire. It is from the French Revolution that we receive the political coordinates of 'Left' and 'Right', even if they have proven to be rather malleable over time.[27]

Early socialist ideas were constructed of political scenarios in which some form of mass political agency (usually led by socialist intellectuals) might overwhelm or overthrow traditional, stagnant, and conservative political orders in order to replace them with more equitable, popular, and accountable forms of governance. Although the Revolution galvanised republican, liberal, and bourgeois politics as well, it also allowed socialists to envision a political prospective in which the masses might come to remake industrial capitalism into something radically changed or even overthrown.[28] It also bequeathed to the state a possibly expanded role in matters of completing socialist projects, an étatisme that in no small part created tensions with the more plebian notion of a people taking historical agency to themselves.

It was only from the 1830s that capitalist industrialisation fully took on a mass proletarianisation through large-scale industrial concentration, and this had massive social effects in those countries where industrialisation was taking place.[29] This was not simply about 'dark satanic mills' but also mining, railways, chemicals, metallurgy, port work, and the construction of urban slums. Socialism drew together a loose set of hostile responses to large-scale industrialisation and the impoverishing proletarianisation that it generated. There was a concern with loss of community and alienation. There was a fear that moral and religious values would be destroyed. There was a concern with the environmental destruction that industry would create, including a worry that people would become divorced from any connection to nature. There was a concern that new industrial bosses were not paying workers fairly. And there was a concern that large-scale employment would create a mass of de-socialised individuals who suffered a lack of social stability and education.

Socialist ideas fed into Marx's writing and activism. And, of course, socialist traditions of political thought flourished after his death. Inevitably, Marxism and socialism overlap and intertwine, sharing as they do an intellectual faith in the supersession of capitalism, a normative focus on the masses, and a shared language about exploitation and poverty. But socialism, as the broader and more ideologically fit-for-purpose tradition, remains the more pervasive ideological reference. From here on, we shall use the term 'socialism' to denote socialist ideas including those in a Marxist tradition; but we shall use a capitalised 'Socialism' to identify non-Marxist socialist ideas. This distinction, we shall see, is quite pertinent to the construction of socialist ideas within PSM. Having established this nomenclature, we can make a sketch that shows how this intertwining played out through the post-Second World War period. Again, this is not only important in itself but also a requirement for any comprehension of current understandings of where Marxism and socialism are in the present.

After the Second World War, (non-Marxist) Socialism expanded and mutated into multi-party electoral systems throughout Europe. This form of institutionalisation – in no small part coloured by the Cold War – brought Socialist discourse into competitive elections as revolutionary communist parties and movements dwindled or were elbowed out of the Labour Party. 'Socialism' served as a positional marker in relation to other parties or individuals. Strategising for a society in which capitalism is superseded became more mantra than active political concern. Socialism shifted towards social democracy, the welfare state, progressive taxation, and corporatism.[30]

As Socialism's expansive set of political ideas attained a broad constituency of support in many European countries and, as a result, instituted itself into the heart of post-war governance, Marxism also experienced what seems retrospectively like a period in the sunshine. From the late 1950s, Marxist thought achieved a considerable presence, not so much among revolutionary leaderships and intelligentsias as it did among humanities and social science university departments.[31] In part as a reaction to Stalinism (and the sense of revolutionary pessimism that this bequeathed), Marxist academics developed a remarkably vibrant, diverse, and complex genre of political theory. Eurocommunism in continental Europe and the New Left in Britain each represented veritable intellectual movements. These 'New Lefts' tended to eschew Leninist vanguardist party structures in favour of more movement-like and unstructured political activisms.[32]

Space prohibits a comprehensive review of post-war intellectual Marxism. We can note selectively (and subjectively) the major thinkers: Georg Lukács, Louis Althusser, António Gramsci (posthumously), Nicos Poulantzas, Ralph Miliband, and Perry Anderson. These writers brought Marxist theory into contemporary discussions of culture, state theory, the analytical relationships between economic structure and socio-political form, and American power. Many others derived from Marx's works analyses of culture,[33] literature,[34] development in the post-colonial world,[35] crisis,[36] and the origins of capitalism.[37] The move into the academy and the broadening of research interest also led to a waning interest in Marxian economics and value theory.[38]

This flourishing of Marxist thought influenced other theoretical traditions. The dour social visions of the Frankfurt School borrowed from Marx,[39] as did the often equally pessimistic Dependency School that theorised poverty in the post-colonial world. Second-wave feminist theory also relied on analyses of the household's articulation to wage labour and accumulation. More broadly, a range of post-colonial nationalisms (most of them authoritarian) drew on Marx's conceptual language to develop ideologies of state based in radical nationalisms.[40] The extent to which these hybridities can properly be called Marxist or even socialist has been intensely debated.

From the late 1970s, socialism's (now in lower-case broader mode) intellectual and political presence alike dwindled through the West. In Britain, the decline of a 'Left' sect within the Labour Party and the rise of postmodern theoretical traditions relocated socialism into an increasingly moderated and contingent position. That is: socialism became a point of reference rather than the master framing of political thought on the Left. By the end of the 1980s, socialism was under siege, not only from a postmodern 'incredulity towards metanarratives'[41] but also a sense that the working class was no longer a historical agency in the sense previously understood[42] and that the end of Soviet communism had settled great ideological debate for good. In the university, 'radical' politics was increasingly articulated through Foucauldian language, liberal optimism was in full flush, and increasingly media-savvy Left-liberal parties such as New Labour moderated the bandwidth of electoral socialism. Bonefeld et al summarise this downturn thus:

> throughout the 1980s ... crisis merely intensified: the resurgence of liberalism and the 'New Right', the accommodation of socialist and social democratic parties to a 'realistic' monetarism and – at the close of the decade – the crumbling of socialist regimes in the East. Marxism seemed to become at best unfashionable and, at worst, outdated.[43]

However, the consensus-building project of the end of history did not last long and in the midst of debt crises in post-colonial and post-Soviet states as well as the rise of the War on Terror, global social justice movements emerged that rekindled socialist ideas, albeit in a range of hybrid forms that also borrowed heavily from anarchism, communitarianism, and a strand of liberalism that advocated a radical form of human rights advocacy. The languages of imperialism, exploitation, inequality and injustice, internationalism, and oppression were sustained through social justice movements that drew on socialist traditions and, in the process, sustained them. Marxism was not a central component in this remaking of socialist politics.[44] Nevertheless, and bringing us up to the present, Marxist thinking has gradually established a place for itself. As noted earlier, this can be seen in the inauguration of new journals and conferences. And, as we shall see, it has contributed significantly to the energies within PSM.

Thus far, we have suggested that Marxism and Socialism enjoy an awkward cohabitation in which the former has a particular theoretical grounding and the latter a more ecumenical conceptual arrangement that is primarily driven by its normative hostility towards capitalism. They share a radical position in their conviction that capitalism is not the only alternative and that the alternative worth advocating is based in some form of mass politics. But, beyond this premise, the overlaps between the two start to stretch. Just as we start this section with Marx disavowing his own name in light of French socialist declarations, we might end with the observation offered by Stuart Hall that Socialists consider Marxism a problem.[45]

This characterisation might seem like an exaggeration. Surely in light of the ideological dominance of the 'free market' and the political Right, Socialism and Marxism both have modern-radical origins that give them much to align over. But, as we shall see, this is an appearance not a substance. When looking in detail at ideological constructions, deeper theoretical concepts matter. Furthermore, we can readily see how distinct Marxism and Socialism are as traditions of political thought if we spend a little time looking properly at what Marx had to say about capitalism and its supersession. This is the task of the next section.

Marxism as theory

Marxism is based in distinct and specific foundations. We shall set them out as concisely as possible here but we need to set out some caveats in the first place. Firstly, any summary account of Marxist theory will be inadequate, mainly because a great deal is still debated and reinterpreted. Secondly, our account has its own selectivity and prioritisation. My own understanding of Marx is very strongly based in *Capital I*, which is his most completed theoretical statement. *Capital*[46] is also the best source to understand most clearly how Marxism deploys a distinct analytical language which is largely absent from Socialist ideology unless incorporated in ways that degrade the original concept. Most clearly in *Capital*, Marx was endeavouring to show how his theorisation was holistic: his understating of value, the commodity, money, surplus, exploitation, wage labour, alienation, prices, and all of the other major considerations made no sense unless taken as a complex and densely integrated whole founded on a strong conceptualisation of materialism.[47] This is why Marx wrote of a *critique* of political economy, not critical political economy: ideas like state and market as separate institutional configurations would not have made sense to him: both state and economy are forms of something deeper, distinct institutional ensembles.[48]

Thirdly, this is an interpretation of Marxism. There is no escaping the fact that Marx was not always clear in his meaning and that some of his texts are at times abstruse.[49] There is a veritable cottage industry of books which seek to interpret Marx's *Capital* and this is in part a symptom of the fact that it *needs* interpretation.

Among the secondary literature on Marx's *Capital*, John Weeks' *Capital, Exploitation and Economic Crisis* offers a concise starting point that emphasises the ways in which deep analytical moves generate systemic understandings of capitalist phenomena.[50] Weeks starts with value, a phenomenon generated by labour but embodied, or made apparent, in the commodity. We immediately hit on a crucial underpinning of Marx's theory: a distinction between appearance/form and essence/abstraction.[51] In plainer language, a thing like a commodity – let's imagine a smartphone – seems an obvious or even plain object, but under an analytical eye, it is a manifestation of deeper social properties that need excavation[52] (what Marxists often call abstraction) in order to understand the full nature of the commodity.[53] The commodity is not simply a thing to be sold, bought, and used. In that latter sense, commodities have always existed. The *capitalist* commodity is a manifestation of historically specific social relations of property and labour. It is a vehicle through which a particular kind of value is generated and realised through money and consumption. And, these relations of property, labour, and profit give a very specific character to the commodity under capitalism which is not present in any other kind of society. In short, it is only at the point at which a commodity is purchased that the capitalist can realise the profit that they make from the exploitation (extraction of surplus value) of their workforce.

The commodity is an endlessly energetic seeking of profit that can only then generate further rounds of commodity production, faster and faster, always seeking to capture the consumer's disposable income. Its tangible or subjective value (what Marx among others called use value) is not what matters most. Nor is the price in itself.[54] An ITV investigation discovered that Amazon had marked 130,000 commodities in its warehouses for destruction because they were considered unsellable. Although most were new, had some use value, and were produced through labour, because they were unable to capture a consumer and realise their surplus value, they were considered absolutely valueless. The only decision was whether to burn, bury, or donate.

One might consider the Amazon example extreme, but for Marxists, it is not exceptional. Rather, it reveals the deep property of the commodity. This was a methodological procedure Marx keenly pursued. The apparent properties of the commodity – its use, price, scarcity – are all important but also impossible to understand without a foundation in their generation through wage labour. Schematically, capitalist wage labour works in the following way, according to Marxists. Workers generate value. Without labour, raw materials remain valueless. The social arrangement of labour – the means through which a society generates values that it can use and enjoy – exerts powerful and even determining influence over all other facets of social life. It involves the allocation of property and wealth, the dispositions of political power (especially the construction of state, civil society, and the economy),[55] the regimes within which people work, the organisation of households, the nature of ideology, the relation of people to the natural world, and so on.

Capitalism's social relations of labour work roughly as follows. Workers labour for capital in return for a wage. That wage is earned during a proportion of the working day, and the rest of the work done during that day is effectively taken by the capitalist, offered up for free, a transaction obscured by the wage labour relation. For example, a worker might produce enough commodities to sell for an equivalent of the day's pay over four hours but work for eight hours. So, in this case, 50 per cent of the worker's productive time is given to the capitalist.[56] This transfer takes place in an occult fashion. Because the capitalist has complete control over the workplace and wage rates, the worker is not directly aware of this form of surplus extraction – or at least not its extent. In Marx's famous simple equation: M-C-M, money (M) spent on materials, technology, and wage labour creates a commodity (C) that is valuable because of the labour embedded in it. The commodity sells at a higher price than that paid to the worker (M) and, as a result, the capitalist accrues profit: self-expanding value.[57] Thus, capitalism is based in the exploitation of wage labour. This is its essence. Workers buy commodities on the market at what is seen as a 'fair' price, but all prices contain this exploitation, this realisation of surplus value extraction. Thus, fair wages and fair prices are opaque and obscuring manifestations of a constitutive inequality.

This is why, for Marx, capitalism was based most fundamentally in the social relations of labour. Capitalism is not simply the free or competitive market but rather a social relation in which a majority are compelled to work for the owners of capital or enter into a precarious, poverty-stricken, and even hunger-filled life. Capitalist social relations are forged and enforced through the dispossession of autonomous labour and the concentration of land, money, plant, assets, and technology in the hands of capitalists.[58] On the basis of this social relation, many aspects of capitalist society might appear 'natural' or consensual. To work for a boss, to have a boss who commands one's working day, to accept that bosses are rich, that you might be dismissed from a job and have to seek whatever other job one can find … these all seem like facts of life, but for Marxists, they are the product of a rather short and unusual period in the history of humankind. And, this state of affairs will only last for as long as these social relations of property can be legitimated and enforced, even in times of crisis and rebellion.

Wage labour is, evidently, based in work for wages, and wage levels are set through a contract to work. This contract effectively puts a price on labour power: one is paid to do certain things for a certain period of time. This is formally consensual, and workers can leave employment if they wish. Employers can also dismiss labour if they wish. These are the premises that allow liberals to talk of a labour market as a broadly postitive-sum and non-coercive realm. But, once labour is employed through wage employment, it becomes a cost for capital. The absolute foundational motivation for capitalists is to get as much value out of labour as possible.[59] Workers each become individual units in a place of work, a factor of production, an expense. The nature of their work is determined by the employer. Each worker generates their wages for part of the day and then works to generate revenue for the capitalist for the rest. Labour is consumed by the capitalist in the process of generating more capital.[60]

Herein, Marxists see how the most common point of reference in mainstream economics – competition – is only fully understood as an apparent feature of the social relations of production. It is not that competition is a sham but rather that it is historically specific to the capitalist mode of production and cannot be seen as a natural, transhistorical, or self-contained social practice.[61] There are two main considerations here. Firstly, workers compete to secure employment. No one is entitled to work. In periods of low profit, workers often take pay cuts or find themselves out of work through no fault of their own. Unemployed workers have the effect of depressing wage claims because they constitute a 'reserve army' of potential labour. In these ways, competition serves to consolidate the domination of capital over labour.

But, competition also takes place between firms who act as 'hostile brothers' in relation to each other.[62] Each producer or service provider must compete with other firms in consumer markets by keeping prices low, producing and selling more, and by innovating product quality.[63] Without this, the capitalist commodity cannot secure its moment of surplus value realisation and, as a result, profit is not made and a firm will be unable to commence another round of production. It will likely go out of business. Competition between firms, then, enforces a general discipline over all capitalists in which each and all push the cost of production down and to relentlessly invest or innovate techniques of production to capture markets. Marxists see competition as a way of socialising the rivalries of individual firms. Wages in specific sectors tend to equalise, failing companies go bust, and the overall pressure of competition means that the ambient tendency is always to seek to pay workers less and make them work more.[64]

So, competition is not only about price setting, marginal utility, and Pareto optimality: the mainstays of classical economics. These phenomena may or may not apply in concrete industries or sectors. What underpins market competition within capitalism is the competition between workers creating the working fiction that labour is an aggregation in isolated individuals who are present in the eyes of capital as a unit of costs. And that competition socialises the disciplinary will of capital in general upon all individual firms on pain of bankruptcy. This is a social relation historically specific to capitalism.

Market competition is not the only general social feature generated by capitalist social relations. There are two most salient features we should note here. Firstly, capitalism has a 'growth obsession'.[65] It cannot reproduce itself over time without seeking to increase the level of production and profit. At every point in the production and consumption circuit of capitalism, the motivation is to increase the velocity of commodities, the quantity of output, the extraction of surplus value. A firm that has a content workforce, a familiar and well-used set of technologies, and a comfortable level of profit will perish as others deploy new technology, push the wage level down, increase output in the seeking of new markets. For Marxists, capitalism has a uniquely 'progressive' property in its restlessness, its willingness to abandon traditional mores, its desire to bring the world into a single energised state. Nevertheless – and in the literature certainly the main focus of attention – capitalism's relentless expansionism is seen as socially destructive, imperialistic, chaotic, and exploitative. This appreciation and despair is not a sign of incommensurate analysis; it is the expression of Marxism's 'agonistic' recognition that capitalism is both modernising and appalling in its DNA: 'Accumulation at one pole is, therefore, at the same time accumulation of misery, the torment of labour ... at the other pole'.[66]

Secondly, capitalism is prone to crises of its own making. The internal dynamics of crisis are complex and we cannot deal with them in any detail here. What we can acknowledge in our brief construction of Marxism as a theory is that competing capitals can generate moments of overproduction, and drastic declines in rates of profitability.[67] Neither of these properties is external to the nature of capitalism, even if government strategies can ameliorate or exacerbate these tendencies.

In summary, capitalism's deep constitution in the social relations of labour generates a political economy defined by historically specific forms of competition, growth, and crisis. But, none of these properties is stable. Indeed, for Marxists, the point of politics is that none of these properties will last and so the challenge is to set out something better. This is because all aspects of capitalist social relations are contested, and contested in a particular way. Capitalism's exploitations, instabilities, and desocialisations are unsuccessfully imposed on working classes that express highly varied forms of resistance to the rule of capital. In the hubris of Marx and Engels' manifesto rhetoric: 'the history of all hitherto existing society is the history of class struggles'.[68] In more academic language, the most important constitutive instability of capitalism lies in its inability fully to dominate the labouring classes that it produces and puts to work and that – as a result of its own failings and the agency of working classes – capitalism will eventually relinquish to a proletarian-led remaking of social relations in which work and sociability will be wrought away from the privations of capital.

Marx wrote about many other things. And, he did not write about many things much: nationalism, the state, the global political economy, gender, and so on. But, the previous section sketches the core of Marx's political economy, his most detailed and mature work. We will progress, recognising the following core features of a Marxist theory of capitalism:

- The foundation of society and its prospects is the creation of value. This is done by people working: applying thought and effort cooperatively to sets of resources.

- Capitalism is defined by the coercive establishing of a large number of people with very little property and an increasingly concentrated group of people who own capital.
- The formal freedoms of labour are underpinned by the inequalities that systemic differentiations in property ownership create.
- All labour is based in an antagonism between labour and capital as capital endeavours to extract as much surplus value as possible from labour and to retain as much of this for its own purposes.
- Capitalism also competes with itself within various forms of market competition.
- The full potentials of human nature are denied by capitalism's exploitations and alienations.
- Capitalism's growth obsession and competitiveness lead it both to impose mass hardship on people and to push forward the frontiers of productivity, technology, and in some degree well-being.
- The state is not a distinct institution from the economy but a form of political authority which – in varied ways – works to ensure that capitalist accumulation remains stable and healthy.
- The historical pattering of capitalist accumulation and politics is endlessly complex but defined by an ineliminable thread of class struggle.

Marxist ideas within political ideologies must, by definition, bear some connection to the theoretical orientations set out in this section. This does not require any formalised correspondence metric in which some ideological traditions are more Marxist than others. The relation between theory and political ideology is far messier and, ultimately, it is unhelpful to proceed with an unchanging truth standard. Although detailed theoretical statements are naturally rare in more political and ideological discourse, an anchoring in labour exploitation, the agency of the working classes, capitalism being responsible for its own crises, the inescapable inequalities of capitalist property relations, and a belief that only a revolutionary change can usher in a fully humane and socialised modernity should be the hill upon which Marxists die on. To relegate any of these foundations to a contingent status is to abandon Marxism for something else, something most likely within the socialist tradition of theorising. Marx's work has served as the source code for a multitude of historically contextual intellectual projects, many of which display salient differences between each other, even if they claim to speak on behalf of the same ideological tradition.

We need to keep these coordinates in mind in the chapters of Part II. We will see how socialist proto-ideologies make reference to Marx and Marxism, and they deploy arguments and vocabularies that draw on Marxism's lexicon. There is occasional name dropping of Marx, Engels, Lenin, and others. There is, as we have recognised in this chapter, an ambiguity in relation to where a Marxist political ideology finishes and a broader socialist one begins. Furthermore, there are grey areas in relation to how socialist political ideologies also draw upon the most vague and moderate discourses of 'Left' and, more specifically, social justice discourse. It is only through a reasonably sound and parsimonious understanding of Marxist theory, Marxism as a tradition of political thought, and socialist discourse that we can have any hope of locating the prolix and volatile ideational work of PSM within an interpretive framework.

The Left

'Left' represents the vaguest of political terms that has some socialist connotation. It is a term that does not have any fixed ideological mooring but rather represents a direction or posture. Retrospectively, historians of political ideas identify a 'Left Hegelianism' that interprets Hegel in a manner positive towards democratic reform. By any modern standard, Left Hegelianism would simply be liberal democracy. In post-revolutionary France, 'Left' identified the place in the National Assembly where republican representatives sat. Although the term comes to associate with democratic reform and a generally redistributive politics, it does not accrue a clear conceptual language and is mainly used relativistically, both over time and between different political positions. One decade's 'Left' might look quite different to another's. The politics of the moderate Fabian left in the 1960s might now seem like a fairly 'radical' Left in the UK's present day. Each country might have an 'extreme' or 'hard' Left as well as a liberal Left. It might even have a 'loony' Left.

'Left' might be used in varied ways to identify positions on environmentalism, rights, monarchy, or development aid.[69] Instantiations of these commitments are varied and positional, which is to say that they require a 'centre' or 'Right' against which to identify. 'Left' in one place and time can be quite different to a 'Left' elsewhere in part because it requires a centre and Right politics against which to define itself. Indeed, there might be a 'Left' within avowedly liberal and conservative political movements.[70] 'Left' is generally understood as a reformist politics: a way to 'civilise' or give a 'human face' to the regulation of capitalism. Left is a spectrum term.

Liberals, Greens, and social democrats can be 'Left'. There are groups labelled or identifying as 'Left' within major political parties. In the UK, *The Mirror* and *The Guardian* are 'Left' newspapers, even if their content hardly betrays any clear and consistent socialist content. In *What's Left?*, Nick Cohen says 'you know the Left when you see it' and sets out an argument that it has lost its way in a morass of liberal moral relativism.[71] In his meticulous analysis of Britain's political economy, Andrew Hindmoor asks again *What's Left Now?* and, in the process of identifying forms of redistribution and equality that are often missed by the 'dour' political Left, he implicitly shows how broad 'Left' is.[72] The Left might connect to any political position critical of 'neoliberalism' and it might be present in any form of fiscal redistribution. Equally, Marius Ostrowski declares that 'the left often come back to a simple general rule: fight for those without and fight against those with', an amply inclusive definition but also one that runs a significant risk of running into the claims of other political ideologies.[73] Owen Jones' analysis of Corbynism and the Left also adopts this moveable signification: not concerned to define 'Left', he uses the term situationally to identify a Labour Left, Left MPs, and Left activists, all of which seem worthy of some distinctions and definitions.[74] Chantal Mouffe's *For a Left Populism* uses the term 'Left' with considerable latitude: against neoliberalism, Syriza, or Corbynite politics, a democratic revivalism, some form of egalitarianism.[75]

The term Left is common currency precisely because of its vagueness and moveability. We will come across it in the next section. What we can recognise here is that, although it is useful as a directional indication, it does not have the requisite conceptual stability to allow us to use it analytically.

Social justice

There is another component to the Left that deserves separate consideration because it poses a specific challenge to our understanding of socialism. Since the early 1990s, and emerging out of diverse mobilisations against neoliberalism, a politics of struggle, resistance, indigeneity, and identity has emerged. Most notably after the global social fora started to be convened, global social justice has become a common reference for those on the Left. It is not like the redistributionist and reformist Left sketched in the earlier section. It does seek to look beyond capitalism. But, its relationship to socialism and Marxism is not entirely straightforward. Let us unpick a little.

The global social justice movement is not founded in a revolutionary critique of capitalism. Rather, it is based in a critique of *neoliberalism*. This is not simply a matter of semantic tidying up. Neoliberalism might be understood as a variant of capitalism, one that is oriented towards a laissez-faire market, deregulation, financialisation, strong state enforcement of property rights, an open global economy, privatisation, and the disciplining of labour. It might be caricatured as a particularly 'nasty' capitalism. Social justice movements tend to focus on the nastiness of neoliberalism more than they develop a critique of capitalism per se. This leads social justice movements to focus on two key things: 'the West' and transnational capital.

The West might mean various things: transnational corporations, America, a roughly figured 'Westernity' that is a culturally arrogant liberalism. Resisting Western power is a major component of social justice movements. It has led to critiques of 'Eurocentrism', imperialism, and racism. It might argue that globalisation is a smokescreen for Western power projection or that transnational companies destroy cultures and communities. Transnational capital might take the form of international companies or global finance and in each case – often rehabilitating imagery originally established by dependency theory schools of development in the 1970s and 1980s – they are dedicated to the impoverishing of Global South labour forces and the extraction of profit back to their Western headquarters.

These foci oriented social justice movements around culture, indigeneity, and political identity: modes of contrast against the West. Explicit references to class were not expunged from social justice discourse, but they tended to be defined as ancillary: conjoined to other categorisations that either had parity or dominance over class. These categorisations were defined by nation, ethnicity, gender, or race. To use a term that became common currency within social justice movements, class is experienced *through* race, gender, and so on.

Social justice discourse generates a radical and critical attitude towards capitalism, certainly. But its relationship towards socialism and Marxism is unstable. It draws from its antipathy towards the West, neoliberalism, and Eurocentrism an image of political struggle that is intersectional. Intersectionality frames the nature of oppression as sited in individuals who embody recombinant oppressions, one of which is – *or might be* – class. Intersectionality might refer to a poor black working-class woman. Or it might refer to a gay Latino man with a postgraduate qualification. The multiple oppressions of intersectionality do not make any prioritisation of class, either empirically or analytically. As we have seen, the entire edifice of Marxism is based not only on a recognition that classes exist, it is based in a set of theoretical steps – a concrete abstraction – that pose class as the difference that makes a difference, the historically peculiar and universal property of capitalism.[76]

If social justice discourse derives from a hostility towards neoliberalism and the West, and it seeks its agencies of liberation in intersectional modes of oppression in which class is possibly present but not prioritised, then it orients the normativity of social justice politics in a way that is also distinct from Marxism and also many Socialist traditions. This might be summarised as a focus on marginalisation as much as exploitation. This is not to say that social justice movements do away with a concern with exploitation; it is rather that they also treat matters of acceptance and recognition as equally important. Civic and cultural *rights* discourse is evoked to support communities that are marginalised and/or oppressed because of their ethnicity, sexuality, disability, and so on. In this regard, social justice movements can overlap with a Left liberalism that has as its telos a market society in which non-discrimination, equal opportunities, and a multicultural mode of governance lock in an equality of individual rights against the prejudices of the powerful.

If social justice politics condemns Western capitalists, it also condemns 'white privilege', some forms of masculinity, heteronormativity, and some form of 'coloniality'. None of these adversaries are defined through class analysis and indeed might define some working-class people as oppressors. A culturalist language might be deployed to create categories of injustice: white folks and black folks, the obviously overstretched and essentialising categorisation of black and minority ethnic people, or Westerner.

Perhaps the dominant trope within this universe of Western neoliberal power, marginalised identities, exploitation, and intersectionality is decoloniality. This is not a well-defined term, but in essence, it suggests that the deep cultural and epistemic modes of colonial thought persist in the present day, erasing other ways of thinking and socialising, reproducing the domination of the West in the post-colonial world. Decoloniality tends to trivialise the winning of independence and it elides historical change into 'the colonial present'. This historiography is based in a principle of continuity: that modes of Western dominance persist or even strengthen and consolidate, reproducing a 'colonial' presence in post-colonies.

Social justice politics has become a mainstay of left-wing mobilisation. It possesses a considerably more radical world view than the 'traditional' redistributionist and reformist Socialist Left. It has drawn on the languages of socialism and it cleaves to a vision in which capitalism is not tinkered with but transformed, a transformation articulated through a struggle against neoliberalism. It shares with socialism as a broad tradition, then, a radical agenda of change. It sees capitalism or neoliberalism as irredeemably unjust. But it does not frame injustice through a theory of class and in its concerns with recognition and rights, it overlaps with liberal justice thinking.

Socialism (with a capital S) is a strong political ideology that bases itself in an egalitarian communalism that seeks to transform capitalism, which it sees as constitutively socially deleterious and impoverishing. It does not base itself on a theory of class as much as a more encompassing set of ideas about community, justice, and education. It is sufficiently broad to encompass a class language and most certainly will express a political sympathy with the working masses, but their place in the political imaginaries that Socialism cleaves to is unfixed. Marxism – the dominant theoretical engine of socialist ideas – cohabits and overlaps imperfectly with Socialism. It is more exacting and parsimonious in its problematisation of capitalism and it insists on a specific historic agency in the working class. Some forms of Socialism are not Marxist. We will use the term socialism to denote an ideological tradition that includes, albeit rather messily, Marxism and Socialism.

We have recognised that, whatever the nuances between Marxism and Socialism might be, they are identified as part of the Left and the Left is certainly the most familiar reference used to encompass socialist ideas. We argued that the notion of Left is not sufficiently robust to allow us to deploy it analytically. Rather, it serves as a mobile and relative signification that is strongly contextual, to the degree that some might even speak of a Conservative Left. Within Left politics in the present, we identified a social justice-intersectionality identity politics that has generated a strong political aesthetic of radicalism and a highly critical attitude towards (a certain kind of) capitalism. But, we noted that the mainstay of this injustice-identity tradition is not Marxist and only partially situates itself within a socialist tradition, bearing in mind that it also encompasses a certain kind of radical rights liberalism. Whatever the merits of these categorisations, they do serve to equip us with a certain kind of categorising clarity that will be necessary in our discussion of socialist ideological work on PSM. Aware of the fast and loose use of language that social media enjoys, this clarity will help us not get lost in the fog of labelling, a practice that is at the heart of social media discourse.

The political moods of socialism

I have used a little licence to keep one core aspect of Marxism and much socialism back in order to segue into this final section. Marx and his epigones have frequently focused on the relation between theory and practice, that is, between the analytical ideas posed by Marxism and their relation to forms of political mobilisation. Outside the doctrinaire habits of Stalinism, socialists reject the dualistic model of formalised and abstract theorisation set up outside of social contestation as a kind of external truth that then leads to questions of how society might be engineered to correspond to properly specified theoretical positions.[77] With varying degrees of commitment and success, socialists wish to understand the theoretical and conceptual tools at hand not only to achieve clarity concerning the nature of capitalism; they also wish to bring something of these ideas into the way politics is done: the strategies, values, communities, and imagery of struggle and contestation. A well-trodden aphorism: 'The philosophers have only interpreted the world, in various ways. The point, however, is to change it'.[78]

Marxism enters into concrete political debate and practice through its ideological forms. As we shall see in the next chapter, political ideologies are 'thought and fought': the source codes of big ideas and great writers are transposed into the heat of politics itself. We can now finish this chapter with a sense of how socialist ideas and theories have manifested in more ideological form. That is, how does socialism look as a way of understanding politics? All political ideologies have a kind of 'form' or set of predispositions that are partially derived from their concepts and logics but also from their normative attitude towards politics. There is always a degree of affect and aesthetic in any public-facing political discourse.

A socialist normativity

As we have seen, socialist traditions rest in the premise that a different and better form of society is possible. This premise might be weakly foregrounded (at the end of a long struggle) and very likely only vaguely sketched, but its presence is necessary if socialism is to resemble something distinct from liberalism's own justice thinking.[79] If the problem is capitalism in itself, then institutional reform, new modes of regulation, and policy making will, at best, briefly moderate the pernicious processes immanent within capitalism. This predisposition gives socialist ideology a besieged quality. Socialists consider their ideas to be so radical and/or heretical that they struggle to get recognition and when they do, they are subjected to all sorts of calumny. Liberals can propose regulatory redistribution and be met with 'reasonable' discussion – a fiscal reform or a change in inheritance laws, for example – and possibly affect the thinking or manifesto pledges of an electable party. Inasmuch as socialists engage in policy reform, they blend into a politics that accepts capitalism's foundations, and they engage with 'the Left' or 'progressives' that have no interest in revolutionary change. In the process, socialist properties are diluted or lost. There are two repercussions here that are relevant to our review of socialism's normativity.

Firstly, socialism's historiographical autobiography is founded on a sense of being 'out of time'. That is, if socialism reveals an essential truth about capitalism that proposes we construct a different society, saying these things in a time when capital is so dominant tends to generate the effect of holding to a conviction that has no clear concrete and present point of reference. It is for this reason that some characterise socialist ideology as either millennial or utopian. Socialism either seeks out a rupture or sublime moment in politics that cannot be prefigured but is necessarily coming, or, socialism is a way to imagine that 'another world is possible', a world that we can imagine through ideal thinking, one that looks appealing but which has no recognisable place in our understanding of the present.

Secondly, this 'out of time' sensibility does lead some socialists (and fewer Marxists) to engage with reformist politics and as they do so, sectarianisms often flourish. For socialists, 'reformist' is a dirty word. Socialists that join a policy think tank or a major political party are, for some, seen as having given up. They stop struggling against and start negotiating with the ruling class. Within this political milieu, different socialist groups identify in part according to a degree of intellectual and political purity, a value which can be held above efficacy or the achievement of concrete change if one insists that socialism's curse, so to speak, is to be right in a time when the world is ruled by those who will one day be on the wrong side of history.

Thirdly, socialism's totalising rejection of capitalism leads it to see how, in order for one political problem to be addressed, *all* problems have to be addressed. An outcome of this is that, although socialists may express lukewarm positivity about particularities – policies, statements, reforms, institutions – they are always couched in a broader sense of discomfiture. That is, even if a political event seems in its own context praiseworthy, it is also limited, contradictory, or perhaps a sop for 'real' change. Consequently, socialist discourse is endlessly dissatisfied. It doesn't know where to begin because almost everything is wrong. Any specific moment of progress is nothing without many other accompanying forms of change.

The triptych vision of socialism

Engels suggests that Marx's work is roughly a combination of German historicism, British political economy, and French socialism.[80] Although one might question the degree to which this fully holds up as a way to understand Marx's work, it does connect Marxism to a clutch of understandings of political change that flow through both Marx's writings and the writings on many other Socialists. We can briefly review these three sources here in order to draw out how socialism has defined for itself a distinctive world vision, a way of seeing that derives from the ideational resources set out in the previous section and which feed saliently into its ideological constructions.

In histories of political ideas, German historicism is associated most closely with a progressive historiography. That is, cyclical and homeostatic notions of history are replaced by understandings of change in which immanent and progressive forces propel complex and profound changes in a singular direction that leads to a state in which some form reasoned modernisation is realised: from 'the circular to the spiral form'.[81] This historiographic orientation was certainly present in Marx's writing: 'the great civilising influence of capital' that drew the world together, gave people a full sense of their social being, and that enabled technological domain over nature.[82] It was also present in the Socialisms of his time and after. For Marx, progress was driven by the class struggle in which capitalists sought to innovate in search of endless accumulation and workers increasingly pushed capitalists beyond their own limits. This is often seen as a dialectic in which forms of antagonism or opposition drive a more general process of change that has an endpoint or telos.[83]

The past reveals how little there was to live for before capitalism, the present shows us how hard life is under capitalism, and the future is revealed to us as a kind of prevailing over the travails of the present. More than any other ideological tradition, Marxism insists that a better world is possible. Key to its realisation is serious ideological work, mobilisation, and 'struggle': tenacious political action against predominant forms of power embedded in property and the state. However, the progressivist historiography of socialism is not that easy. Indeed, for some, socialism might be seen as a political tradition of doom and gloom. Socialism might be trapped in a permanent despair at the present and it might, as a result, only be able to see how things are immanently to get worse. This temporal framing tempts some into something of a historiography of despair in which the totalising rule of capital is made a permanent present, an endless seriality of exploitations, environmental disasters, political crises, and war. Inasmuch as this dour historic sensibility connects to Marxism, it is through variations on another familiar historiographic tradition: the tragedy.[84] In short form, this understanding of progress reconciles itself to the fact that the disruption and privations intrinsic to capitalist accumulation also create the conditions within which technological progress, economic growth, and social change take place: 'something very important is lost at every stage where humanity "progresses"'.[85] Strictly speaking, this is not tragedy in the classic sense[86] but rather a recognition that there is a kind of paradox or irony in the nature of change: crisis creates resistance and rebellion; capitalism digs its own grave.

What Engels meant by British political economy was the development of systemic thinking about the economy and economic policy. The works of Smith, Malthus, Ricardo, Bentham, and Mill each and all construct images of a *systemic* political economy. Indeed, these authors and others in correspondence with them originate the phenomenon of 'the economy' as a national entity that has systemic properties which are amenable to scientific analysis to promote growth and/or reduce poverty:[87] specific policy contentions formed around demography, trade, technology, and money to realise systemic thinking about economic matters.

Marx wrote within this milieu. He was most clearly influenced by Ricardo's mode of abstraction in relation to value and engaged with Smith (in relation to primitive accumulation) and Bentham (in relation to bourgeois visions of the market economy) among others. Marx took on the conceptual language and epistemology of political economy: its focus on relations between prices, factors of production, and the source of value and the ways in which these relations constructed systemic entities. Marx understood 'that the world is a unity and that things within it are what they are because of their place in the whole'.[88] But he also profoundly rejected the premises of all major thinkers to such a degree that, as we have noted, the entire discipline of political economy was, he argued, based in erroneous logic.

The 'British political economy' influence on socialist political ideology pushed it towards meliorist system-thinking. The political economy of the late 19th century was, for Marx and most socialists, the world view of the elite or bourgeoisie and, as such, it combined characteristics of reformist zeal that might seem radical with a deep commitment to property rights and 'free' labour. From Hume onwards, 'classical' political economy was defined by socialists as a form of conservative and capitalist ideology.

Once one defines one's area of study and debate as the 'capitalist mode of production', the more reformist discussion of liberalism or cautionary arguments of conservatism seem like nothing so much as rearranging the deckchairs on the Titanic. Systemic and/or revolutionary change (however defined) become the master-norm by which all other developments are measured.

Thirdly, French socialist thought brought into political discussion the crowd as an agency. The masses or proletariat were conceptualised as antagonists against an incumbent and oppressive elite, whether the latter were landed, monarchical, mercantile, or industrial. A certain kind of historic choreography was established within French socialist thought after the Revolution: a people and a ruling class in which the former had both the forces of history and the moral case and the latter the wealth and power. Both the terms 'bourgeois' and 'proletarian' were deployed in this tradition and popularised in Marx. Marxist ideological projects are necessarily conditioned by this choreography, both analytically and normatively. In relation to the former, there is a prioritisation of the (potential) mass agency of the people, the masses, the working class. This prioritisation is based in the premise that mass agency is most likely to challenge capitalism and seek its supersession with something better. In relation to the latter, there is a normative core to Marxism that the major injustice or antagonism within capitalism resides in the dominance of the bourgeoisie over the proletarians. Amid all the debates[89] about the nature of this structuring domination and inequity resides a normative purpose to advocate on behalf of the masses.

Socialist affect

Socialism is fixed within a historical vision of modern progress, an understanding of history that is systemic and open to conscious change and an identification of the mass working poor as the historic agent of that change. This generates a heroic historiography. It understands history as essentially progressive, politics as a project of emerging rational agency and control, and a condensation of epochal change in the rise of the proletariat as a class that will do away with the limitations of capitalist dominance. It is well recognised that this heroic or optimistic prospective was profoundly undermined between 1914 and 1945 and it has hardly undergone a significant renaissance since, even if one is generous about the 'spirit of 68'. As a result, socialist historiography has something of an 'obstetric' quality.[90] That is to say, being a socialist means living a life in expectation (or perhaps trepidation) of profound rupture. This has diverse normative relays. It might mean seeking out the green shoots of a new world in the present, carrying out heavy ideological work to make a case that these shoots augur in a rupture in capitalism that creates the conditions of possibility for socialism. It might mean focusing on the 'morbid symptoms' of the present, portraying the world as in the midst of an indeterminate period that requires socialists to mobilise and capture the future direction of politics away from other retrogressive forces such as populism or fascism.[91] Or, it might evoke a kind of melancholia in which socialists are destined to roam the world armed with critique but not prognosis, knowing that their cherished political future will not take place in their lifetimes and that history only tells tales of defeat.[92]

In all of these cases, the impact on socialist political ideology is to generate a kind of parallax. History and its expectant agency of revolutionary change run along two disconnected pathways, observing their own time, one of present dominance and one of innate potential.

In summary, we can connect Marxist theory to a socialist attitude towards history. Based in systemic concrete abstractions concerning capitalism, it sees politics as a dialectic form of progress, defined by a hopeful expectation that eschews the reformism of the Left, acknowledges the achievements of the bourgeoisie, despairs at the wreckage left by the very same, and sustains a faith in mass democratic working-class agency.

Conclusion

Recognising that socialism is a complex and often fraught tradition of political thinking, we have taken stock of its key categorisations: the theoretical dominance of Marxism, the egalitarian and democratic impulses of Socialists. The cohabitation of these is not easily schematised and can only leave us with a partial sense of distinctiveness and also a great area in which Socialist and Marxist ideas intermingle and cross-fertilise. In everyday political discourse, the term 'the Left' is probably most familiar and certainly most fungible. We discussed the limitations of 'the Left' as a way of thinking about socialism, and we identified a relatively new social justice tradition within the Left which manifests a different kind of radical vision to some Socialists and many Marxists. These distinctions are, as I have insisted throughout, not clean-cut. But they do anchor key contrasts that allow us to make sense of the 'noise', hybridity, and conceptual dirtiness that infuses social media. To use all of these traditions as broadly synonymous, to speak only of 'the Left' as a broad direction of travel, or to assume a comity of thought and value between these different traditions would be to lose considerable analytical purchase in the next part. Finally, we sketched out attitudes that socialist political thought has generated. These derive from an understanding of history and the nature of capitalism that is progressive, systemic, and – at least declaredly if not in substance – optimistic.

In the next chapter, we will explore how we might develop some analytical tools that will allow us to take socialist political thought and consider the means through which it has endeavoured to construct political ideologies, and most pertinently, how ideological work can be understood as an important source of political work in the present. The notion of an end to ideology or of ideological decline are insufficient lenses through which to understand what is a vibrant and contested political present.

4

Proto-Ideologies

> The mass media, social movements and networks, and popular
> political language have disseminated new vehicles and forms
> of ideology, and the notion of a 'post-ideological' age is itself a
> masking device. Ideologies mutate regularly, their boundaries are
> porous, and ideological delocalization is countered by cultural
> decentralization. Yet the fragility of particular ideological
> arrangements must not be confused with ideological fragility
> in general.[1]

This chapter will make a selective excursion through the literature on political
ideologies. It does so in order to set out an analytical framework for the
case study chapters that follow. In Chapter 2, we made a case that PSM has
enabled the development of a rich body of political ideas and debates. What
we need to do here is make some clearly delineated steps to treat these ideas
and debates analytically. We are not simply arguing that people still debate
politics or that the internet is a vibrant and exciting place. Rather, what we
are aiming to do is treat bundles of ideas as more substantive than simply a set
of texts, signifiers, or discourses. In other words, there has been a *qualitative*
development in politics as a result not only of growing content provision on
social media but also that PSM has in turn nurtured these bundles of ideas.
PSM has served as a seedbed for the cultivation of sustained and concerted
ideological innovation.

Making this argument requires two things: in the first place, an
identification of evidence; secondly, a procedure through which the traffic
of social media is extrapolated from its immediate environs and analysed.
The commonest way of analysing a body of concepts and ideas is to treat
them as an ideology. We shall see how this term is both very frequently used
but also treated with no small amount of license. Nevertheless, the term
offers the best starting point both to identify how concepts, arguments, and
terminologies articulate and also to set out a clear way of assessing their

properties. Thinking about ideologies nudges us away from the intellectual culture of social media within which ideas are generated. This is important because we do not want to evaluate the internet left on the terms of PSM itself. This would involve, as we argued in Chapter 2, a rapid and exaggerated factionalism and contrarianism which would not be appropriate to the aim of deepening analysis. Extrapolating from the procedures of social media allows a certain kind of analytical 'cooling' in which we treat bodies of ideas 'academically' rather than through attack, counter-attack, and hard position taking.

Nevertheless, we should not build into our methodology an answer to the question. We will not, in other words, declare that the internet left is generating new ideologies of critique or opposition to capitalism and then set our categorisations to fit this argument. What we shall do is establish an understanding of political ideology that, with a little manipulation, allows us to talk about *proto*-ideologies. This takes away the determinism or teleology at work in treating new discourses as ideologies or ideologies in the making. All we need claim is that there are the materials for genuine ideological construction within the internet left and, having established this, analyse what is out there in these terms. Any conclusion that follows will be suitably moderate and provisional.

Political ideology

Ideology as politics

Political ideologies are theoretically informed arrangements of concepts which display some internally systemic relations between different ideas and categorisations. A political ideology is not a set of floating signifiers, endlessly nimble and contingent. It is more robust than what those of a post-structuralist bent might call discourse or grammar. Political ideologies modify and adapt their concepts, but they have to undertake specific intellectual labour to do so: to demonstrate that an ideology remains fit for purpose. But, what purpose?

Political ideologies are bundles of ideas, concepts, premises, and propositions arranged for the purposes of combat. They are partial and partisan, and they are products of their time. It is somewhat of a tautology to accuse any political argument or publicly declared position as being 'ideological', analogous to accusing a dog of acting canine, and there is no merit in imagining that the realm of politics can be anything other than ideological. Politics without ideological content is emotion or administration. Claims that politics can (or should) be the non-ideological rational administration of the state by experts is itself ideological.[2] This is so because it relies on a normativity, a sense of how power should work, as well as a perception of what human agency is. These considerations are no less important than whatever formalised and logically framed arguments technocrats might make about rationality, efficiency, neutrality, utility, and other contested terms.[3]

Political ideologies intrinsically and constantly seek to make themselves relevant and attractive to broader publics in the context of constant political change and uncertainty. But this endeavour is never perfected. Political ideologies might find new modes of expression as politics changes, but they might also lose favour because their essential features fail to fit with the times or to maintain much of a presence in the public sphere. Most accounts of the history of neoliberalism demonstrate this. Ideas that emerged in the 1920s and 1930s were marginalised by variants of Keynesianism and other forms of regulatory governance.[4] The ideological project of neoliberalism was nurtured in relatively cloistered communities until the late 1970s, sustained not only by private funding and intellectual determination but also with a shared sense that the times will come when the fundamentals of the free market and the strong state would return to historical salience.

Political ideologies are like axes: both tools and weapons. They create analyses that have a normativity that argues how politics should be done and why other ideologies are wrong. They seek to understand and interpret through conceptual work but also to do so in ways that seek to show how much better they are than their rivals and that, in doing so, they should serve as the paradigm through which politics should be practised. This means that any basic definition of ideology should pay attention both to the substance of the ideology's composite ideas and its historical endurance and relevance.

Political ideologies have always sought out adversaries in order to gain public attention and (hopefully) support. In constituting themselves, they contribute to the constitution of their adversaries. They assemble concepts that can be put to work not only to demonstrate their own intellectual merit but also to undermine rivals. Political ideologies more or less realistically seek political authority or influence of some kind.

Political ideology as practice

There is a profoundly pragmatic property to political ideology. Terry Eagleton's *Ideology* offers a nuanced and broad treatment of ideology that has at its heart an interest in its purposes. He itemises those purposes as follows: unifying, action-oriented, rationalising, legitimating, universalising, and naturalising.[5] We shall make an adaptation of these for our own purposes.

The unifying property of a political ideology relates to the efforts made to generate a *coherent and encompassing* political narrative. As with any theoretical work, this means simplifying, selecting, and generalising in order to create a singular point of view. The critique one sometimes reads that an ideology does not account for everything is more a recognition of what a political ideology is than a critique. Political ideologies are holistic and integrative. They are not niche; rather, they aim to make a claim about what really matters and to construct world views through this claim. 'Ideologies offer us a picture of the world complete.'[6] In doing so, political ideologies construct political constituencies and, in the process, also their own unique entreaties to people to cleave to this particular ideological tradition. Class, nation, individual, gender, and ethnicity are all ideological categories of mobilisation which require a drawing together of people.

The *action orientation* of a political ideology denotes those properties in its concepts that direct towards political agency. They 'claim both to describe and prescribe' political change.[7] The normative properties of political ideology construct agency out of an identification of a wrong and the stipulation of a putting right. This commonly involves languages of justice, liberation, duty, propriety, order, and struggle. Ideological action orientation is politically richer than the social movement concept of framing which tends to focus on the resource and organisational aspects of mobilisation.[8] If there is something material-logistical in political ideologies' action orientation, there is also something provocative. Political ideologies do not only frame; they narrate a political totality based in an ontology of humankind and some metaphysic concerning power, right, and order. The possible demands this makes on people's behaviour can be considerable.

An ideology's *rationalisations* relate to its ability to demonstrate how its conceptual components collectively perform explanation. As Eagleton argues, a political ideology's rationalisations are always normative, that is, they offer up explanations as *justifications*. If explanation tells us why things are the way they are, a political ideology also tells us why things should stay the same or this is why things should change. Explanation itself is a key property of an ideology, not only in itself but in its rivalries: what better way to contest a political issue than through the establishing of a superior explanation?

Political ideologies are forged in contest, and that contest fundamentally revolves around the relative merits of *legitimacy* claims. A political ideology's ability to generate public support depends not only on its analytical insight or correctness but also on its ability to articulate with a range of normative positions: justice, stability, liberty, equality, community, harmony. Any connection to these positions is as much cultural as logical. Legitimacy is thicker than correctness. Acts of ideological legitimation require an identification and advocacy of those who, it is claimed, can realise the normative aspirations of an ideology, and also the key adversaries who are characterised as tyrannous, corrupt, callous, mendacious, and so on. It should be clear that the contestation of legitimacy is heavily aesthetic. One can only support a political ideology that is, among other things, attractive to oneself.

All political ideologies need a core truism or article of faith that is immutable and *decontested*. By claiming that this core pertains to all humankind (is universal) and that it is a priori or natural (not subject to debate that questions its existence), a political ideology fixes some of its components beyond fallibilistic possibility. These core components become transhistorical and pre-political. Immanent debate about the conceptualisation of class within a Marxist ideology is commonplace but the proposition to abandon or relegate class as a concept to some external or contingent condition is impossible. Arguments about the end of class are left to Marxism's adversaries. This decontestation is not a weakness or failing. Without some foundational a priori, a political ideology will struggle immensely to maintain its *differentia specifica* or to fare well in debates against other political ideologies.

We should add another purpose of our own to Eagleton's list, if only to draw out a facet of his analysis that is particularly germane: *combat*. Political ideologies seek to present themselves and generate political commentary in ways that seek to win. This is partly about making a convincing account of some political phenomenon, but it is also about making that account in ways that are rhetorically effective. One can only articulate the conceptual language of a political ideology in ways that are assertive and contain attacks on other traditions. The tone of these articulations can be very significantly varied, from modest to shrill, persuasive, or condemnatory. But there is little point in a political ideology, even a well-made one, in hosting a conversation only among its own adepts. Nor is there much political energy in establishing a parsimonious and well-evidenced ideology; indeed, it is not obvious that this would pass muster as a *political* ideology at all. Ideological positions seek to intervene in politics on their own merits and against the claims of others.

Morphology

Concept building

Eagleton's work identifies a set of ideological purposes, but it does not use these to develop analytical tools of a kind that would allow us to identify conceptual components, their relations, and the nature of the ideology that they construct. If we are to explore the development of ideologies through social media, we need to not only understand their practices but also identify and assess the 'DNA' of an ideological project: the internal conceptual arrangements they make to understand politics. The best-known framework that aims to do this is Michael Freeden's morphological approach.[9]

Freeden understands political ideologies as 'complex constructs through which specific meanings, out of a potentially unlimited and essentially contestable universe of meanings are imparted to the wide range of political concepts they inevitably employ'.[10] It is the structure of conceptual arrangements that establishes a political ideology. Freeden wishes to analyse political ideologies through a bio-spatial metaphor in which they have a unique form and content. Each political ideology has a form set by the arrangement of its internal conceptual components. Ideologies have core, adjacent, and peripheral concepts that shape their contours. We will set these three properties out briefly before considering how they might be deployed.

The *core concepts*[11] of an ideology are those that are ineliminable to it and are 'indispensable to holding an ideology together'.[12] To relate back to the previous section, core concepts are those which aspire to a state of what Eagleton calls decontestedness. The presence of core concepts is non-negotiable in that, if they were to disappear, the ideology itself would no longer hold together because its concepts would lose 'intelligibility and communicability'.[13] It would, in effect, transition from ideology to a cluster of ideas articulated through speech. For Freeden, this does not mean that core concepts are unchanging. They might be ineliminable but their nature can change and it is also possible that their importance might wax and wane. The prominence of core concepts in the articulation of an ideology might vary: they need not be announced frequently. Cores can be expressed in cognate ways or associated with other concepts differently.

Core concepts will condition the nature of other concepts within a political ideology more than vice versa. *Adjacent concepts* are endowed with meaning in relation to the core, but they are also equally important to a political ideology. They 'are crucial in finessing the core and anchoring it'.[14] These concepts give the core distinctions of a political ideology their character, their political valency. More flexible, colourful, and less concerned with their essential meaning, adjacent concepts make an ideology seem timely, convincing, and ambitious.

Freeden categorises adjacent concepts as *logical* and *cultural*. Logical adjacents are those which have 'necessary options and permutations' in relation to core and possibly other adjacent concepts.[15] The key word here is necessary: that core concepts entail some inevitable choices in terms of their adjacent connotations. Although not necessary in a pre-emptive and determinist fashion, core concepts are related to logical adjacents through relative autonomy: there is a logical constraint on the field of these adjacent concepts.

Cultural adjacents are those concepts that carry out more normative and aesthetic work which derive from their 'temporally and spatially bounded social practices, institutional patterns, ethical systems, technologies, influential theories, discourses, and beliefs'.[16] Cultural adjacency might often evoke a historically specific understanding of human nature in order to connect to and support other political concepts. Culturally adjacent concepts do not have to meet a logical and analytical standard but might rather have some association to other concepts that is mainly bolstered through legitimacy which is, in itself, in part aesthetic. The aesthetic will be found in the customary content of a concept: its concrete socio-historical setting.[17]

Adjacent concepts weave together to present the core of an ideology as worthy of public attention. They are more motile than core concepts; their relative presence and presentation varies. Some adjacent concepts might disappear and new ones emerge without doing mortal damage to the ideology. Furthermore, adjacent concepts might be shared by different traditions of political ideology, even if logical and cultural content is distinct and likely antagonistic.

Peripheral concepts are, as the name implies, more remote and less essential connections and associations: 'moral, marginal and ephemeral'.[18] Inasmuch as a political ideology aspires to speak to as many aspects of a political sphere as possible, it will need to say something about things it is not centrally interested in. Freeden divides peripheral concepts into *margins* and *perimeters*. Margins are those concepts that are insubstantial for the ideology itself;[19] perimeter concepts/components are those which are only very weakly figured to a degree that they might well not be concepts but rather 'specific ideas and policy proposals'.[20] Peripheral concepts have a 'boundary location' that shapes the 'configuration, flow, and layering of meaning' within a political ideology. Peripheral concepts are a manifestation of how political ideologies cannot exist as closed systems.

Conceptual practices

Freeden's setting out of these three morphological components is intricate and nuanced. He presents the framework as one primarily tasked with identifying and describing the concepts that constitute a political ideology. There is a sense that each political ideology is defined by a dynamic interaction between core, adjacent, and peripheral concepts which includes graduation or relegation from one space to another. He argues that political ideologies are historically and culturally varied and are composed by different kinds of authors for different kinds of audience.[21] In his treatment of specific political ideologies, one gets a detailed account of conceptual development through intellectual innovation and the writings of specific authors. The morphological approach is valuable as a way clearly to identify how an ideology is constructed, and this is vital for our interest in proto-ideologies. But, it also needs some adaptation. There are three considerations here.

In the first place, Freeden's work does not give a strong awareness of the dynamics of combat. Although he speaks of persuasion, there is relatively limited reflection given to how political ideologies encounter one another for the purposes of contestation. Freeden is mainly concerned to explore political ideologies immanently – in terms of their own discrete properties. The kind of image that Freeden presents is more of a public sphere replete with political ideologies which present themselves to citizens with the aim of winning their fealty. The possibility that ideologies might do this in the act of debating against each other is less present. In this sense, the images of a political ideology presented by Eagleton and Freeden seem rather different: an ideational-pragmatic organisation of concepts for the purposes of contestation or an internally arranged and justified set of concepts maintained by political thinkers. We need both images. The 'history of political thought and argument [is] … about the history of political organisation and struggle'.[22] We will unify these approaches – which are not incommensurate – in our presentation of proto-ideology later on.

We shall pay particular attention not only to the internal arrangement of concepts and their robustness in terms of logic and structure but also to the degree to which they are articulated in ways that make them ready to engage adversarially with other political ideologies. A political ideology with well-ordered conceptual components that mutually affirm one another might appear secure in its values, but if its concepts are not purposed to critique other traditions or develop strong incisive comments in relation to political controversies, then it might well lose ground to less elegantly composed but aggressive political ideologies. This might mean that simplicity, reiteration, and the establishment of strong and tight positive or negative associations can get a political ideology a long way. It will also mean that peripheral concepts might be doing a lot of work for an ideology, even if they are not so easily assessed by their conceptual properties or strong connections to the core of an ideology.

Secondly, although in the chapters that analyse ideological traditions Freeden readily recognises how ideologies are constructed and modified over time and that 'clusters of thought claiming' to be political ideologies emerge,[23] he is concerned with the historical analysis of completed ideologies. He does not consider how political ideologies might be contemporary and active projects, composed from incomplete, tenuous, idiographic, or idiosyncratic political resources. They achieve their ideological status at least in part through curation rather than some immanent and definitive achievement stage. If we recall that political ideologies are a form of practice, it becomes clear that practice is present in the very coinage of a political ideology. And that coinage can only be effectively and successfully performed by drawing on a significant enough pool of ideational resources that pre-date the ideology's inauguration.

It remains essentially contested when cultures of political thinking, the emergence of key works of political thought, the actions of specific individuals, and the socialisation of all of these things become an ideology that one can use with some categorical certainty so that we can talk about, say, liberalism as a discrete historical presence. And, in the final analysis, the establishing of a political ideology is a matter of canonisation. That is to say, to some degree, the establishing of a political ideology depends on the sociology of intellectuals. Whether, when, and how concepts are named is in good measure a matter of research and debate.

Furthermore, it is not enough to identify the threads that came to weave the political texture of an ideology which, once named, achieves a clear and stable identity. All political ideologies continue to shift and twist as they adopt and adapt to ideas and texts which may or may not declare for that ideological tradition. In other words, the practices of curation and naming do not dissipate as a political ideology matures but rather remain as its intrinsic properties.

We need a way of looking at bundles of concepts as *possible* ideologies, or – although this generates twisted historical methodologies – ideologies that don't yet know what they are. We need to see how concepts are being actively composed and tested, and we need to think about the ways and extent to which those concepts look like establishing a political ideology, a tradition of thinking coherently about politics with a view to garnering authority, support, legitimacy, and influence.

Thirdly, we shall take aesthetics more centrally into consideration than Freeden. Although Freeden acknowledges the centrality of historical relevance and cultural resonance, these are fairly formally presented. There is no attempt to explore the internal properties or dynamics of the representational and how they might affect the ability of a political ideology to win public attention. This is not only about ideological connections to history and culture but also about rhetorical form, the dissemination of imagery, and that slippery analytical term: affect. Although affect is not a term that sits easily in political analysis – more purposed to literary studies perhaps – there is no denying that political ideologies are received in part as emotive propositions. 'The emotional and affective register is a vital dimension of motivation and thus a necessary and inextinguishable aspect of practical political thought and action.'[24] Shared emotions do important work in mobilising a group of people to act politically. Outrage, hubris, solidarity, despair, enmity, and sympathy all connect people to political ideologies. Each of these emotions is also in part a motivation: an encouragement to advocate, publicly identify with, and act. In each respect, the textual or visual symbolism relayed through a political ideology intensifies this motivation. This is more clearly the case for insurgent or rebellious political ideologies.

The morphology of uncertainty

Thus far, we have highlighted three key features of political ideologies. A political ideology requires a robustness that distinguishes it from political discourse, and it derives this robustness from the transparent and detailed defining of logically articulated concepts. Secondly, the construction and sustenance of political ideology is something that is based in a set of intellectual practices that secure a 'bond between the present and the future':[25] establishing a broad and coherent political narrative; orienting the narrative towards political action through a 'transformation of ... subjectivity';[26] giving justification to those (prospective) actions; setting political practice and its normative embedding in a broader presentation of legitimate politics; arguing that a specific and small set of political goods are not up for contestation; and organising all of the former within the ambition to win public attention over and above other rival political ideologies.

Thirdly, the analysis of particular ideological constructions is best carried out via the morphological approach in which political ideologies are understood as collations of core, adjacent, and peripheral political concepts. Because we are interested in the construction of political ideologies in the context of intense contention, we make three modifications: to consider not only the logical connections and prioritisations of concepts but also their organisation as a means to assert meaning vis-à-vis other ideologies; to recognise more fully that the inauguration of a political ideology is historically blurred and that, as a result, ideological traditions might exist, so to speak, as ideologies in the making; finally, to pay more attention to the political aesthetics of the concepts within a political ideology, most importantly because these can have strong mobilisational effects.

But, we are not there yet. Although we have a framing to explore the ideological possibilities of socialist PSM, we need to take care that we do not assume too much or too little. In relation to the former, we need to ensure that we are clear – and duly moderate – in the claims we are making as to the ideational creativity within PSM. A novel cluster of ideas shared between blogs does not an ideology make.

If we recall that political ideologies are compositions that emerge possibly chaotically from multifarious sources, we can accept that many ideas, or texts, live and die with little impact on the canonical ideologies that define so much of our understanding of political contention. The possibility of failure is always present in any political project and it certainly pertains to the projects explored in the next part of this book. We are analysing *aspirational* ideological projects, not successful ones. We shall refer to these as proto-ideologies.

In relation to the second caution – assuming too little – we need to recognise that we should not consider ideological labour as failed if it does rise to dominant or canonical status. We have recognised that political ideologies are changeable and constantly subjected to an influx of new concepts and ideas. They are internally differentiated, and especially in relation to the larger and longer-lasting ideologies, they bifurcate into distinct sub-traditions. In this sense, any political ideology should be treated as a set of proto-ideologies, each of which sustains a 'school' that, notwithstanding a shared foundation in core concepts, sets out distinct conceptual arrangements. Within this perspective, we should not pre-emptively trivialise or condemn an aspirant proto-ideology that seems limited in influence. Not only are its prospects not foreclosed, its effects on broader currents of political thinking cannot be discounted.

Proto-ideologies feed into, influence, and provoke other proto-ideologies and, in the process, they contribute to and modify the canon and its dominant traditions. The two proto-ideologies we shall explore in the next section have their own successes and limitations, but beyond this, they have both affected how we engage with and discuss socialist political thought. In summary, concrete and present-day ideological work is proto-ideological work that contains two cardinal properties: an aspiration to dominant status within its ideological tradition and a feeding into the warp and woof of that ideological tradition more generally.

Proto-ideologies

Restlessness

Political ideologies are traditions. As such, they rely on origin narratives – a 'need for ancestors' – which are retrospectively constructed.[27] A 'biblical' text, the birth of a zeitgeist, the life works of a specific individual, or the epochal changes (supposedly) wrought by an event infuse traditions of political ideology with their sense of autonomous historical presence. These origin stories are always in part fictions, fictions that require enough people to believe them in order to activate the political ideology. Furthermore, as they develop, political ideologies develop different points of origin as splinter groups, different 'schools', national-cultural traditions, or particular charismatic public intellectuals emerge. In the previous chapter, we saw this pattern in relation to socialism. To be a political ideology is to be in constant revision. Indeed, to some degree, a healthy political ideology is an unstable and multiplex one. Political ideologies do not want to become doctrines. If they do so, their energies dwindle as debate collapses into iteration.

The point here is that political ideologies require nurturing if they are to avoid collapsing into doctrine or cliché. If we are working with a morphology defined by core, adjacent, and peripheral concepts, we need to understand that – no matter what the innate merits of these are – they require inputs from outside their immediate field. These inputs might be revisions to existing ideas and texts, neologisms with conceptual ambition, the presentation and interpretation of new evidence, the capturing of a cultural-political zeitgeist, or the resuscitation of an idea previously considered defunct.

The modifications we made to Freeden's model all speak to this representation of political ideology. We argued that, regardless of its conceptual arrangements, political ideology is defined by its ability to contest vis-à-vis others, its ability to change and strengthen in response to the activities of other ideological projects, and its ability to generate and reflect powerful cultural symbols.

All of this suggests to us a morphology of political ideology that is not only an order of concepts but also a 'dendritic' one. That is to say, ideologies have roots from which they draw up new ideas and perspectives, and all ideologies develop new branches or thicken some existing ones. The figurative use of a tree-like form serves to present political ideologies as discrete but hardly autonomous, defined according to the nature of the discourses that feed them and the ideational work that allows them to grow and, in the process, change. These features of a political ideology are especially salient in a proto-ideology.

Building ideologies

Proto-ideologies are intellectual projects that are driven by a desire to energise and improve a political ideology. They carry an obvious ideological affinity to a parent political ideology. Proto-ideologies have four characteristics. Firstly, and most obviously, they are in construction. They are not completed or named as one might expect from a dominant or established political ideology. The proto-ideologies offered in the next section might be familiar but they will not signal an established conceptual arrangement. This means that concepts might not be clear or stable. Authoritative intellectual foundations – texts of individual writers – may not be present. One would find it difficult to write up a reading list for an undergraduate module for these proto-ideologies. Being in construction means that it is necessary to be ambivalent about their prospective qualities or success. We cannot know how these proto-ideologies will fare. Only a reified idealism would expect that the 'best' or 'correct' ideas ascend to pre-eminence on their own merits. Instead, we will cleave to the 'too much, too little' guidance: a proto-ideology is not necessarily an ideology in the making but it aspires to be, and this has real effects that go beyond its own intellectual community.

The second characteristic is aspiration. The aspirational quality of a proto-ideology is qualitatively different to the generic combativeness of political ideologies. This is because proto-ideologies need to prove themselves, to establish themselves. Socialism, Marxism, or Gramscianism are not going anywhere: they require no exceptional effort to remain extant in intellectual circles. Some ideological traditions – fascism, for example – are intellectually moribund but remain, unfortunately, very present in political discourse. Not so for proto-ideologies. We shall see that these display an exceptional and constant aspirational energy: to develop, persuade, argue, and to establish bona fides.

Thirdly, proto-ideologies sustain an exceptionally energetic and distinct form of combativeness. The energy derives from aspiration, and the nature of contestation has a particular twofold character. Proto-ideologies take up intellectual arms not only against the enemies of their own political tradition but also against rival schools and proto-ideologies within their own tradition. They might even desire to tear down a regnant tradition, at the risk of causing more general damage. There is a 'within–against' quality to proto-ideologies that stems from the fact that aspiration is not only to contest against other ideologies but also to achieve stronger ideological status for itself, a status it can only achieve immanently.

Fourthly, proto-ideologies are – for all of their upwardly mobile abrasiveness – nurturing. They serve as innovative and even daring sources of new ideas, vocabularies, and aesthetics of political analysis and debate. A canonical political ideology with many vibrant proto-ideologies is a healthy political ideology. Even strongly phrased critique of established ideas can be taken as constructive work. Conceptual testing, rearrangement, redefinition, and even some jettisoning only serves to sustain the dendritic qualities of an ideology.

Proto-ideologies and social media

The highly active, aspirational combativeness of proto-ideologies makes social media an ideal venue for their work. Access, exposure, and dissemination of argument are hypermobile; the clustering of ideas into sub-provincial venues or silos through cross-posting is routine; immediate connections to attention-spiking political issues is intrinsic to PSM.

We should note the key ways in which the presence of proto-ideologies within PSM define our approach to research. In the first place, we argue that proto-ideologies can be analysed morphologically. They do claim to be based in logical arrangements of concepts. But, we need to carry out more interpretive work to discern these concepts. Concepts within proto-ideologies are not fully delineated or generally accepted. We have no textbook point of reference from which to set out their conceptual morphology. Conceptual arrangement and development are being actively performed via the prolix medium of PSM. The robustness of a morphology is ambiguous.

We shall base our analysis on a heuristic approach that derives from a deep reading of content in the context of that proto-ideological tradition's own conceptual history. We should also recognise a point stressed in Chapter 2: the intensity of traffic, volatility, and affect within PSM. This form of venue facilitates and even encourages proto-ideological activity in a way that previous practices never could. Pamphleteering, public speeches, branch meetings, door knocking, and banner holding now seem rather cumbersome ways of developing public recognition of political ideas. Subscriptions to blogs and podcasts, online meetings, Twitter and Facebook followings, and the aesthetic tools of social media (the memes, the imagery and its manipulation) are the context within which we can understand the vibrancy of socialist proto-ideological work.

Analysing proto-ideology
History and genealogy

Thus far, we have established proto-ideologies as contesting branches of political innovation that feed into their parent ideologies with a view to achieving dominance. Proto-ideologies show us that political ideologies are driven by the political energies that aim to define the meaning of an ideology as well as its ability to win public support. This means that political ideologies in their concrete manifestations are intrinsically unstable and incomplete. It is the inability of any particular rendition of a political ideology fully to command its meaning that leads to a constant and intrinsic divisiveness, a divisiveness which is not a symptom of some kind of dysfunction but rather the very energy which allows a political ideology to flourish.[28]

Proto-ideologies endlessly seek to occupy the dominant 'place' within a political ideology. They do this in conditions of endless multiple currents of sectarian ideas which can only be understood both in relation to the conceptual merits of those ideas and the modes of address through which they take form. All of which nudges us towards a historical approach to proto-ideology: a means to integrate dynamic, contested, and pluralised ideological formation that takes place within ever-changing contexts of governance and public culture. Both proto-ideologies that we explore in detail are historically specific refusals of neoliberal dominance and, equally prominently, an expression of a case that socialism is not dead.

As we have noted, the canonical list of political ideologies is quite familiar, at least in its major traditions. Each of these has achieved its place as a result of two interrelated historical processes: an assemblage from varied proto-ideologies which did not clearly identify as being part of a grand tradition of political thought, and subsequently, an ongoing nutrition from proto-ideologies that sought to make their imprimatur on that political ideology once it had established itself as a major tradition of political thought.

Freeden's approach to political ideology – one that categorises and analyses the content and relations of concepts – is mainly based in political theory.[29] Another approach is to explore the history of political ideas. Research into the history of political ideas is not separate from political theory, but there is a difference in the mode of analytical procedure.

Historians of political ideas generally adopt a genealogical approach in which political ideas are understood as products (and part) of historical change. The socio-economic circumstances, lives of intellectuals, changes in global order, and the instabilities of sovereignty and statehood all feed into the fortunes of political ideologies as they weave through the textiles of political contestation.

It is more likely that historians of political ideas will ask: 'what are liberalism's origins?', 'how was the new liberalism of the early 20th century constructed?', or 'how did liberalism adopt or reject imperialist ideas?', rather than 'what are the core concepts of liberalism?' or 'what does liberalism mean by freedom?'. Histories of political ideas more readily reveal the proto-ideological within the ideological: the fortunes of an ideology's progenitors, the sectarianisms that flourish within an ideology, the historical moments of rupture, the ascendance of one school over another. If political ideas are part of historical change, they are also intrinsically changeable: coined, adopted, contested, and reinterpreted.[30]

Extrapolating concepts from contest

PSM is not a propitious venue for the academic appraisal of clusters of ideas. And yet, it is within PSM that we find the most widespread, energetic, and engaged political discourse. This book's interest lies in treating the ideas that emerge within PSM not only on their own terms as part of the serial contestations of social media but also as something with greater ambition. As we shall see, Left discourse on PSM has a Janus-like quality: looking out towards the currents of opinion within social media and also looking inwards towards a desire to construct something more like a world view that requires abstraction, a conceptual language, and a sense of intellectual standing.

Of course, one can acknowledge that PSM has enabled an explosion of political debate and ideas and that it has done so with some ambition to innovate how we see politics without troubling oneself with how one might analyse these debates. One can select what seems useful and, if one wishes, also follow the trails of debate that are valuable in themselves. In short, one can go with the flow and follow or engage in the endless critique that is at the heart of PSM. As noted in Chapter 2, PSM tends to be purposefully combative: identifying double standards as a sign of moral fault, accusations of authors' hidden agendas, exaggerated renditions of positions to heighten the argumentative stakes, and a range of opaque associations between a post and other ideas or normative positions. And, all of this with the intent of getting the upper hand in a skirmish, not necessarily reaching a consensus or even a sense of the nature of dissensus before 24 hours pass and attention moves on.

But there is something frustrating about this. It is both too critical and not critical enough. That is to say, although PSM is replete with critique and might be said to be centrally driven by mutual attacks on different positions, the overall nature of this critique is that it does not need to, and rarely does, establish how some ideas might be more valid than others, or what exactly the problem is with one position in relation to others or in relation to a particular political issue or question. Critique is in-the-moment response. Its purpose does not go beyond this. As a result, it is not easy to derive political reflection and insight beyond the texts in motion themselves.

Furthermore, engaging in PSM requires that one take on its normative vernacular. To raise a question is to take a position. To disagree is to attack. To agree is to be 'one of those people'. A point once made is open to a set of (unfavourable) associations which are not explicitly present in the point itself. It might be that aspects of one's identity or experience are drawn into discussion: for example, one's 'race' or gender identity. The positionality of the author or researcher is, of course, also part of the critical framing of debate in academia, but the frame tends to be socio-historical, not personal. The fact that gender, nationality, and period matter to political perspective is distinct from the more personalised and normatively antagonistic consideration of authorship in social media.

One might summarise the 'noisiness' of social media meta-discourse (the rules within which different discourses are articulated) roughly as follows:

- A tendency towards polemic. This is exercised not simply through extreme and hostile responses (triggers) to posts – this is something social media displays generally and we are concerned with a more select ecology (PSM) in which certain forms of moderation are present. But, there is a tendency to identify camps, shorthand positions, and in the process generate what might be called familiar oppositions (hence the use of the term polemic). Algorithms that process likes, followers, and hashtags consolidate this.
- A strong imbrication of discussion with broader identitarian and culture war difference and dispute. This is a natural part of the fact that there are distinctive venues through which to post but it seeps deeper into discourse as a result of the fact that everyone can review everyone else's previous commentaries, 'friends', endorsements of other texts, and so on. In other words, each post or blog is easily rendered intensely biographical in a way that is quite different from academic journals and books. If one posts something disagreeable to others, one's social media archive might be trawled.
- As part of the necessity of working within a competitive attention economy, posts are often 'heightened'. That is, the claims made, the challenges set, and the oppositions taken are intensified and integrated into necessarily brief texts. The room for nuance is radically truncated. The internal logic of a blog or other post is to 'message', not analyse. The language of PSM is often an awkward hybrid of tabloid journalese and airport book titles aimed at an 'informed' public: 'why we should forget about ...', 'why I am no longer ...', 'what's wrong with ...', 'the end of ...', and so on. Within the text, there might well be an attempt

to meet the demands of an eye-catching title, and some caveats squeezed into the sparse remaining words. This represents a tension or perhaps incommensurability between the protocols of academic research and those of a social media driven by the logic of brief attention spans and a seeking out of 'hot takes' and 'cutting edges' within a media that is endlessly amnesiac and desperate for likes, follows, and comments.

- Finally, there is a lack of referencing and extrapolation. There is little time/space to make connections to broader ideas, to acknowledge other authors, to draw back from the matter at hand to something broader. Acknowledgements of what might be called a canon (a set of authors) or genre (a tradition of thinking) are, at most, a brief nod rather than a connection. Although most academics enter into PSM after years of detailed and voluminous reading and reflection, they present themselves as if they have coined a discrete and original take on something.

The outcome of all of this is that, although one might get a few hours of intense debate scrolling through posts and responses on social media, it is unlikely that one would come away with the impression that anyone is any the wiser. If we are to treat PSM as a host for proto-ideological projects, we need some form of abstraction, a way to transpose text from its fleeting and polemic context into an analytical field in which it can be considered in relation to concept building.

We shall endeavour to collate currents of PSM, identify their key properties, and then ask a set of questions of them which will allow us to put them under consideration as aspirant ideational systems or ideologies: proto-ideologies. We shall connect to the following questions throughout the case studies, albeit not in a strict or formulaic way. The questions derive from the discussion earlier:

- What is the proto-ideology? We shall identify and analyse the core, adjacent, and peripheral political concepts. We shall explore the latter's content and interrelations.
- How is this proto-ideology being constructed? We shall pay attention to identity: what the proto-ideology claims as its distinction and how it constructs 'others' against which it also defines itself. This leads to a subsequent line of inquiry into its principal modes of combat, that is, the wherewithal it has to critique, claim superiority, or engage in contention over specific political issues.
- What are the proto-ideology's political aesthetics? We shall explore the two major components of this discussed previously: the affect of a proto-ideology and its historiography. In relation to the latter, we mean to explore the structure of historical explanation that storifies temporal location. This pertains biographically – how the times we are living in

74

are historically placed – and autobiographically – how the proto-ideology tells us about its own origins.

- Each of these is a line of inquiry, not a questionnaire template. They will be treated interpretively. Different proto-ideologies will be keener on some aspects than others. But, by keeping to these cues, we can sustain a comparative set of analytical reflections that will allow us to keep to the core motivation of the book, which is to demonstrate the value and energy of ideological projects within a socialist tradition.

This section has argued that the post-ideological and generally dour mood of contemporary political vision is exaggerated. Even within a political realm commonly seen as symptomatic of political decline, it is possible to identify tenacious counter-currents to political defeatism. And, within this counter-current, it is possible to identify an energetic intellectual community that sustains an ideological tradition commonly commended and belittled: socialism. Socialism's own history lends itself well to crisis: it is a political ideology that expects more from progress and modernity than capitalism can offer. It is systemic, conceptually sophisticated, and combative. It is also highly internally differentiated. It has its own historic sense of outrage and expectation. In these ways, one can see how socialism's withering away is frequently and prematurely presumed. To understand the political ideology of socialism in the present day, we have to identify and assess its conceptual arrangements; but, more importantly, we need to study the dynamics of these arrangements: their assemblage, curation, and revision. This in turn involves struggles against and within: against rival ideologies and within as different proto-ideologies claim to have a superior way to deploy socialist ideas. The notion of a proto-ideology enables us to transpose text generated within PSM into an analysis of content treated as ideology in construction. In the next part, we shall explore two case studies in this fashion.

Part II

Democratic Marxist Nationalism

DMN is a strong candidate for a proto-ideology. It has generated a considerable archive of commentary on a range of political issues. It has done so in a way that is anchored around a set of core concepts. It also contains within it a political purpose or advocacy and a sense of difference contestation in relation to other ideological traditions.

DMN is a proto-ideology that fundamentally seeks to retain a Marxist political tradition and adapt it to a recent past and present that, it claims, has been disrobed of the deadening effects of liberal and social-democratic managerialism. Its leitmotif is a recrudescence of politics as a historical venue for confrontation and progress. It puts class at the centre of this return of the political. Articulating a certain narrative about democracy and the nation-state, DMN sketches a vision of struggle based in organised mass agency and the possibility of new political parties. Its analytical lens might be described as realistic in the sense that political theory uses that term: cautious about political moralisation, cognisant of political incommensurability, and aware of the unique political resources offered by state sovereignty.

DMN is generated through a core set of writers, websites, and campaigns. Although each author might contest their collation here as co-authors of an ideological tradition, mutatis mutandis, there is regular cross-referencing and shared reaction/position taking. Writers share online publication venues which themselves cross-endorse each writer. Spiked,[1] the podcast Bungacast, the blogs and news sites The Full Brexit, Northern Star, Compact,[2] Damage, and the publisher Zero Books serve as the core platform for DMN.

Core concepts
Democracy

DMN's most fundamental core concept is democracy. Democracy is that good in itself that founds discussions about the merits of all political phenomena that revolve around it. It is Archimedean. This is a normative foundation which establishes a mode of assessment for a wide range of political phenomena. It is decontested in that it either trumps other political values or it articulates those values as best realised through democratic procedures. Of course, democracy is arguably a core normative concept for many ideological traditions. But DMN deploys this term in ways that allow it to bind together its own unique constellation of core concepts. Democracy is central to DMN for two reasons, one immanent and the other more relational.

Immanently, it considers politics only to be legitimate and authoritative if it is based in democratic procedures. Democracy is articulated through some familiar associations. Most centrally, democracy is rule of 'the people' who are assumed to be, broadly speaking, working class or to represent some form of majoritarian mass or popular view. The key means through which the people exercise power is through the election of their representatives. DMN is not strongly invested in developing new models of democracy as many interested in civil society, citizens' forums, and cosmopolitan democrats have. DMN makes a case that existing mechanisms of representative democracy should be reinvigorated. It sees the fundamental crisis of politics as one in which the people have become increasingly disillusioned with parliamentary politics. It argues that the parties who claim to represent their constituencies have become increasingly disinterested in the people.[3] As a result, democracy has depleted. Politics has become driven by elite 'bubbles'; people consider politics less of a way to influence government and more the business of a distanced elite. DMN holds popular representative democracy as its core value because it establishes its main motivation to engage in social media and the contestation of political ideas more broadly: to rail against elitist, technical, and 'unpopular' forms of political practice.

There is a second facet to the intrinsic valuing of democracy: freedom of expression. DMN considers freedom of expression to be unconditionally a political good. It does so on the grounds that individual expression is intrinsic to humankind. It is in this sense decontested. DMN also values freedom of expression in two extrinsic ways: firstly, on the assumption that censoriousness tends to be nefarious, and secondly, that the open expression of contesting views creates better political discourses. We shall return to these matters when we discuss the concept of liberty later.

Relationally, democracy is set at the core of DMN because it underpins its normative affiliation to Marxism. The value of Marxism lies in its theoretical and political connection to the working class as a historical agency. This is based in an assumption that the working class are a mass and popular constituency. Indeed, this is foregrounded a lot more than a discussion of the agency of the working class is in relation to the achievement of socialism. There is a premise that current modes of governance marginalise the working class and that the political ideas and perspectives of the working class are often distinctively valuable for a well-functioning democracy. DMN understands democracy as having been won by working-class mobilisation. It sees democracy's most dangerous enemy in the West as elites that constantly try to securitise popular democracy from power. International treaties, technocratic policy making, and the centralisation of governance are all understood fundamentally as ways to dampen, erode, and delimit the possibilities of a more vibrant popular democracy. As such, the core commitment to representative democracy is very strongly associated with the commitment to Marxism. Democracy also sustains other aspects of DMN which reside in the adjacent concepts, as we shall see.

Marxism

Unlike democracy, DMN's core conceptualisation in Marxism is largely implicit. But, it is nevertheless a core concept in that it is decontested and it cannot do without it. Although there are scattered namechecks of Marx or Marxism, this affiliation is rarely brought to the foreground and one might imagine a good part of this is because of the general indifference or hostility to Marxism within the popular or central ground of politics.

Marxism is articulated within DMN through a terminology and set of arguments that are Marxist, but often implied more than declared. In the first place – and connecting closely to the normative a priori of democracy – the working class is the foundation of DMN's normative motivations. The masses, the proles (a term used ironically to ape what is seen as middle-class contempt for the working class), and ordinary citizens are all synonymously used to assign a class constituency. The working class is also identified as the collectivity that is most hard-working, most poor, and most exploited. Marxism assigns class as a category without caveats. A Marxist core allows class an autonomy: in itself and for itself. As we shall see in Chapter 6, not all socialisms do this, preferring to articulate class in a more 'auxiliary' fashion.

Marxism's core status derives chiefly from its ability to arrange its adjacent concepts. The declared commitment to democracy – which is far more prominent – is articulated through a conceptualisation of class relations. A democratic conceptualisation of a populist 'people' or a liberal civil society are disallowed by this Marxist understanding of class. As a result, Marxism quietly performs vital underlabour for this proto-ideology.

Nationalism

Both democracy and the politics of working-class liberation are expressed through the political locus of the nation. The nation is strongly connected to the state not only through the commitment to representation but also through the fact that states have proven to be the most effective territorialisation of authoritative and (to some degree) legitimate power.[4] DMN holds an incredulity to transnational and intergovernmental institutions which it sees as exceptionally elitist, unrepresentative, and only able to impose a patchy political vision.

The positive valuing of the nation derives from the fact that the nation–state represents the geopolitical outer margin of meaningful political ambition while also being realistically articulated to the demands of democratic accountability. The nation–state offers the 'shell' within which the broadest, most democratic, and most effective possibilities of socialist transformation might take place.[5] Within this strong valuing of mass democracy resides a faith in – or ambition for – mass working-class political ascendance.[6] We shall return to this association with a mass working-class constituency and its historic role within democracy later.

There are other important aspects to the characterisation of nationalism that we should note here. DMN has a preference for 'thick' politics. It takes politics as being at its most effective or valuable when it is infused with culture and community. This is not for conservative reasons to do with family or land: thicker political values are not essentialised or static. Rather, it is argued that any tenacious or ambitious political endeavour must matter deeply to people.

The contradistinction here is with 'thin' politics that might derive from the symbolisms or intellectualisms which are perceived as aesthetically pleasing or ideally perfected. New social movements and identity politics are commonly dismissed and lampooned in large part on the grounds that they are not seriously connected to long-steeped political experiences of marginalisation, hard work, and exploitation which are commonly situated in locality and history. They are instead portrayed as unmoored political discourses that seek the symbols and neologisms of the current, the fashionable, and the performative.

Relatedly, 'thick' national politics represents a counter-balance to 'thin' trans/intergovernmental politics. Intergovernmental and transnational politics is characterised as blandly legalistic, technocratic, abstract, and idealist.[7] It is associated with an elitism that combines authoritarianism, liberalism, and a moral economy of marketisation. Inasmuch as the transnational politics of trade agreements, human rights, and currency unions impact upon a nation-state, they repress the possibilities of robust, working class-driven progress and replace this with the caprice of elite green room meetings and international bureaucracy.

In sum, the nation serves as the entity within which meaningfully democratic politics is practised and it is also more appropriately connected to the more thickly valued political beliefs of communities within its borders than intergovernmental institution could be. However, it would be erroneous to suppose that DMN is national*ist*. Its nationalism sits within parameters set by its two other core concepts. DMN has no interest in defining a nation qua nation. In fact, one could use the term internationalist as much as nationalist to encapsulate DMN's core. The image of the world that DMN portrays is one of increasing globalisation, but this globalisation is not one that one would describe as cosmopolitan. The distinction is best encapsulated by a phrase sometimes used within DMN discourse in relation to Brexit: love Europe, hate the EU. Solidarity and cooperation between peoples are advocated on the grounds that peoples who express their broadest political values through representative national democracy should encourage and enjoy an international politics that would look very different from a world of introverted and autonomous nation-states, one based in mutual respect between sovereign peoples. In short, DMN's nationalism is not a valuing of the nation against other nations; it is a valuing of national intercourse through sovereign states and against transnational governance.

DMN's 'thick' nationalism is not an ethnonational one. Although there is clearly an argument that 'traditional' national identities, associated with the 'white working class', or with communities in marginalised parts of the country, or people who derive political values from the oral histories and norms carried through multiple generations of living through change in one place, DMN does not advocate a greater valuing of these political identities over other British ethnic identities or against those who have arrived more recently. There is some debate around this, which we shall return to, but we can mark here that, in spite of some representations of DMN as ethnonational, it is not.

Adjacent concepts

Working class

The working class (and synonyms thereof) is deployed within DMN not so much as an empirical socio-economic category as it is an ontology. In other words, the working class is understood as a theoretically deduced category that contains within it certain properties and potentials. One might call this proletarianism. The working class contains conceptual properties that ground an analytical position in relation to manifold political arguments and viewpoints. A sensibility that the workers are an implied democratic majority is sustained not through sociological evidence but rather an aesthetic-normative affinity to the proletarian-popular.

'Working class' serves as something of a normative orientation, something concerning the vernacular-authentic, the impact of economic change and deindustrialisation, and something about the alienating effects of the anti-democratic proclivities of elites. All of these facets have differing connotations. As such, the working class can be understood as an adjacent concept: grounded in a Marxist core, the working class is evoked to make arguments about snobbery, neoliberalism, and 'the void' at the heart of democracy.

Freeden makes a distinction between cultural and logical adjacency. The concept of the working class is deployed within DMN more culturally than logically. That is, the concept of the working class is immanently defined by specific aesthetic, normative, and pragmatic properties.[8] This is different from simply saying that any definition of the working class is in some fashion 'cultural'. Rather, it is that the working class is an adjacent concept that contains the properties it does in order to buttress and advocate the core concepts of DMN.

What might these cultural adjacencies be? The working class is a social repository of a set of denials. These denials are tightly interconnected and relay back into the democratic core of DMN: representation, accountability, and participation. Each of these values – which float freely between various ideological traditions – are, for DMN, fixed within the working class as a kind of subject denial: these values are important precisely because they are only as good as the working class's ability to struggle for them.

The working class increasingly denied political representation because the party system is dominated by the bourgeoisie and middle class. The Labour Party's connection to the institutionalised expression of some working-class interests has been severed. The Conservative Party might capture working-class votes but is unable to keep those votes as it is in the thrall of a financial oligarchy. There is no accountability to the working class because governing elites across parties concern themselves with the more politically active and demanding middle classes, the signals issuing from financial markets and creditors, and the regulations and norms of international governance. This leaves working-class votes constantly on the precipice of disillusion, cynicism, and hopelessness – powerfully demotivated to engage with politics.

There are three core properties of the DMN's working class. Firstly, DMN's proletarianism focuses on the community. Working-class people are articulated to narratives about being deeply embedded in a place, being products of a rich and thick history. Working classes are also seen as exemplars of what might be called DMN's aesthetic of a rugged society, which we shall also return to. Secondly, and in a more formally analytical fashion, DMN frequently articulates the socio-economic marginalisation of the working class with neoliberalism. Thirdly – as we shall see later – the working class is understood aesthetically as an attitude: as a repository of common sense or no-nonsense political judgement, as a collective agency that works hard and has no time for the flimflam of new social movement or identitarian posture.

There is an understanding of the working class here as a historically 'in and of itself' class. The cultural adjacency here is implicit, but analytically vital. It is these approaches to the working class that set up other social distinctions as equal to class – race, ethnicity, gender, and others – and serve a regressive political purpose because they downgrade through relativisation the particular historical agency of the working class (singular), ignoring the Marxist foundational categorisation of class.[9] Indeed, a great deal of DMN discourse works to destabilise the notion that race or gender are absolute necessities to an account of working-class subjectivity. It insistently rejects talk of intersectionality.

Middle class

Enter the PMC. Across the West, the PMC enjoys a high degree of integration, both sociologically and culturally. Their use of social-media platforms, particularly Twitter, and cultural conformity help promote a coherent identity; the nongovernmental organizations they almost exclusively staff help to train them in the modes of activism, protocols, and language necessary for their collective political action. They see themselves as the political conscience of the whole of society.[10]

The adjacent concept of the middle class is equally articulated as a conceptual category that bears considerable cultural meaning. And, as with the conceptualisation of the working class, the middle class is a concept that acts as a kind of moral vector, channelling a purposeful and broad-ranging argument about the state of politics more generally. If the working class is the concept that orients DMN's sense of championing, the middle class evokes its principal sense of enmity. We will move soon to identify the cultural characterisations that enable this enmity, but we should start with some understanding of how the categorisation 'middle class' is defined.

For DMN, the middle class is defined by its relative affluence and the nature of its work. The middle class earns salaries not wages; they are relatively well paid and are occupied in knowledge work. They are employed by capital but are relatively educated. In some DMN text, the term *professional managerial classes* (PMC) is used.[11] The term PMC has been used mainly in the US to discuss the rise of a certain cadre within the middle classes that are 'skilled', earning relatively good amounts of money, and enjoying 'comfortable' lifestyles. They are also employed in positions in which they are tasked with organising workers, finances, and information on behalf of capital. As such, they are aligned with the purposes and imperatives of profitability. They are not only middle class but also working with rather than working for capitalists. In other texts, the middle class are a kind of intelligentsia that revolves around the media and university; they are a 'chattering class'. They are also associated with residential property ownership, or maybe property with a garden ownership.

The middle class is, then, loosely defined analytically as the relatively 'skilled' and affluent workers who display some combination of the following social traits: a sense of social differentiation from lower-paid and 'unskilled'/ manual workers, a commitment to the technologies that define capitalist strategies of labour and resource management, and a strong sense of their own lifestyle and value. These cultural significations endow DMN's middle class with a sense of privilege and *en haute* social purpose.

What matters is not only the relative material privilege but also – possibly more so – relative political power. The political expression and organisation of the middle classes has captured a considerable amount of attention from politicians, most of whom are also middle class. As a result, middle-class views of politics are seen as views of politics in general.

'Middle class' also relays a set of political values for DMN. This is important in relation to the ideological tradition within which DMN operates. For DMN, what conceptually fixes the middle classes is a patronising moralisation of politics that is based in a snobbish antipathy[12] towards the working class. There is very close antagonistic adjacency between the working class and middle class in which DMN's advocacy or the former is inextricably and intensely connected to the opprobrium visited on the latter. The middle classes treat the working classes as infants: lacking knowledge, unable to execute rational thought.[13] They treat them as morally corrupted: racists,[14] vengeful, mean. They treat them as socially ill-equipped: immobile, blinkered, spewing inappropriate phraseologies.[15] Within DMN proto-ideology, these morbid properties attributed to the working class by the middle class enable a kind of moral conversation among the middle classes about what 'we' should do to socially engineer 'them' into the correct practices of civic life.[16]

The patronising and moralising attitudes assigned to the middle classes in relation to the working class are given intensified normativity by the association of certain cultural features to the middle class. They are seen as cosmopolitan in the sense of being socially unmoored and mobile and at most partially committed to a national popular politics. They are seen as being narcissistic in their presentations of self and in their consumption habits. They are seen as individualising, that is, not only as individuals but individuals who constantly reaffirm the value of the individual. This is why the politics of the middle class is, in DMN's view, irredeemably liberal. It is based in the sanctity of a kind of individualism which is connected to a faith in the free market and human rights. Both of these core liberal credos are so deeply couched in a sociology of relative privilege that when they are undermined, all manner of panicky authoritarianism emerges, what one writer considers bad liberalism.[17]

They are seen as being meticulous, disciplinary, and prurient about the use of language. They are seen as elitist, looking to a gaggle of celebrity intellectuals for their political orientations rather than some more grounded, dirty, and popular politics. One might be tempted to shorthand all of these cultural features as '*Guardian* reader',[18] and *Guardian* headlines often pop up in DMN Twitter feeds for hard-nosed lampooning. For DMN, the middle classes have dinner parties with organic food and top-shelf Merlot to discuss the insights of Greta Thunberg and fret about how to deal with the pervasive racism in football fans.

The conceptualisation of the middle classes does considerable cultural work to bolster other adjacent and core concepts in its ideological formation. It is the working class–middle class antagonistic dyad that drives the sense of injustice at the core of DMN. It is the supposed weak and capricious middle-class attitude towards nation and popular democracy that gives normative strength to two of DMN's core concepts. However, in relation to the third, it is important to note that there is nothing in the pathologisation of the middle classes within DMN that speaks directly to the merits of Marxism, a feature that we will return to.

Common sense

'Simple facts, plain arguments, and common sense.'[19] The sentiments of Thomas Paine are reflected in the adjacency of the common-sense concept within DMN.[20] DMN shares with Paine a founding faith that society or the masses are the repository of political virtue and that the state or a governing elite – most especially those that are unrepresentative of the people – are the source of political woe.[21] DMN holds a particular conceptualisation of what good politics is. Common sense serves as a validation of a political orientation that has the following properties.

Firstly, the popular view is very likely to be the nearest thing to the right view in relation to a political decision or issue. Secondly, that simplicity is the key guide to political intuition. This implies a cynicism of sophistication (perhaps an association with this term's original meaning) and excessive nuance. There is an association of phrases like 'this is a complex issue' with an elitism in which politics is portrayed as something best managed by elites.[22] There is an antipathy towards 'word salads'.[23]

Thirdly, plain speaking is honest speaking and, even if erroneous in some fashion, still politically valid. It is through the open and direct contestation of core ideas that the political good emerges. DMN is strongly against censorship of undesirable political language. Declarations that a certain form of speech or statement is unacceptable are always a partial shutting down of fulsome political discourse. When speech is racist or homophobic, DMN responses are as likely to call it 'stupid', the voice of a 'few idiots', rather than unacceptable and triggering a discussion of censorship. Common sense connects closely to matters of freedom of speech and expression, discussed later.

DMN wishes to allow all political commentary and opinion; it wishes all voices to speak as plainly as possible, and it expects that brusque, direct, open political contestation will drive political progress. Common sense is, then, something that can only be achieved through open contest. It connects to the notion of a rugged society mentioned later in that a common-sense politics is a rough-edged political discourse in which idiots are called idiots, hypocrites are called hypocrites, and so on, not only for the purposes of endless social media contrarianism but because there is an underlying faith that the telos here is an emerging rough consensus that, at the heart of popular open political debate, is a popular consensus of what constitutes the political good.

Common sense sets a tone and it establishes a procedural method for the preceding adjacent concepts – the working class have it; the middle class do not. It also provides a telos for its core concepts: common sense is what allows a comity between democracy, nationalism, and Marxism: that each and all are a priori justified by their essentially popular nature, a nature that is in turn connected to a conceptualisation of the political good. Common sense, then, serves to decontest the core concepts. What Marxist would not wish openly to argue that good politics should be popular and right?

Liberty

In liberty, we have a final adjacent concept. Adjacent concepts can be purloined or shared between ideological traditions and there is a convincing argument that liberty lies within a great many ideological traditions. The term is most familiarly of liberal provenance: 'liberty has held the stage in the monodramas of liberal history'.[24] But, although this is undoubtedly true, liberty has proven to be remarkably fungible. We have already noted its place in French Socialist political ideas. Liberty has connotations of active and powerful individual agency which can go beyond a core liberal belief in freedom from state oversight. Republicanism's seeking a 'powerful and vigilant citizenry'[25] that ensures no one is dominated by external agencies evokes liberty. And, libertarianism sees liberty as its most fundamental concept value to a degree that it pervades practically its entire discourse.[26]

DMN, as a proto-ideology, relies on the evocation of liberty in a way that draws on liberal, republican, and libertarian normativities. Liberty resides somewhere in a space defined by the staunch advocacy of the freedom of the individual, a certain kind of enmity towards the state, and a commitment to the nurturing of a public culture of non-domination.

DMN's core evocation of liberty (or its close synonyms) is non-interference. Interference is articulated through an associated adjacent concept. The capture of policy making and lobbying by the middle class has created a habit of governance in which the state – in a paternalist mindset – intervenes in the lives of the masses as if it was a pedagogical, tolerant, but disciplinary parent. It seeks to tell people what to eat, what cars to drive, what sources of information to believe.

Liberty is also the driving force behind its advocacy of freedom of expression. Unlike much contemporary liberal agonising over the line between freedom of expression and harm, DMN seems close to an unconditional say or write what one wishes. This connects to common sense and the peripheral concepts of a rugged society that we will explore later. Unpleasant ideas are allowed because liberty is a higher-order value than freedom from being offended.[27] Saying offensive things should not be met with censoriousness but rather robust counter-argument. The faith is that unencumbered, plain-speaking, mass politics will subdue xenophobia or sexism through debate and challenge. Furthermore, because 'offence' is hardly an easy thing to define, it tends to meld into a code for things 'woke' middle-class people dislike.[28]

Liberty's normative orientation is, in turn, conditioned by other concepts within the core and adjacent spaces. It is the liberty or ordinary people against an overbearing government, against a patronising middle-class cadre of educators, against transnational organisations that wish to legislate away the sovereignty of the nation-state that DMN rails.

DMN's adjacent concepts are certainly proto-concepts. Liberty draws on different ideological traditions, working-class agency is assumed to have a certain historic role, and the middle class is portrayed as much as bête noir as it is a socio-economic group. But, together, they do present a well-integrated mise en scène, almost a morality play in which political contestation is realised through the difference between a proletariat and Guardianistas.

Peripheral concepts

Peripheral concepts, we should recall, are those least clearly figured and connected exclusively to a specific ideological tradition. Freeden uses the term 'concept' loosely and interchangeably with other rough synonyms when discussing peripheries. We should also note that peripheral concepts/terms tend to emerge in the heat of contention. In other words – and also recalling our analytical emphasis on contention in the process of ideology building – peripheral concepts' presence in a proto-ideology is as much about contesting issues as it is the intrinsic intellectual merits of a term. Per Chapter 4, we will treat peripheral concepts as less analytically substantive but more mobile and public-facing terms, terms that reveal the combative nature of a proto-ideology.

Education

Debates over curriculum design and cultures of learning are frequently engaged with by DMN. Over the last ten years or so, education (and especially higher education) has become the main focus of the 'culture wars' in which a set of positions concerning the symbolic meaning and merit of certain practices, vocabularies, and symbolisms have generated often polemic arguments concerning the value of education.

DMN harbours a strong incredulity and cynicism towards a certain kind of political correctness that it labels as 'wokeness'. This is not so much the project to regulate and modify language to reject racialised and gendered slurs and associations which emerged in the 1980s but rather a subsequent more complex and meticulous regulative/modifying project in which a broader range of cultural and historical language practices are identified as problematic. This project of speech-act regulation has become increasingly nebulous: not only concerned with the use titles and symbols that were gendered and racially coded but also with dress, memorialisation, performance/behaviour, and implicit/micro gestures. For now, we can note the adversarialism that it has generated within DMN as a conduit to explore this proto-ideology's interest in education.

There is an increasingly prominent and influential political movement within universities, schools, some political parties, and campaign groups to 'decolonise' the university. It is difficult to identify exactly what makes universities colonised or what decolonisation means[29] – and this is perhaps key to its expansive fungibility. Whatever definition might underlie decolonising the university/curriculum, it is clear that it has led to a series of critical reflections over the curating of readings, the languages of teaching and learning, the practices of pedagogy, the revision of curricula, and the relationship between lecturers and students.

It is this project that DMN rails against. There are four key components of its critique, each of which connect back to core and adjacent concepts. Most fundamentally, DMN believes that decoloniality is a variant of 'wokeness' that wishes to expunge or add 'trigger warnings' for historical and political content that is perceived as problematic because it is part of a system of 'white'/male/Western domination. This violates DMN's strong commitment to liberty and free speech.

Secondly, decolonising/wokeness is seen as an elite language game, defined by a kind of intellectual self-regard. It judges those who do not use appropriate terminology as morally compromised and/or in need of correction. Most prominently, it is seen as a weapon through which the middle-class instructors problematise or even demonise the working class. This is most extant in DMN's general demeaning of claims to historical injustice which are represented as rather pious and didactic conjurings of events long passed in order to educate a broader population about the nature of injustice.

Thirdly, it is seen as a way to generate a justice narrative based in identity politics. Wokeness/decolonisation focuses on intersectional identities that tend to generate their own profusions and individual positionalities. The values of individual recognition and respect are articulated through a normative field in which each individual is a site of a specific form of oppression and/or marginality. This obscures the possibilities of mass or class-based political mobilisations. In DMN's perspective, identitarian politics in this form also situates itself in a middle-class culture of self-affirmation which does not connect effectively with broader and more popular cultural identities.

Fourthly, decoloniality in the university undermines the ability of students to engage fully with the facts of politics and history by attempting to censor and redact the content of syllabuses. This is seen as patronising and hostile towards a healthy process of independently minded inquiry. The premise within DMN is that students should engage freely with all ideas in as unmediated a fashion as possible in order that they will – not without some risk and some troubled engagements – come to their own understanding. There is particular opprobrium for arguments that black students should not read too many 'white' texts as this would be oppressive or even racist. This premise rests on an expectation that students are better off when 'stress tested' in their learning rather than protected from ideas that they might find unpleasant. This connects to our next peripheral concept/term.

Resilience

DMN does not so much advocate rugged individualism as a rugged society. It believes that society is more resilient and dynamic when the tenaciousness of all of its individual members is realised. Social resilience is, then, a property held within the ruggedness of its members; the whole is greater than the parts. DMN sees this property as generally left in abeyance by political elites who – through one form of paternalism or another – endeavour to cosset social groups, think for people, or constrain the scope for people to take risks, or hold a predilection for victimology.

Consequently, DMN holds an adversarialism towards the cultures of professionalised therapy and lifestyle advice, which it sees as ways to repress the full nature of humankind: adventurous and not entirely without the troubles and scars of having lived.[30] DMN easily identifies therapy discourse with an elite middle-class culture of personhood which is, to use a stylisation, 'comfortable'. In this class context, declarations of victimhood are not entirely trivialised but are downgraded and relativised in relation to material scarcity and the demands of hard work.

The ontology of victimhood means that people with considerable affluence can play the sleight of hand of occluding their privilege behind a language of therapy.[31] DMN is incredulous towards declarations of celebrity and middle-class guilt at their own wrongdoings. If a rugged sensibility would be to 'try again and fail better', DMN identifies and condemns a kind of publicised introversion that derives from a meticulous delving into the soul.

DMN argues against various forms of victimology[32] in two other ways. Firstly, because it is an ontology of passive political agency that evokes pity. Secondly, it generates a culture of increasingly individualised reflections on the self and its vulnerability. Individuals might feel themselves subjected to injustice as a result of cultural appropriation. They might feel the need for safe spaces or concern themselves that safe spaces have been invaded. They might identify microaggressions which might be manifested in gestures, dress, and cadence of voice.

DMN tends to emphasise or celebrate the fact that ordinary people work through political issues through a day-to-day negotiation, in work and leisure. It sees communities as a source of strength and untapped political energies. Cultures of therapy and victimhood and their articulation to images of (near) perfected well-being do not speak to this. If we think back to the politics that Marxism has relied on, we can see how DMN would wish for a hard-nosed, collective, and combative political self; in the Marxist vision of class struggle, this is also present. The spiritual or psychological balance of the individual is at best irrelevant or at worst a distraction.

Double standards

Perhaps DMN's most malleable normative weapon is the highlighting of double standards. DMN aspires to a foregrounded and carefully maintained consistency of moral standards. This is something that is deeply embedded in its notion of common sense. 'Double standards' is offered here rather than hypocrisy, although the latter is certainly part of the repertoire. This is because a good deal of DMN's attacks on other political positions derive from a critique of middle-class politics for its being based in certain levels of affluence, education, and lifestyle. This leads middle-class commentary to condemn Brexit voters for not realising how valuable immigrants are for the service economy. It leads to a mild affirmation of lockdown lifestyles as enabling home baking as well as smart remote working. Double standards here is an attack on the fact that middle-class political and cultural normative commentary is based in the assumption that everyone has a living salary, high levels of education, some relative affluence, and, consequently, a cultural more that enables a sense of political virtue that is, in fact, exclusive.[33] Thus, the critique is aimed not only at bare hypocrisy but also consistent and sincerely held middle-class values based in an ignorance of how other people live.

Secondly, a closely related form of double standards which is regularly the object of DMN's ire is corporate wokeness. As we have seen, 'woke' serves as a floating referent for a great deal of what is wrong with elitist politics. In this particular instance, DMN accuses large companies with strong 'woke' branding. This might relate to 'inclusiveness', rainbow politics, Black Lives Matter, or various ethical consumer standards. The double standards accusation takes the form of a contrasting of declared virtue against the ways that these companies treat workers or cohabit with regimes that carry out widespread and systematic human rights violations.[34] There is sometimes a suggestion that corporations deceive in their self-representation as justice seeking. There is an accusation that companies' social conscience is expedient, strategic, and aligned with prevailing middle-class consumer sensibilities. There is also an argument that more substantive and important matters relating to companies are missed: the nature of work and the liberties of the people. This is a general property within DMN's attack on double standards: that the standards of the middle class are in some rather effete, too easy, too pleasing. In a word, hippy.[35]

A third and less-mentioned area in which double standards are identified and condemned relates to Britain's actions internationally. Foreign intervention is very strongly attacked, and the basis of this attack is always the difference between declared aims and realities. This might simply be the lies told in the pursuit of military intervention. It might also be the narcissistic declarations of intent that go with humanitarian intervention and aid in which Britain is saving distant others.

There are two different articulations to core and adjacent concepts at work here. In relation to the double standards of the middle classes, the principal connection is that there is a majority-experienced common life shared by the working classes that, it is strongly implied, should be the foundation for one's reflections on the values one takes as those generally shared by the nation's people. The critique derives from the sleight of hand of assuming a minority affluent life is a generally shared one, or one in which those that don't share matter less or don't deserve it.[36] The morality of the middle class is, DMN claims, strongly and implicitly defined as a universal morality which – as a result – asserts itself over the often more 'common sense' or more important moral issues experienced or raised by working-class people. In instances where middle-class commentators criticise facets of their own oppression, DMN is keen to identify how the more important matter at hand is a lacuna in relation to an engagement with working-class oppressions. A salient example here is that 'middle-class' public protests were considered proper public events and that 'working-class' protests were seen as riotously dangerous to public health.[37] Concern about sexual harassment is framed within a larger concern for the sexual exploitation of working-class women.[38]

The second – which more closely resembles bare hypocrisy – connects to the premise that the best political shell for democracy is the nation-state and that this requires a robust popular sovereignty. A world of popularly sovereign nations in which governments are accountable to their people is negated by intervention which always erodes the connections (even if weak) between states and their peoples. Thus, the consistency that underlines and defines the attack on hypocrisy is that there is a consistent internationalism in which nation-states serve as the most amenable arrangement for democracy to be practised and intervention by strongly sovereign nation-states in others serves to reproduce their weakness and lack of democratic potential.

Progress

Thus far, one might have the sense that DMN is a rather spartan proto-ideology. Its texts might seem commonly dedicated to the bursting of more idealistic and flowery middle-class social justice bubbles. But this is not entirely correct. DMN often goes into battle with other ideologies and discourses on the basis that they have history wrong. DMN maintains a sense of optimism about the future which contrasts strikingly with prevailing Left-leaning discourses on the environment,[39] demographic change, the prospects for democracy, Brexit, and COVID-19. DMN tends to see the future as a set of possibilities for the realisation of greater technologies, economic growth, and more nice things for more people. It is explicitly a child of Enlightenment optimism, or perhaps more aptly, progress.

DMN sustains a strong rejection of the misanthropy that some Left-leaning commentators have,[40] especially in relation to the human impact on the planet, the 'Anthropocene', and so on. Contrastingly, DMN asserts that humanity is generally winning history: finding solutions, harbouring the energies of the planet, pushing frontiers. It sees humankind not as another species of animal that cohabits with others and has roughly the same value as other species but rather as the principal subject of all history and value. This world view, in relation to DMN and more generally, is described as Promethean.[41]

DMN also condemns the fearfulness that dystopian future building generates. It maintains a keen eye for prognoses that have proven to be apocalyptic rather than born out by evidence. It seeks out the empirical questionability of predictions by elite organisations concerned with climate change, 'peak' oil, and so on. It wishes to argue a case for something more Promethean in its future histories. This peripheral concept connects least clearly to the core and adjacent concepts set out earlier. One might construe that the progressivist attitude derives from an aspect of Marx's work which holds that the capitalist class is historically progressive inasmuch as it promotes gains in productivity, innovates, and expands. But, this is not extant in DMN texts.

Conclusion

Having established a constellation of concepts we should finish by considering what kind of morphology DMN is: what form does it take? DMN has a deep, wide Marxist base upon which rests a more prominent and broader

Figure 5.1: Schema of DMN's morphology

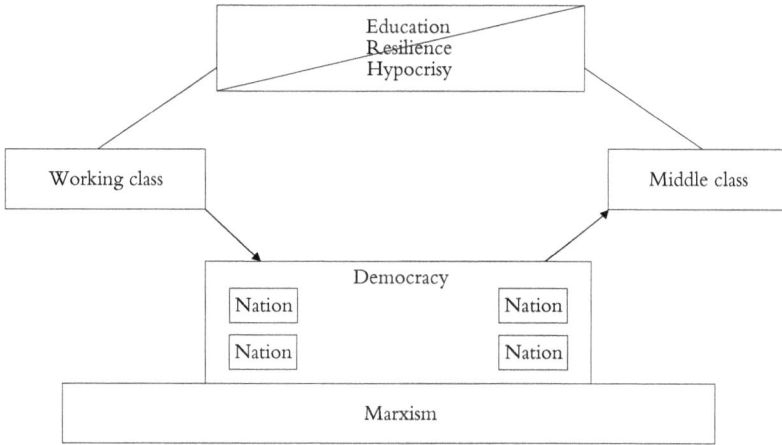

democracy which rests at the centre of all other concepts (see Figure 5.1). Inside this democracy is a very deeply nested nationalism which fills democracy through multiplication into multiple nations. Intersecting with the Marxist foundation and democracy, but on opposing sides, are two class concepts: the working class and the middle class. These are opposing and have no overlap. Their antagonism derives from the fact that the working-class concept relates to democracy positively and the middle class one negatively. The two classes do, however, connect as adversaries in relation to a set of overlapping cultural-aesthetic concepts, rendering the latter schismic through a class antimony: education, resilience, and hypocrisy.

6

Identitarian Socialism

Introduction

Identitarian Socialism is a proto-ideology in which a range of social injustices are drawn together through an association of oppressed identities with a left-of-centre politics. Its critique of capitalism is that it is based in an elitist politics that exploits, oppresses, and marginalises a society composed of various social groups. Its aspirational world view is that a diverse coalition of identities will push the political centre of gravity radically to the Left through a multi-sited and diverse set of political activisms. Deploying the core concepts of socialism, intersectionality, and populism, Identitarian Socialism would construct a socialism that understands class as a property expressed through situated cultures or resistance and activism.

Identitarian Socialism is oriented around a group of individuals who share some connection with Novara Media. Novara Media was set up in 2011 by Aaron Bastani and James Butler. It is perhaps the best known and most popular socialist news media outlet, which started as a podcast and has grown into a network of political commentary, driven by its Facebook and Twitter profiles. These social media profiles are not only disseminated by Novara's own accounts but also the accounts of its main spokespeople who have achieved considerable public profiles that have brought them into TV appearances and columns in *The Guardian*. Identitarian Socialism also weaves into the content of other websites such as Tribune, Stats for Lefties, Left Foot Forward and New Statesman.

Core concepts

Socialism

In Chapter 3, we explored how the term socialism was both historically changeable and therefore varied in its relations to Marxism. At the end of the spectrum, socialism seems like a synonym for the rather vague and relativistic 'Left'; at the other end, it seems like a synonym for Marxism or communism. We distinguished between a Socialism that was not Marxist – the anarchism, social democratic, and romanticisms of those seeking to find a better life beyond industrial capitalism – and a socialism which was broader, encompassing these trajectories as well as all the variations of Marxism. Identitarian Socialism's socialism is lower case. Indeed, as we shall explore, there is a discernible ecumenicalism to Identitarian Socialism that evokes Marx, even if it does not go far beyond the act of evoking itself.

Novara Media declares its remit as addressing 'the issues that are set to define the 21st century, from a crisis of capitalism to racism and climate change'.[1] The signalling of a crisis of capitalism, qua capitalism, fixes the socialist core concept: there is within capitalism a tendency to crisis that can only be properly addressed through its surpassing. Crisis sets the possibility of a post-capitalist world and – as with socialist conceptualisations generally – this premise is decontested and rendered axiomatic within Identitarian Socialism's political argumentation. Capitalism is crisis.

Novara's statement of identity's allocative structure is not simply a common or garden socialist declaration: 'from capitalism *to* racism and climate change'. Racism and climate change are not clearly located within capitalism but rather as its possible co-equals, or maybe slightly less central but autonomous and important concerns. In other words, they are not put within capitalism in a way that would render them dependent or second order. Indeed, the kernel of this statement is that Novara's concerns are *crisis*, racism, and climate change. The foundational presence of capitalism becomes ambiguous. A critique of capitalism is co-equal with race and environmental concerns. The term 'capitalism' is restricted to an *implication* of a systemic world view, not a specification that establishes its foundational status as a category. Socialism connotes something that requires both a diversity of struggles and a diversity of agencies: identitarian, issue-based, and based in workers' conditions.[2]

But, in this conceptualisation, socialism still holds considerable radical promise. Socialism is conceptualised as a collective noun, an insistence that capitalist crisis (that crisis qualification remains) frames a set of 'struggles against', even if it does not analytically unify them or endow them with a singular revolutionary agency or intent. We have seen how 'Left' doesn't carry sufficient conceptual weight for ideological construction. For socialism to serve as a core concept, it will require sufficient detail, fixity, and decontestedness to anchor other concepts. Let us explore how this is so.

Identitarian Socialists are often happy to use the term communism and also to endorse Marx. The most iconic moment in Novara Media's history is Ash Sarkar's response on *Good Morning Britain* to Piers Morgan's jibe about Barack Obama's being her 'hero'. Sarkar's response – 'I'm a communist, you idiot ... I'm literally a communist' – gained millions of views[3] and led Novara to produce a T-shirt with the same text.[4] There is also a Novara T-shirt sporting the single bold-letter word, 'Marx'.

These references to Marx and communism are not substantive enough to be understood as fully conceptual work. There is one specific way in which the term communism is used in a manner that displays conceptual underlabour, which we will discuss later; but for now, we can recognise that 'communism' and 'Marx' resemble signifiers rather than concepts. Marxism and communism are articulated as self-identifications that do not come with clear explanations of historical analysis or the primacy of class. The 'Marx' T-shirt is on sale on the Novara merch website along with a similarly logoed water bottle for the gym.

So, how does the concept of socialism work? It locates Identitarian Socialism as a radical-Left tradition. In other words, socialism serves as a core concept that sets a *general* orientation towards a systemic critique of capitalism in order to signal a *radical* position within the political spectrum of the Left. The radical property of socialism is that it bases itself on the premise that another world, not currently visible, is possible. This alter-possibility property of socialism orients Identitarian Socialism in a radical-Left stance in relation to any current affairs issue: political parties, the media, inequality, and so on. The conceptualisation poses the question of what this other world might look like.

On *Newsnight*, Aaron Bastani offered a concise and clearly Marxist definition of communism based on the abolition of the wage labour relation.[5] But, more generally within Identitarian Socialism, the prospective of a world after capitalism is not articulated to a Marxist theory of history in which class struggle drives a historical movement towards the graveyard of the bourgeoisie. Instead, *marxisant* language is combined with a more open sense of historical progress which resembles that of social justice movements.

As we have seen in previous chapters, the conceptual morphology of a proto-ideology will contain lacunae and ambiguities that are not only a manifestation of the fact that there are no perfected ideologies but also that these are ideological *constructions*, work in progress. Identitarian Socialism absolutely requires its socialist core in order to establish and maintain its radical credentials, but the intent and meaning of socialism is ambiguous: partly critique of capitalism, partly Marxist, and partly an injustice concern that may or may not involve a holistic critique of capitalism.

In Identitarian Socialism's media output, socialism is situational. Its radicalism exerts a kind of gravitational pull, but its force varies. Identitarian Socialism has used its socialism to support Corbyn, Momentum, and less well-known Left-leaning groups within the Labour Party[6] while also maintaining its sense of alterity in relation to the limited prospects of parliamentary parties. This locative indeterminism – of being in and outside, near and remote to parliamentary politics – was most clearly revealed in the broadly Remain messaging communicated by Identitarian Socialism, based in an acknowledgement of the 'neoliberal' nature of the EU but also a judgement that a push leftwards was more likely within this regional organisation than without it. Identitarian Socialism's ambiguous radicalism leads it to spend a good amount of reflection considering how engagement with Labour can effectively move its centre of gravity leftwards. A good example of this is Owen Jones' account of Labour under Corbyn.[7]

Intersectionality
Introduction

Intersectionality is a concept that emerged as part of a critique of liberal visions of justice, the main critique being that equal opportunities approaches to law making did not properly account for the multiplex nature of oppression, especially the particular injustices visited upon black women. Feminist researchers in particular used the term to disaggregate categorisations of 'women' and 'race' in ways that had two main effects: to combine forms of oppression and marginalisation in their analytical categorisations, and to increase the focus on the particularities of oppression and marginalisation on individuals.

Intersectionality is 'the notion that subjectivity is constituted by mutually reinforcing vectors of race, gender, class, and sexuality'.[8] Individuals were perceived as embodiments or sites of manifold injustices. Broadly structural concerns with race and gender became increasingly 'recombined' with each other and also with other facets of marginalisation and oppression: sexuality, disability, specific ethnicities, and so on. This had the effect of intensifying the focus on individual experiences of oppression, a phenomenon sometimes called positionality in the literature.

As a result, the notion of intersectionality has established the political identity of the subject as its founding ontology. Political identity sets a sense of justice-seeking agency that is based on variegated, diverse, and 'positional' or 'multi positionings'[9] (that is, personally experienced) coming together for the purposes of broad campaign issues.

Intersectionality is a term that has also been integrated into social justice discourses.[10] Injustice is articulated as something like a web or *nébuleuse* of particular oppressions. As a result, the politics of class is always also a politics of gender, race, ethnicity, region, age, and so on.[11] To some degree, this always exerts a qualifying and calibrating effect on the way class is conceptualised. It is not a singular and autonomous concept; it becomes a classification that requires a further classification. In much of the intersectionality literature, class is rendered as a state of poverty that is one part of a list of modes of oppression: 'poor, black woman', for example.

Intersectionality encapsulates an important shift in the broad terrain of left-wing politics. It foregrounds political identity as a diffuse and individualised experience and it has pivotally contributed to the rise of a social justice discourse that is inclusive, issue-based, networked, and protest-oriented. Its salience for our purposes is that it provides a context within which Identitarian Socialism establishes in its core concepts a connection to a broader universe of resistance politics. This can be seen, above all, in the central treatment given to matters of political identity, selfhood, and multiple forms of oppression and marginalisation.

Intersectionality as concept

Discourses of intersectionality have fed into Identitarian Socialism in a way that is rather diffuse. If political identities are multiple and interconnected, intersectionality tends to create broad political fields which are analytically 'flat'; that is, they do not base themselves in an essentialism, a priori, or abstraction that specifies a phenomenon that matters most or matters in a higher-order way. Perhaps, then, intersectionality might be very present within Identitarian Socialism but it does not really deserve categorising as a concept.

But, the term intersectionality not only encapsulates a good deal of Identitarian Socialism's discourse, it also endows that discourse with a unified analytical normative meaning. Analytically, it serves to bind together variegated forms of social mobilisation and struggle. In other words, intersectionality works within Identitarian Socialism dialectically: its disaggregates are re-aggregates. Identifying the (individual) subjects of injustice by representing them as multiplex concatenations of oppression, intersectionality then proceeds to draw those subjects into a broader field of political contention.

Normatively, it produces a notion of injustice that is based in a combination of demands for recognition and rights and demands for material improvement. As a result, the apparent diversity of text within Identitarian Socialism is more substantively serving to develop a concept of intersectionality that holds that diversity within a single normative field.

Identitarian Socialism produces a consistent stream of content concerning ethnic minorities, immigrants, LGBTQIA+ people, disabled people, and other identity-based groups. What connects this reportage – what gives these different experiences a commonality that allows concept building – is that they are articulated as instances of a shared injustice. Intersectionality is presented through Identitarian Socialism as a concept that generates a powerful normative affect concerning injustice. Injustice has a twofold characteristic for Identitarian Socialism. It is both a normativity that concerns itself with a lack of recognition: of fundamental rights or, more ambitiously, social recognition and validation of the cultural expression of an identity. It is also an injustice steeped in matters of poverty and inequality.

Intersectionality, then, corrals a set of political issues together and, as a result, generates a sense of political contention that is both very productive but also rather ambiguous. It engages with a diverse set of identitarian struggles for recognition and rights and qualifies each of these with loosely class-related concerns with poverty and inequality. As a result, things like overwork, struggles to pay rent, lack of benefits, precarious employment, and poverty are articulated to racial, gendered, and other oppressions.[12]

This lends Identitarian Socialism a kind of maximalism in its radicalism. It aims to overthrow all forms of social prejudice and injustice and, because they are all interconnected, scope of ambition overwhelms analytical prioritisation. Either/or is far less prominent than both/and.[13] One effect of this is to render the notion of class as less analytically distinct and to some degree auxiliary, that is, only present in its material effects on forms of identity injustice. Novara has carried some articles that explicitly reject Marxism as a foundation for progressive struggle, even identifying it as a kind of distraction from the project to dismantle racial capitalism.[14]

Intersectionality's normativity

We have identified intersectionality as a core concept that most centrally serves to define a justice politics for Identitarian Socialism. Injustice and its interpolation through intersectionality generates a rich field of opprobrium.

Prejudice. Identitarian Socialism accommodates the mainstay of inter-sectionality politics, which is a concern with prejudice against certain social identities. This is something that it shares with many liberals who consider justice as founded in equal treatment of all individuals. However, in order to push leftwards on matters of prejudice, Identitarian Socialism presents its intersectionality not as matters of rights or the formal indifference of law and government to the specificities of individuals' identities. Rather, it connects them into systemic forms of political domination which serve the interests of the elites. The main relay of this radicalisation of prejudice is the suffix phobia, for example, islamophobia or transphobia.

The phobia suffix stipulates that there is a systemic prejudice at work. In the sociological sense, a phobia is not an individual, cultural, or psychological condition but rather one that supports a systemic form of oppression. This is a powerful trope. It intensifies the very real prejudices that, say, trans people suffer. Intensification is an important means to achieve campaign success: legal or institutional reform are not up to the job of tackling historically entrenched social oppression.

But the characterisation of social prejudices as social phobias within Identitarian Socialism is not entirely coherent. If there is a systemic phobia against a group of people, any socialist tradition of thought will likely ask: cui bono? What purpose does this systemic prejudice serve in the pursuit of power? In response, it might be tempting simply to gloss an elite as prejudiced because they are, well, an elite. But this is weak beer for a socialist tradition and it does not feed well into Identitarian Socialism's radicalism. After all, many liberals (and especially Left-liberals) would also argue that social prejudice is widespread, elites are bigoted, and there needs to be a cultural shift (likely through education) to right these wrongs. The sense of a loss of *socialist* focus is only exacerbated by the tendency sometimes to see social phobia as a popular phenomenon: held by white, working-class people.[15] At the point in which systemic prejudice is understood to be widespread or popular, manifestations of an ethno-proletarian whiteness, it undermines the class component of Identitarian Socialism. Consequently, intersectionality demands further intellectual explanatory work to suture its own conceptual arrangements.

Injustice might be framed as a *marginalisation* of specific identities. Consider the following commentary on international football: 'for the rest of us – that is, for most English people – there has always been one form of exclusion or another to contend with, and some degree of ambiguity around our connection with the team'.[16] This is not simply a recognition that there is racism in football fandom. It is articulated as an experience held by gendered and racialised individuals: just before the quotation, the author defines the 'rest of us', the marginalised, as non-white, non-male, and non-heterosexual. The dynamics of exclusion are themselves multiple. The author focuses on racism but also later problematises the form of masculinity at the cultural heart of football. They conclude with an entreaty to a multiple-identitarian coalition: 'there are many different struggles to expand that collective in a variety of ways. All of them are connected to and dependent upon each other'.[17]

Ash Sarkar reflects on her own realisation that 'the exclusion of trans and non-binary people goes far beyond toilets and changing rooms: it's at the heart of all the other issues I derived my political identity from caring about'.[18] Here, we see clearly the exclusion–inclusion dynamic resolved into a generalised social justice identification, articulated with emotional affect. A class-based prioritisation based in a critique of exploitation is eschewed in favour of a justice narrative focused on exclusion, marginalisation, and the rights claims this evokes.

Intersectionality is a concept that allows Identitarian Socialism to connect to a diverse range of political struggles and movements, more so than DMN. The recombination of class and identity within social movements and community groups lends itself to a 'grassroots' framing of political struggle in which spokespeople's voices and the witnessing of meetings and protests are more present. This has an aesthetic effect on Identitarian Socialism in the way that it generates a persuasive imagery of livelihoods as politics, as we shall see later on.

Pluralism
Anti-vanguard

We have seen how the concept of socialism locates this proto–ideology in a radical position in relation to matters of the Left, and we have seen how intersectionality enables a breadth of political advocacy through combinations of political identity, recognition/rights, and class. Pluralism sets these two concepts within a refusal and affirmation which provide essential coordinates for the way in which Identitarian Socialism understands political prospects.

Let us start with the *refusal*. Here, pluralism is a strategic concept that orients Identitarian Socialism against Leninist notions of political struggle.[19] There is no desire to identify a single organisation or party, to seek out a vanguard leadership, to work towards a single 'line' in relation to the achievement of socialism. It would be conceptually impossible for Identitarian Socialism to align itself with a 'party line' of any kind. Political practices derived from anarchism and localism guide political activism towards procedurally and normatively pluralistic politics: deliberative, open, and networked. Forms of political action are celebrated in their diversity, not assessed in terms of their correctness.

This leads us to pluralism's *affirmation*. Identitarian Socialism's political agenda – as implied in the previous section – is manifold. It does not prioritise 'the struggle' in a Marxist sense that sets something intrinsic to class relations as its essence but rather defines a set of injustice issues within a 'coalition of coalitions' politics that sees war, migration, climate change, racism, gender oppression, legacies of imperialism, policing, and other issues as all equally urgent and important.[20]

Conceptually, pluralism is not only a strategic orientation but also a principle, and it sits at the heart of Identitarian Socialism. Pluralism rests at the core because it feeds into key adjacent concepts which, without a pluralist imprimatur, would be considerably more difficult to interconnect. Pluralism *enables* a kind of tolerance for what are ostensibly significantly different forms of political mobilisation and demands. If an organisation has some radical/socialist potential, fights against elites, and maintains the aesthetic form of the underdog, it is likely to receive some endorsement from Identitarian Socialists.

Pluralism operationalises most clearly in the way Identitarian Socialism engages with a field of social movement and other organisations which display sufficient Left-leaning tendencies or potential to be brought into the Identitarian Socialist ambit. Most prominently, Identitarian Socialism displays considerable positivity regarding Extinction Rebellion: 'the left should vocally support this movement'.[21] It reports warmly its occupation of public spaces and its affects of pleasure and spectacle.[22] Criticisms of Extinction Rebellion there certainly are. Some actions are judged to have been self-defeating, exhausting, and anti-political. The suggestion that underlines these criticisms is that Extinction Rebellion's prospects lie, crucially, in its ability to become more fulsomely embedded in a movement of movements, a coalition that will allow its praxis to become more politically sustainable and popular with the public.[23] The pluralism of a social justice movement establishes a form of political comity which is anchored to the articulation of socialism outlined previously: as a diversity of struggles.[24] In other words, Extinction Rebellion's politics overlaps with socialism inasmuch as they identify climate justice as part of a systemic problem with crisis-capitalism. It is pluralism that enables and expresses these kinds of association.

As already noted, Identitarian Socialism does not allow support for a single party. It's relationship with Labour is framed by the socialism concept already outlined: a critique of moderate forces and an advocacy for a more radical-Left position that led to support for Corbyn and Momentum. Momentum itself enjoyed particular support. As a movement based in grassroots membership, and having emerged from a youthful ingress of Labour Party members during the leadership contest that elected Corbyn, Momentum not only propounds a clearly left-of-centre position within Labour but also chimes with the social movement and youthfulness signals that Identitarian Socialism is based in. Identitarian Socialism can also support other political parties. Consider Identitarian Socialism's treatment of the Green Party, a 'small 'leftist party' which is increasingly taking the radical ground from Starmer's Labour.[25] The Greens also key into the Identitarian Socialist understanding of a critique of capitalism as being multi-faceted. If capitalism's essential and fatal properties are its exploitations, racisms, and environmental violence, then a party that focuses centrally on climate change is not missing the point, as a 'class first' position might argue, but rather addressing one of three roughly co-equal issues of contention. If the Green Party captures a more left-wing constituency than Starmer's Labour, it also captures a bundle of environmental issues in a way that Labour does not.[26] Finally, the Green Party's shift from a strong environmental focus towards a social justice focus also keys into the core concepts of Identitarian Socialism. Its increasing focus on localism and citizen assemblies, its promotion of trans rights, and indeed its increasing discourse on social justice articulate with Identitarian Socialism's intersectionality and pluralism.

Similar kinds of assessments can be seen in relation to Occupy, Black Lives Matter, and a set of smaller localised community-based struggles. Extinction Rebellion, the Greens, Momentum, Occupy, BLM, and grassroots movements are critically supported as parts of a diverse political landscape.

To summarise, Identitarian Socialism's core concepts define a proto-ideology that is distinctly positional or, more positively, agile. It maintains socialist normativity not so much to define a position but rather a direction: that many political groups and contestations should move leftwards. It considers the injustices generated by capitalism as defined by class, but not class in itself. The structured economic inequality that is at the heart of pretty much any definition of class (including those within a Marxist tradition, even if the analytical underlabour is distinctly different from other traditions) is manifested within concatenations of social identity. The radical intersectionalities of class generate a cognitive field that is unavoidably diverse, and this requires a conceptual orientation that is tolerant of considerable difference. Pluralism conceptualises political struggle in ways that resemble the ontology of social justice movement literature and politics: let a thousand flowers bloom.

Adjacent concepts

Crisis

> In the truest sense of the word, crises are apocalyptic.[27]

This statement comes from Novara Media. As we would expect, there is some loosening of meaning as we move to consider adjacent concepts. Nevertheless, crisis is not simply an empirical referent – a financial crash or a pandemic – that is simply given passing focus of attention during a piqued media interest. It does conceptual work because it contains within it a particular historical narrative.

Crisis endows Identitarian Socialism with a prospective vision. This vision is composed out of three components. In the first place, a sense of conspiracy or co-production, that is, that discrete crisis tendencies are interconnected and mutually intensifying. The mode of analysis here is something like: this seems bad, but if one understands it in relation to these other processes, it seems disastrous.

Secondly, the choices that crisis establishes are extremely time-constrained.[28] We might recall here the political sensibility of apocalypse, discussed in Chapter 2. There is some similarity here: a framing of political futures through a kind of compression. At a certain point, there will be no return; at a certain point, the ability to address a problem will disappear; at a certain point, we will enter a world that will be radically and categorically worse; things are changing quicker than we think. It is the historic sensibility of approaching a precipice.

Thirdly, crisis is a kind of clarity. Crisis (again like apocalyptic politics) is a kind of revelation in which financial bubbles bursting, forests burning, viruses mutating, masses migrating are all *revealed* as symptoms of the crisis of capitalism. It is increasingly clear, as the saying goes, that it is socialism or barbarism that the world faces. Let us explore how these themes are manifested in content.

Aaron Bastani hosts a conversation with Andreas Malm in which one can see clearly how mutual intensification works. It is worth starting with Malm's general world view, best expressed in his *Corona, Climate, Chronic Emergency*.[29] In this book, Malm argues that climate change and the COVID-19 pandemic are only apparently dissimilar. More substantively, they are manifestations of the same synthetic crisis, a crisis resulting from carbon capitalism. The interview commences on the basis of a consensus that 'we all know and constantly articulate the scale of the crisis and what this means and it is existential in the long term'.[30] The breadth of scale enables a constant connectivity between disasters or impending disasters in Identitarian Socialist discourse: 'threats should not be viewed in isolation from one another: a world of rising temperatures, and further deforestation, also means more pandemics. Threats should be viewed as additive rather than distinct'.[31] In another article by Bastani, extinction, COVID-19, and global warming are connected together, leading him to conclude that 'it's clear time isn't on our side'.[32]

There is, of course, substantial evidence to back up the kind of associations made between climate change and the environmental damage done by fossil fuel-driven accumulation. But, it is debatable the degree to which these combinations generate crisis and it is also an open question how governments or movements should respond. There are two salient facets to the Identitarian Socialist framing of crisis response, both based in a firm belief that – as just outlined – crisis is major and immanent. Firstly, the framing of crisis is global. A simple perusal of Identitarian Socialism content reveals that it has a greater focus on global politics than DMN by virtue of its emphasis on crisis as a maximal framing. As with all matters of global crisis, this generates a kind of aporia in which the scale and force of crisis substantially mismatches with any credible form of political agency. Identitarian Socialism critiques and opposes the liberal architectures of governance: UN organisations, intergovernmental agreements, and major international non-governmental organisations. Crisis framing is intrinsically anti-reformist and, as a result, Conference of the Parties (COP) and other forms of liberal intergovernmental environmentalism are seen as woefully inadequate. As a result, it frames a form of apocalyptic global political concern that struggles to identify an agency that puts the crisis into a zone of contention in which some form of response is possible.

There is within Identitarian Socialist proto-ideology a kind of agonism that global-historic crisis is here, creating a historic precipice that has no redeeming political agency to meet its challenge. In proto-ideological mode, the crisis concept – by virtue of its maximal articulations – frames an existential political challenge which has no discernible political solution. This leaves a gap which aspirational political entreaties only partially suture.

The distinguishing feature in this aspirational response is that the obstetric historic sensibility of socialism, discussed in Chapter 2, is not attached to revolution but rather *salvation*. The intensity of presence of crisis narrative subdues the hopeful and combative facets of socialism – we organise to make a vastly better world for all. In its stead, the expectation is that somehow a popular politics will save humankind from disaster, and any slight (distributional) improvement on the present is a bonus.

Bearing in mind how prominent crisis sensibility is, one might wonder whether Identitarian Socialism's morphology demands that it serve as a core concept. But, evocations of crisis are not essential to Identitarian Socialism. Rather, crisis acts as an intensifier and it might attach itself to varied political prospectives which include not only climate change, disease, and the carbon economy but also ageing, humanitarian disaster, and economic collapse. Crisis is a concept that needs core concepts to manifest in a particular way across issues: a capitalist crisis that requires radical critique and a commitment to pluralised social movement politics.

Technology

As with crisis, technology's apparent descriptive-empirical nature develops into an adjacent concept within Identitarian Socialism's morphology. Science, engineering, and specialist tech knowledge is rendered as a set of valued social practices. Technology is a form of power: it focuses on how techniques of production can be put to the use of a socialist programme through its embedding in a set of political relations. Technology, then, can be conceptualised.

Identitarian Socialism understands technology as smartness and social vision. That is to say, it celebrates the wondrous progress in scientific research and its application as a *via media* towards a more socially just world. The conceptualisation of technology is therefore generally positive. It contains within it a strong aesthetic property in which intelligence, youthfulness, and improvement are combined. For Identitarian Socialism, technology is understood in a radically different and more optimistic way than either Marx's critique of 'machinofacture' or Frankfurt School destructivism. Technology is innovation. It is about creative responses to problems and it carries with it a progressive prospective.

There is a second coordinate to the conceptualisation of technology that articulates more closely with Identitarian Socialism's radicalism. Technological innovation – and a belief that technological advances have recently been remarkable – offers up a way to imagine a world beyond capitalism. Technology plays a central role in addressing the tyrannies of wage labour, and it does this through automation. This argument is set out in detail in Bastani's *Fully Automated Luxury Communism*,[33] an influential work that has also echoed through Identitarian Socialism's social media.[34] The body of the book is an overview (a fairly sanguine one) of major technological advances in processors, energy use, diet, and raw material supply. It is accelerationist in that it sees rapid or even exponential growth in the supply and efficiency of these things, leading to a state of excess. This state of excess – a bounty of supply – is secured through automation in production and it is through this that the established capitalist-industrial mode of labour can be surpassed.

Technology has four key characteristics in Bastani's work. It is *liberatory*: it provides the wherewithal for people to escape the constraints of capitalism and to realise their potential. There is a clear assonance with a well-known thread of Marx's writing here. Marx's understanding of human nature was consistently based (albeit with greater or lesser emphasis) in a critique of capitalism as constraining the full flourishing of human sociability and creativity. Marx identified in the history of capitalist accumulation a tendency for a divergence between the forces of production and the relations of production. The essence of the argument here is that innovation and investment powered by capital would be undermined by its own obsession with profit maximisation and competition.[35] This would create the conditions of possibility for a socialisation of productive technologies to liberate them from the capital relation and to put them to a full use of all people. For this reason, Marxist projections of a future socialism have often dedicated central attention to the ways and means of putting increasingly productive and remarkable technologies to better use.

Secondly, for Identitarian Socialism, technology is commonly associated with professional and knowledge workers. Bastani's book is consistently focused on those who might be described as already *tech-savvy*. The kind of society Bastani imagines is already part of the tech revolution he reviews. This evokes a longer tradition of 'knowledge economy' writing that demonstrably pays negligible attention to those who work in deskilled, precarious, or 'traditional' jobs that have not been strongly integrated into the frontiers of technological change.

Thirdly, technology manifests concrete but *optimistic* accounts of the future. People are liberated from work; poverty is overcome by new technologies of production; the capitalist-environmental crisis mentioned earlier is conquered by technological fixes. It shares something of the Prometheanism of DMN here. What it also does is provide a counter-position to the adjacent concept of crisis. Remembering that adjacent concepts have less stability and a degree of contingency, we can note that there is a kind of creative inconsistency between the more apocalyptic narratives of crisis and the more progressivist accounts of technological innovation. In terms of historical narrative, what this does do is provide a scenario in which – however one balances the odds – the best hope for a world beyond capitalism lies in the hands of an intellectual elite with the skills innovatively to deploy cutting-edge technology. The 'thousand flowers' are absent.

Finally, technology is *déclassé*. This might seem counter-intuitive to the quotations of Marx's discussion of machine technology and forces and relations of production. And, very clearly, Bastani identifies the technological future of luxury with a surpassing of capitalism. But there is no class struggle in Bastani's futurology. In short, the working class has little agency in *FALC* and it most certainly does not have the agency that Marx insisted it did if the overthrow of capitalism was to be achieved. This point touches on a general aesthetic orientation of Identitarian Socialism which has been averred to earlier but is also present in some of its other conceptual architecture: lifestyle.

Lifestyle

We should recall at this point the distinction between logical and cultural adjacency. If technology resembled a more logical adjacency – defined by corollaries of the core concepts concerning post-capitalism – then the lifestyle concept within Identitarian Socialism is more clearly cultural: relating to social habits, ethics, and values. Lifestyle, as it is used here, connotes a series of closely interconnected aesthetic discernments about the good life. For Identitarian Socialism, a good life is not something that concerns the internal properties of virtue in the self but rather a series of attitudes and leisure pursuits that, for want of a more academic term, are cool.

This might not seem like much of a concept. But, lifestyle contains both a consistent set of properties and those properties clearly serve to enhance the value of other concepts within this proto-ideology. Lifestyle commentary does conceptual work inasmuch as it works an aesthetic value judgement into Identitarian Socialism's arguments and the strength of its other concepts. It also influences the discursive forms of Identitarian Socialism. It is common to find narrative text using the first person and confessional mode. This leads to a certain amount of playfulness in narrative style. Arguments with other ideological positions might, as a result, become freighted with irony or sarcasm which are not simply generic weapons of PSM intercourse but also statements of identity. Of course, all PSM has to consider the medium and the message. But, Identitarian Socialism takes its mediatisation very seriously. It is intrinsic as well as extrinsic: the imagery of Identitarian Socialism tells us something about its internal properties as well as its ability to achieve attention. Let us explore the manifestations of the lifestyle aesthetic within Identitarian Socialism.

It is striking how Identitarian Socialism contrasts with DMN in its appearance. DMN's main podcast vehicle, Bungacast, is audio-only. Identitarian Socialism's main podcast vehicle, Novara, has podcasts, video, and YouTube. There are hedonistic references in the ways these are presented: TyskySour podcasts reference a beer; the ACFM podcast is curated through recreation drug language of trips and microdoses.[36] Videos have a set of production guidelines: clean backgrounds, simple casual clothes, smartness, smiling faces.

On Novara podcasts, commentators sometimes move from political analysis to a playful critique of other media forms, a practice that generates a 'hot take' or satirical affect that plays to a constructed coolness. For example, when watching a promotional video of Keir Starmer driving an HGV, the presenters (who you see watching the clip) begin:

'You saw the moment his soul just left his body, it's just awful!
  "Go left? Well, I'm not sure I want to go left – I'm always told by my other advisors not to go left." Then he crashes into the bit of concrete behind him, he's told "you've failed".'[37]

Beyond the rather familiar collapsing of the metaphorical and the spatial meaning of 'left', the video bolsters a sense that Identitarian Socialism derives some of its strength from an aesthetic coolness and some of its critique from the clunky, unfashionable, or unattractive nature of less radical politics. Another podcast responds to self-styled contrarian Jordan Peterson thus:

'I've got two words for Jordan Peterson if he's watching, which is: eat carbohydrates. Stop this whole meat diet, because you've got the low-resolution thinking. You could see he was thinking really slowly and he's just really tired. Jordan, have a bowl of pasta. Have a sandwich. Have some rice.'[38]

Some Identitarian Socialism spokespeople post holiday or celebration pictures, intermixing what are largely political Twitter feeds with a scattering of selfies. Politics is lifestyle is aesthetics. 'Ah god why am I thinking about the Labour Party it's the weekend' declares one tweet.[39] Hedonism is associated with a kind of progressive politics or at least affect, or perhaps an act of resistance to the core form of domination, already identified as a tight combination of capitalism, racism, and patriarchy: 'partying as resistance'.[40] Resistance is connected to the intersectionality concept explored earlier: a way to escape and/or challenge cis-heteronormativity, to celebrate and perform identity. It connects to the ways in which carnival is articulated within social movement cultures. Leisure/pleasure is youthful and attractive.

Most notably within Twitter feeds, Identitarian Socialism discourse is determinedly vernacular. An argot of 'streetness' is used. And, there is a constant seeking out of neologisms or recent and high-uptake coinages. This manifests itself in a range of specific ways. Firstly, a 'too cool' response to the arguments or attacks of others. Secondly, a deployment of street or slang phraseology in the midst of political discussion. Thirdly, for some, a generous interpolation of profanities.[41] And fourthly, an edginess that expresses itself in references of sex[42] and drugs.[43]

Any lifestyle representation necessarily requires a sense of being part of a group. This is what makes a certain kind of life into a lifestyle. Identitarian Socialist discourse is relaxed about certain kinds of celebrity association. Indeed, Identitarian Socialism's cultural adjacency is arguably built on the kinds of public resonance that celebrity can achieve through the portrayal of lifestyle. Identitarian Socialism tweets might comment on celebrities, music, and film, or a range of mimetic cultural artefacts, and this sutures with the playful coolness of its phrasing. RMT leader Mick Lynch is 'Ross Kemp in an industrial dispute'.[44] Any spats with celebrities, or intellectuals, are enthusiastically addressed through sassy commentary.

The mediatisation within Identitarian Socialism lends it a mode of address which lies somewhere between intensification and exaggeration. This is about being heard, maximising impact of argument, and adding rhetorical panache. The orientation of core and adjacent concepts already serves to create a world vision in which crisis and struggle are ever-present, but this proto-ideology does not rest there. There is also a proclivity to dramatise, to search for the most evocative or provocative of phrases and association. There is a desire to achieve rhetorical flourish. One tweet accuses author Lionel Shriver of using the logic of Nazism.[45] Again, an association with Axis powers: the image of 'Boris Johnson being dangled upside down from his ankles by an angry mob'.[46]

Crisis, pluralism, and lifestyle each contain an empirical focus combined with underspecified analytical meaning. Respectively, there are kernels of analytical insight that argue for combined and holistic analysis, a strategic assertion of progress that is multi-directional, and there is a discursive strategy to combine argument with cool. These concepts work roughly together and they buttress core concepts. But they do so in ways that seem incomplete. Most strikingly, these adjacent concepts do not strongly and directly focus on class and class struggle.

Peripheral concepts

Post-coloniality

Post-colonialism is a concept dedicated to understanding how the structures of power forged through colonialism persist and furthermore remain dominant and prevailing in the present. In the academy, this orientation has led to all manner of theoretical reflection. For Identitarian Socialism, the concept is used as a historical orientation. Although post-colonialism enjoys weighty academic baggage, Identitarian Socialism deploys the term frequently but *en courant*. It is used as a kind of historical preamble on the way to making a critique of the present.

The concept of post-colonialism seeks to find the origins of present-day political problems in the period of empire. The principal purpose and effect of this is to intensify the problematisation and critique of the issue at hand, commonly through a presentation of Western power and its endurance. In short, the deeper the historical roots of a political phenomenon the more powerful or radical the critique.

Post-coloniality is a concept designed to critically address racism and nationalism. It is a critique of presence and absence. Its presence resides in the persistence of national grandeur, and especially xenophobic or ethnonational versions of this. These public renditions of nationhood are critiques as the pernicious legacy of empire. The absence refers to the cleansing of national histories of their manifold brutalities and exploitations. Post-colonialism insists that romantic narratives of nationhood should be corrected into recognising the mass violence of settlement, slavery, forced labour, racism, torture, and so on.

Post-coloniality mainly serves as an entrée to discussions of racism. It is the legacy of empire that provides the raw material for the articulation of racism in the present day. Post-coloniality gives racism a structural feature that gives the politics of race a particularly intense importance within the intersectionalities of oppression and exploitation set out earlier. If there are concerns about immigration, these are a product of an imperial/ Commonwealth system and its legacy. If there are celebrations of Englishness/ Britishness, these are often racialised through romanticised references to empire. 'The scars of empire still run deep. It is this history that followed [England football player Bukayo] Saka, as he walked up to take his fateful penalty at Wembley – a stadium that was originally built to house the British Empire Exhibition in 1924.'[47]

This racial ideology operates at the level of elite fantasy and the everyday: in the former as 'symbols of domination, exploitation, empire' and in the latter 'an increasingly reactionary and paranoid majority'.[48] There is an overarching location of Britishness as a petty island mentality, a post-imperial melancholia[49] that has within its cultural properties a kind of bathos. This historical cautionary also articulates to critical discussion of the British government's foreign policy which is driven by some combination of racial paternalism and 'colonial violence'.[50]

Post-coloniality is, then, a historic orientation that serves as a mobile critical response to matters relating to nationalism and a certain kind of populism, as well as British government action overseas.

Livelihoods

As with post-colonialism, the concept of livelihoods has a well-established conceptual status within social science, especially development studies. Chambers and Conway offer an early and representative definition: 'a livelihood comprises the capabilities, assets and activities required for a means to a living: a livelihood is sustainable which can cope with and recover from stresses and shocks, maintain or enhance its capabilities and assets'.[51] As this definition suggests, livelihoods contains within it a normativity which expresses a concern with poverty, precariousness, and overwork. Livelihoods is a concept that loosely assembles an affirmation of the community, intersectionality, and the detailed and complex nature of injustice. It also enables a validating seeking out of the agency of ordinary people. Livelihoods, then, has material fixing. One might say that the poor and the working classes have livelihoods and the wealthy have lifestyles. For Identitarian Socialists, livelihoods means a normative commitment in which local sociability is strongly valued.

The livelihoods concept makes a case that it is the lived experiences of ordinary people that are the ultimate and surest measure of a political issue. This case is made by identifying how specific policies impact upon poor and marginalised communities or individuals. The livelihoods concept is articulated in what might be called a livelihood reportage: coverage of community groups and local activisms in which material hardship or political marginality are expressed through day-to-day actions. Local mobilisations and ordinary voices are valued and advocated.[52]

The use of livelihood reportage also enables Identitarian Socialism to foreground the importance of intersectionality, and in this sense, the livelihoods concept has an especially strong adjacency to intersectionality.

Figure 6.1: Schema of Identitarian Socialism's morphology

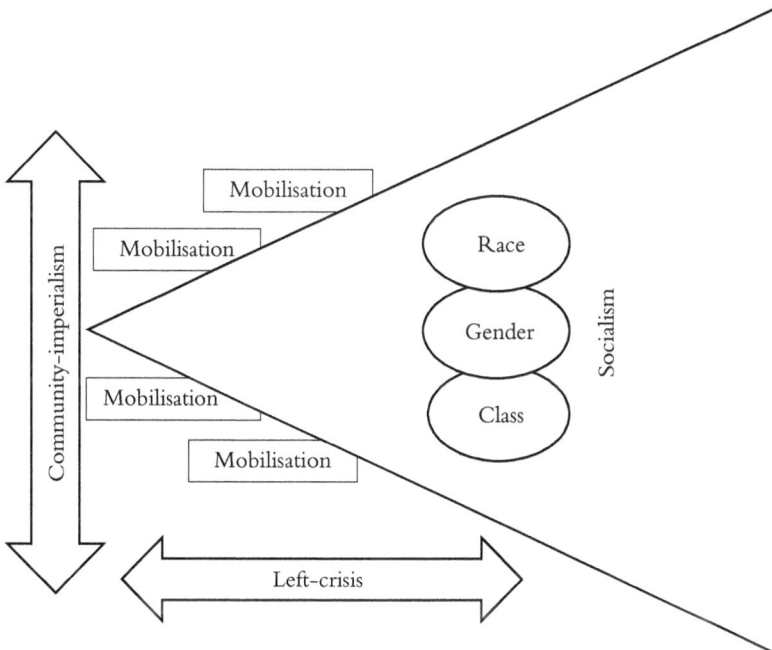

There is also, finally, an aesthetic in Identitarian Socialism's livelihoods concept. The kinds of people represented in livelihoods imagery are *well* presented. They are not angry, dirty, or desperate. They are articulate. They relate to the matter at hand in ways that articulate well with Identitarian Socialism's proto-ideology.

Conclusion

Identitarian Socialism is founded in a radical-Left positioning which contains different orientations in relation to socialism. Its sociological gaze identifies justice causes intersectionally, and these causes are aggregated into a world view that is pluralistic: the revolution will be diffuse and horizontal (see Figure 6.1).

Identitarian Socialism's morphology is presented as less foundational and more directional. Its core conceptualisation of socialism works as a constant 'Left pull'. Within this orientation, agency is conceptualised through a Venn-like intersectionality of oppression. It is the radicalisation of these that progress takes place, meeting crisis with left-wing politics. Each mobilisation is a unique instantiation of these political dynamics, producing a plurality in a political field framed as bottom-up against top-down.

7

Contention

Introduction

We have set out two proto-ideological projects that seek to reinvigorate socialist political ideology. Each has conceptual arrangements that help make sense of the world and establish arguments as to why and how socialism remains an active and valued way of thinking about politics. These chapters have been mainly descriptive: apprehending the shape of each political ideology as it lives in PSM. This chapter seeks to focus on the nature of ideological construction in more detail and in the midst of live political contention. As we have argued, proto-ideologies are upstarts: combative insurgent traditions that wish to elbow into public spaces not only in relation to their ideological foes but also their fellow traveller traditions. It is the latter that we shall focus on. The main reason for this is that it is in the midst of debates for the meaning of socialism that the most intense political contention resides. If, say, a spokesperson for the Institute of Economic Affairs announces that rising unemployment is a necessary effect of market competition, then it is of no great interest to explore how any socialist tradition might challenge this. It would be neither surprising nor intriguing to see voices of opposition from any socialist position.

What is more interesting and instructive is the contention between DMN and Identitarian Socialism. As socialist proto-ideologies, both necessarily have to deploy similar political devices in their contentions, even if their meaning and their intentionality – the purpose to which those devices are put – are dissimilar. Both seek to establish an ascendance in relation to the meaning of socialism, which makes them rivalrous. And, in exploring the interactions between the two, we can see how much of the morphology set out in the previous two chapters is activated to generate affective and aesthetic tools which, as we have argued, are especially central to a proto-ideological project.

Weaponry
Aesthetic and affect

We will explore two bones of contention: Brexit and COVID-19. In each case, these two proto-ideologies articulate substantially different and antagonistic views. These views were clearly based in each proto-ideology's own distinct concepts. Before we move on to do this, we need to return to the aesthetic and affective components of our model as set out in Chapter 3 in order to detail how they will be deployed.

Socially mediatised and in construction, any resilient proto-ideology will need to develop robust concepts but also develop tools of deployment. That is, a proto-ideology will need to go beyond a proofing of logical coherence or fit with evidence and find modes of address that *persuade*, and do so within the milieux of social media which – as we noted in Chapter 1 – has a grammar of 'sarcasm and irony, and sharp-eyed attacks'.

We emphasised the aesthetic and affective. Aesthetic content is that which conjures imagery that bolsters an argument, defence, proposal, or refutation. All political rhetoric manipulates implied or evoked imagery. Persuasion requires a full-bodied aesthetic. By this, we mean a series of interconnected images that work to 'brand' the proto-ideology. Aesthetics have to be consistent and speak to the identity of the proto-ideology itself. This might be the obvious stuff such as frequently used words or repeated references to well-known people or things. Or, it might be more implied aesthetics built into language, style of imagery, or organisation of webspace.

Closely interconnected, the aesthetics of a proto-ideology will endeavour to generate affect. In other words, any text will have both an analytical and emotional relay. To accept that a point is correct is one thing; to have it resonate with oneself – to be convinced – is another. We derive from identifiable rhetorical and aesthetic turns of phrase an immanent emotional vector which *seeks to* resonate with others. Whether it does or not is beyond the remit of this book. One can only assume that sustained emotional appeals of one kind of another that are enacted within densely social spaces of political intercourse will have some effectivity.

Devices

We can sketch the principal modes through which proto-ideologies generate imagery and emotional evocation before we flesh out their instantiation later on. These devices come in two forms: humour and intensification.

Humour is, of course, remarkably ubiquitous and polysemous. In the midst of PSM, Terry Eagleton's aphorism is apposite: 'the opposite of comedy is destiny'.[1] In other words, the mainstay of humour on PSM is, in one sense or another, an effort to veer away from a path dependency, a consensus, or orthodoxy. This might involve the lampoon: to exaggerate an argument and, in the process, weaken the logical or evidential scaffolding within which it rests. A sub-species of lampooning is reductio ad absurdum; another is caricature. There is also the ribald exposure of double standards or inconsistency. The essence of humour is inconsistency and so one would expect within these devices some misrepresentation. But the intent within this misrepresentation is to *reveal* something, a truth. As such, humour might seek affect in the form of a grievance or accusation. Humour is also a means to generate 'rightness': a sense of who is right and wrong through satirical attacks on the fools, the complacent, the patronising.[2]

Intensification pervades PSM. In the flat seriality of text, there is an innate imperative to get noticed, even for five minutes. There is little merit in simply being right and a palpable demerit in being right in a cautious and nuanced fashion. The ferment of ideological contestation is (thankfully) not Rawlsian political theory. Intensification overlaps with humour in the form of exaggeration. It might also involve personalisation: identifying specific individuals and attributing the nature of certain arguments to their online persona. It might involve the use of language which amplifies a specific assumption or repercussion in an argument. It might involve the juxtaposition of an image to an excerpt of text.

Humour and intensification, and the weapons that they hold, allow our two proto-ideologies to assert themselves in relation to each other. Each of them is punching sideways in an attempt to present a case that the socialist project and its ideological reconstruction should follow one pathway, not another.

Thematics

Contestation between proto-ideologies is not a brawl. We can set out the themes – choreographies – within which debate takes place. We should start by recalling that PSM is not the bunfight that characterises a lot of social media generally; it broadly follows the guidance of deliberation, as we set out in Chapter 2. More specifically, contention is oriented around four themes.

Firstly, contention revolves around *smartness*. A great deal is staked on being empirically right. This will, of course, involve matters of historical record and evidence. Being right is also, of course, a matter of interpretation: there are no facts that speak for themselves, and in cases where facts are presented thus, they are nevertheless unable to escape from the normativity of the narrative in which they are embedded. Indeed, the trope of 'getting real' or seeing things as they are is a significant resource to deploy in the midst of debate. Being consistent, having a full understanding of an issue, being concise and pithy ... all of these properties enhance the combination of smartness with effective engagement within PSM. This might seem commonsensical, but we will see how the articulation of smartness can generate different political propositions and postures. It is a common property within PSM to read contrasting texts and at first blush judge that both are right.

Secondly, debate and the conjuring of evidence are significantly enhanced if they are woven into the proto-ideology's own *identity*. In other words, strong argument is made stronger if it is in part a statement about the proto-ideology's specific conceptual arrangements. This is not only a formal exercise in correspondence – this theory does the best with the best evidence – it is also aesthetic. The deployment of the concepts owned by one proto-ideology to present evidence both speak to correctness and a particular narrative tradition over another: a sense of fit and fitness. On the terrain of ideological contestation, being right and being Marxist or socialist are indistinguishable.

Thirdly, as we noted in Chapter 2, the master framing for political debate is crisis. Socialist and Marxist traditions are well equipped to discuss crisis as both see capitalism as crisis-prone, not equilibrating. The nature of crisis analysis within PSM is not centrally guided by the best crisis theory but rather the best *crisis response*. In short, debate consistently revolves around which proto-ideological tradition is most fit for purpose in a political time when crisis is either here or immanent.

Fourthly, contention revolves around how each proto-ideology responds to the question of *representation*. Socialist and Marxist thought both have to make a claim to be speaking on behalf of the working class, and we have seen how each of our traditions has articulated that representation differently. There is in both traditions a form of practice that might be dubbed ventriloquism: the 'speaking on behalf of' in which a voice of the working class emerges not directly from a certain constituency but rather through the interpretive efforts of those engaging in debate.

In summary, we have set out guidance as to how to understand how proto-ideologies contest and in the process self-construct. This builds on the comparative analysis of conceptual morphology in the previous two chapters which illustrated how two ostensibly sibling ideological traditions have established considerable dissimilarity in their concepts. The rest of this chapter will explore how this dissimilarity is also a productive antagonism. By deploying aesthetic and affective text, using humour as a mode of combat, and organising around a set of thematic procedures that locate contention within the remit of PSM, we can see how contestation has played out in two of the biggest political events of the last decade: Brexit and COVID-19.

Brexit

Brexit according to DMN

After many years of sluggish growth and deindustrialisation,[3] the party political system disintegrated as established political constituencies fell apart. Membership of the EU was not a counter-balance to this drawn-out process but part of it. The EU reduced nation-states to member states and used transnational constitutionalism to lock in neoliberal regulatory infrastructures in the name of regional integration.[4] Labour was losing its working-class fealty and the Conservatives were losing to UKIP. The referendum on EU membership was principally an attempt to revalidate EU membership and, in the process, hopefully cement a degree of stability in the party system and, for both parties, to exorcise anxieties about the sovereignty and economic constraints of EU membership. It was, at heart, a referendum that MPs hoped would staunch the question of EU membership and the democratic deficit this created.

The vote to leave was a mass democratic expression of preference. It was a shocking rebellion in which the masses expressed a desire to reinvigorate sovereign politics by taking back control (here, not a pejorative phrasing).[5] It was an instruction to political elites to be more accountable to the people (not to Brussels).[6] It was also an expression of a desire to push political elites to perform better: not simply to use market-conforming 'technopolitics'[7] but to intervene, to protect, to serve a common good. The 52 per cent had voted for a new sovereign politics that moved away from member-state status and neoliberal regionalism.

Remainer voters responded to the referendum outcome with shock and disbelief. Deriving from a middle class, and often south-eastern regional social milieu, Remainers went into a state of denial, asking for another referendum and insisting the outcome was 'advisory'. A social prejudice quickly emerged that Brexiteers were 'information-scarce' or plain stupid. That they were xenophobic or racists. In short, Brexit triggered the open expression of a latent cosmopolitan middle-class snobbery about those who voted for Brexit.

With a Westminster Parliament filled with Remainers on both sides and the preponderance of Remainer discourse close to the halls of power, leaving the EU was a fitful, delayed, and botched affair in which the hopes for a revival of sovereign politics were quashed. Amid this protracted interregnum between 2016 and 2019, Remainer arguments stressed the economic damage that leaving the EU (presented as a regional free trade bloc) would cause. A political sentiment sense of national self-loathing emerged.

Since leaving, UK politics has not seized the possibilities of independence from the EU. And, in any case, by the end of the year of leaving, another political disruption had commenced that will be treated in the next section.

Brexit according to Identitarian Socialism

The referendum's outcome represented a major political regression.[8] It was a manifestation of an 'unstoppable force of an angry, Brexity majority'.[9] This had two components. In the first place, Brexit was a manifestation of widespread xenophobia in British – or often English – culture. Voting to leave was principally about stopping immigration; 'take back control' was a dog whistle for 'keep foreigners out'.[10] Brexit was a kind of lightning rod that exposed how insular and backward a good swathe of English/British culture was. It was also an expression of a continuing imperialism.[11] Two Identitarian Socialists removed themselves from a speaking event that included Eddie Dempsey, probably on the grounds that his pro-Brexit views were racist.[12]

Secondly, Brexit threw into sharp relief how a mass group of ordinary people suffered from such long periods of political marginality and a lack of education or full perspective that people voted Leave in spite of the fact that it was irrational: against their own interests.[13] The negativity of Brexit was, in this interpretation, a judgement on the state by the working masses that was itself a result of decades of social decline.

This latter point – more nuanced than a singular 'working classes are bigots' one – led Identitarian Socialists to judge that many people had made the wrong decision because they were not given the right facts clearly enough. This led some Identitarian Socialists to be warm to the idea of a second referendum (a people's vote to ratify the exit agreement) for a period, although not all did so.[14] It also generated a representation of ordinary working people not as capable voters expressing a rejection of the state of current politics and a loss of sovereignty but rather a rather inchoate and problematic constituency, not to be condemned but to be, in a sense, solved: perhaps given another try.[15]

Membership of the EU was associated with a public culture of liberal tolerance. The multiculturalism of major cities and the general association of these cities with Left-leaning political ideas was articulated to a Europeanness that was multinational and Left-leaning. This cultural intuition was expressed thusly:

> The Corbyn project now has an opportunity to rekindle its relationship with one of the biggest social movements in Britain today: the move-ment against Brexit. The remain movement is broadly left wing … remain voters fit more easily within the progressive bloc. … Brexit is dominated by the right – *and a quasi-fascist right* at that.[16]

Additionally, Remain was culturally associated with youth, the latter categorisation being ostensibly demographic but substantively cultural: the young as liberal, Left-leaning, 'tolerant', progressive, and urbane.[17]

Within this association, again, negative representations of England[18] enabled a portrayal of the EU as an enlightened and tolerant bloc. Brexit was, embarrassingly, an exposure of how un-European the UK was.

As a proto-ideology more interested in maintaining Left-radical positions in relation to the Labour Party, Identitarian Socialists largely supported the party's Remain campaign. But, the lukewarm and inconsistent 'seven out of ten' attitude of Jeremy Corbyn generated some ambiguity herein. Corbyn, and Momentum's rise, was celebrated by Identitarian Socialists. His historical cynicism about European economic integration did not allow pro-European Corbyn supporters a fully coherent position in relation to Brexit during the campaign as the referendum approached.

The main way in which this was sutured was through the 'remain and reform' argument: that the problems with the EU could be best solved by organising with partner movements throughout the EU to reclaim the 'social' and bridge the democratic deficit in the EU project.[19]

A consistently critical attitude towards Brexit was sustained by attacks on the Conservative Party's handling of exit negotiations and the general chaos within Theresa May's cabinet. Dour predictions of economic recession, a collapse in international trade, rising xenophobia, and global isolation quashed any possibility that Identitarian Socialist analyses of Brexit would entertain any space for the notion that the British state would no longer be locked into EU law. Indeed, a kind of elision fed into the critical analyses of Brexit as negotiations towards Article 50 proceeded in which Brexit became a general context for all manner of different issues and crises. Characteristically, Identitarian Socialism's penchant to see a synthesis of problems and difficulties as part of a major crisis scenario performed strong affective work here, but the exact role of Brexit as a factor in creating crisis was far from specified. 'Brexit' served as a curating term to assemble critical concern about the environment, national defence, land ownership, and trade, and in doing so, it shifted from its own specific mechanics into a general framing.

Brexit contentions

Democracy

For DMN, Brexit was first and foremost an expression of mass democracy. For the first time in a long time, the people had spoken. This was the principal contention for DMN: that a democratic expression of political decision was superordinate to everything else. Contrastingly, Identitarian Socialism's concerns with the conditions within which the referendum was undertaken were delegitimised as attacks on democracy. There were lies during the run-up;[20] people were duped; voters were voting against their own best interests; young people did not vote; the decision was too momentous to be decided by a single referendum … these were all, at heart, expressions of anti-democratic sentiment according to DMN. There was a double standard at work in which democratic choice was valued by Identitarian Socialism, but when the 'wrong' outcome was produced, this value was not absolute.

For DMN, the Brexit critiques of Identitarian Socialism were an expression of its paternalism towards the working masses. Identitarian Socialists revealed the limits of their commitment to democracy as a polity based in majoritarian decision making. DMN constructed ironic representations of those who voted for Brexit as stupid bigoted proles with the aim of exposing or exaggerating through caricature Identitarian Socialism views of the (white) working class.[21]

Identitarian Socialism was not averse to using the term 'gammon' in and around Brexit. This term was sometimes offered humorously, but as we have set out previously, these humorous devices were also weapons.[22] The use of the term sought to make an association between some Brexit votes and xenophobia or small-mindedness. This was enough to break down the majoritarian approach to the referendum into something more pluralistic, as per its own pluralistic and identity-based conceptual morphology. A referendum outcome was against working-class voters in London and some other cities. It was a threat to ordinary people who were not white. Those who voted for Brexit were elderly, affluent working-class or middle-class people, or Tories. In short, the referendum outcome was a positional challenge in which different groups had aligned around the referendum in different ways, in ways that required socialists to consider how some factions of the working class had voted erroneously.

Identitarian Socialism's response to DMN's assertion of democratic legitimacy was to evoke minority rights as a way of making particular points about the effects and outcomes of Brexit. The rights of the non-white British and immigrants were the main focus of attention.

Culture and aesthetics

Identitarian Socialism's aesthetics concerning Brexit were oriented around a validation of a multicultural sociability. The notion of a 'rump' British nation, made up of little Englanders, insular and unchanging, was articulated by some in the Identitarian Socialist camp.[23] For Identitarian Socialism, Brexit was a moment in a longer imperial/post-imperial British history. Voting Brexit was perhaps a bathetic expression of national pride, a last hurrah for a national grandeur that had long passed. The multicultural communities of some urban areas were the positive legacy of empire: the cultural conviviality described by Paul Gilroy,[24] a shift in Britishness away from ethnonationalism to something more pluralistic and more tolerant, more associated with Remain.

DMN's historiography is more post-Keynesian. It started its analytical narratives not in empire but rather with the class war prosecuted by Thatcher and the mass deindustrialisation that this created throughout Britain. Empire and its legacies were, within this optic, largely irrelevant. What reason would a 20-something working-class woman from Darlington have to reflect on the colonial projects of the late 1800s and their presence in her own lifeworld?

DMN focused on the poor working-class people in provincial towns and cities who had little hope of a decent job or any upward mobility and who had been let down by Labour. DMN avoided a pluralistic approach in which Remainer communities were validated and 'traditional' working classes were wrong or xenophobic, preferring to identify a working class deeply damaged by neoliberalism and now taking revenge against the elites that championed it. The DMN narrative was more 'political economy' and less 'community': quantitative survey data and economic indicators.

Identitarian Socialism could portray DMN as indifferent to the oppressions of race and ethnicity and it tended to perform this aesthetically through an association of 'traditional' with 'white'. This was rarely explicit; but it is hard to understand the nature of contention regarding the cultural relays of Brexit without this subterranean racialisation. At heart, the difference here is an expression of the core and adjacent conceptual morphologies of the two: class not race and other social identities *contra* class through race and other social identities.

Representation

At the heart of a good deal of the contention between these two proto-ideologies concerning Brexit is the fact that they offer rival representations of the working class. Within a socialist tradition, both absolutely need to claim their foundations in this act of representation. How they do so is not straightforward and, unsurprisingly, follows the contrasts set out earlier.

Identitarian Socialists framed Brexit as a victory for UKIP and the Conservative Party. There was plenty of critical commentary on the EU as a neoliberal regionalist project, but leaving the EU was seen as a worse outcome from two unpalatable options. Leaving would mean losing the 'nice things' EU membership contained and being subjected to a supercharged Right shift in British politics. The focus on the Rightward shift in party politics served to situate Identitarian Socialism's critique away from a more fulsome consideration of the agency of the working classes.

One way in which Novara Media represented ordinary people was through vox pop podcasts in which the overall message was that Brexit voters were anti-immigration. Although not always treated adversarially,[25] and sometimes asked to give their justifications, the purpose of the vox pops was to extrapolate into a broader socio-economic morbidity that was narrated by the Novara interlocutor. In Aaron Bastani's podcast *Is This England's Referendum?*, after interviewing Brexit-voting people in 'pale' Bournemouth, he extrapolates the following judgement: "for me, it basically betokens a sense of loss and regard to empire – no Britain does not treat the rest of the world like a beach ball they can just play with". None of his respondents mentioned empire.[26]

In summary, Identitarian Socialism's representation of the working class was bifurcated. An urban multicultural plurality was contrasted with a provincial-urban and small-town working class, defined through its morbid symptoms. DMN represented those working-class people who voted to leave as expressing a rejection of the neoliberal consensus in parliamentary politics and a positive desire to reinvigorate representative sovereign politics. This keys in with the generally positive attitude that DMN has towards national sovereignty and its potential as a mode of mass political representation. Democratic Marxist Nationalists insist, against more cosmopolitan attitudes, that national sovereignty in the state and people is still the best way for democratic accountability to be realised.

This working-class sensibility was assumed as much as demonstrated. '[Leave voters] were primarily driven by hunger for political change, after decades when the political elite had scorned and ignored most ordinary people.'[27] Other similar phrases gloss working-class attitudes in ways that – while not necessarily untrue – seem to express the political sentiments of DMN writers as much as ordinary people.

Additionally, DMN accounts would also deploy survey evidence to contest the racist/xenophobic/conservative gloss given to mass leave attitudes.[28] There is indeed plenty of evidence that British mass society has become generally less racist with the passing of time, and that this trend is extant across socio-economic categories.

The argument that racism is in decline allows DMN to establish a certain distinction between concerns with immigration and racism. That is to say, it becomes possible to explain – and in part validate – concerns with immigration not because of a fear of foreigners but because labour markets have been subjected to wage repression and casualisation as immigrants (note here that I do not mean causation) have entered into employment in the UK. Within the DMN optic, there is a class filter at work here in which middle-class liberals say immigration is good for the economy because it makes service and public sector industries cheaper and more dynamic and working-class communities see construction, plumbing, and service sector work taken by people willing to work for lower wages in worse conditions.

But, the use of survey evidence and arguments about changing labour markets do not give a strong figuring of the working class. Hence the ventriloquism of working-class voices and – rather paradoxically bearing in mind how much store is set on basing its values in a proletarian historical agency – DMN engages less with working-class identities than its more liberal and pluralistic adversary.

Identitarian Socialism's lower-order prioritisation of class is framed within a focus on identity, livelihood, and intersectionality. This means that although its advocacy and analytical prioritisation of class is less foundational, it has a morphology that more easily lends itself to vox pops and cultural identity.

Its aesthetics of 'streetness' also enable a kind of engagement reportage that is absent from DMN.

DMN makes a more robust defence of class in relation to Brexit, but this is an analytical defence with far less aesthetic import. Its position on Brexit is deduced from empirical data, an analytical account of the impact of neoliberalism, and a theoretical premise about the role of class in politics. As such, it presents a proto-ideology that derives its strength from its approximation to a theoretical project rather than an ideological one.

In summary, DMN and Identitarian Socialism disagreed about Brexit, generating strong positive and negative reactions to the referendum. DMN's advocacy of democracy and national sovereignty, combined with a foundational unifying categorisation of the working class, framed Brexit as an expression of popular condemnation of neoliberalism and elite politics. Identitarian Socialism's pluralism, cynicism towards popular nationalism, and intersectional understanding of class led it to understand Brexit as a recidivist act. Each perspective structured contention between the two: DMN as 'paleo'; Identitarian Socialism as snobbish and anti-democratic.

Lockdown

Lockdown according to Identitarian Socialism

Identitarian Socialism treated COVID-19 epidemiologically. That is to say, the virus had its independent agency, best understood through scientific research.[29] This gave it an externality: a natural disaster that required a scientifically instructed and concerted emergency response from government.

The pandemic elicited two orientations from Identitarian Socialism: firstly, a demand that the government take radical action to deal with the spread of the virus, and secondly, that it was vital that there should be a universal and harmonised social response to the epidemic.

Identitarian Socialists took the virus's threat to public health very seriously and drew from this gravity of analysis a consistent demand on government to take measures that reflected the extremity of the perceived public health threat.[30] Lockdown came too late and was ended too early or too quickly.[31] It needed strong enforcing.[32] Opening up too early was a risk. Social control via track and trace was necessary. Vaccination campaigns needed to be universally enforced. The government was, thus, a constant target for Identitarian Socialists' ire because of its inefficacy.[33] The government was portrayed as incompetent, erratic, and riven with cronyism. It was cavalier about the nature of the threat from the virus. Idioms of a failed state or a 'plague island' ran through Identitarian Socialist content that fused a critical approach to the Tories with a desire for more effective and muscular state action.

Secondly, Identitarian Socialism saw in the pandemic a kind of challenge in which something of its social vision might be realised.[34] COVID-19 imposed the conditions of possibility for a new sociability in which people cared for each other, obeyed socially responsible rules, and expressed a kind of human solidarity. The hardship of lockdown was, in a sense, celebrated: lockdown itself was not questioned[35] but rather the ability of people to endure it was validated as an expression of people's fundamental social conscience. To stay indoors was an act of social solidarity. Those who broke lockdown guidelines were treated as anti-social.[36]

Vaccine roll-out, the opening of schools, and the removal of restrictions of social events and working practices were all treated cautiously by Identitarian Socialists. The persistence of a scientific narrative concerning resurgent spikes in infection remained and government 'responsibility' during the gradual *abertura* remained Identitarian Socialism's primary narrative.

Lockdown according to DMN

The virus was not treated epidemiologically in the same way that Identitarian Socialism treated it. DMN sustained a critical understanding of scientific knowledge. This was not a denial of science per se but rather a recognition that there would always be dissensus within scientific research, that elites would manipulate scientific data and select from the advice given by scientists, and that scientists make poor political decision makers. In short, Democratic Marxist Nationalists commenced with an incredulity towards the notion of a scientific consensus that was created out of a value–neutral exploration of the virus.[37]

DMN saw the pandemic as, in large part, a political construction. This even evoked some favourable references to a Foucauldian tradition of analysis, especially the work of George Agamben. The pandemic was a form of securitisation, an exercise of state power over people. This was the central leitmotif of DMN's account of lockdown. *Contra* Identitarian Socialism, lockdown was not a bold and responsible way to make sure society stayed safe but rather an unprecedented exercise of state power over ordinary people whose effects on liberty were extremely worrying.

This left DMN with a rather equivocal attitude towards the Tory government. Identitarian Socialism's positional-Left and consistent attack on the Tories contrasted with a narrative in which a certain libertarian tendency within the Tories was actually preferable to the mainstream contests between Tories and Labour to see which could be most lockdown-bombastic. The focus was less on the Tories and more on the nature of the state and its elites: their disdain for ordinary people, their love to bureaucratic fiat, their desire to emaciate the sociability of public space.

Scepticism of the claims that there was a value-neutral scientific consensus and concern about overweening state power led DMN to condemn lockdown as based in poor or partial scientific evidence and driven by

an authoritarian political reflex. A similar view was offered in relation
to mask wearing and the exclusion or brutalisation of those not wearing
masks. Those not wearing masks were painted as 'deniers' by mainstream
liberal-Left opinion. Independent thought, heterodoxy, and the freedom
not to obey led people not to wear a mask, which validated Democratic
Marxist Nationalists' support of non-wearers. Not wearing was seen as a
kind of stress test of what liberty is: doing something that many people
do not like.[38]

Attitudes towards the public health crisis reflected its 'rugged society'
concept.[39] Following the Great Barrington Declaration, emphasis was put on
protecting discrete vulnerable groups and allowing a general herd immunity
approach in relation to the general public. Becoming infected was not seen as
a disaster for those under 70 and without chronic health conditions. People
were tough. Getting the virus would improve one's immunity. The virus
would not go away and zero COVID-19 was seen as preposterous.

DMN was more aware of the damaging effects of lockdown on the
economy and public services now being de-prioritised as a result of
the emergency response to COVID-19. The profound disruption to the
economy and the falling apart in healthcare services were specifically focused
on. A resilient society that kept working and mobile would push through
the pandemic and, in the medium term, emerge better off as the socio-
economic damage of lockdown would have been avoided.

The image of a resilient and mobile sociability that kept the economy and
public culture active was given sharper delineation through contrast. DMN
portrayed the locked-down condition as one supported by, or favourable to,
the middle classes.[40] Evoking the aesthetics outlined in Chapter 4, the middle
classes were portrayed as enjoying a lockdown lifestyle. Home cooking,
home schooling, pursuing hobbies, gardening, and so on were conjoined
with white-collar professional jobs that could be done remotely: designers,
lawyers, lecturers, IT consultants, banking, and so on.[41] A caricature (not
entirely unrepresentative) served to lampoon those seen as most supportive of
lockdown as a kind of fantasy life in which work and home leisure pursuits
were only interrupted by the occasional Amazon or Ocado delivery.

COVID-19 contentions

Society

The public health emergency that was COVID-19 pivoted around differing
conceptions of society. Any public measure, or any prediction as to how
those measures would play out, depended crucially on how each tradition
understood social dynamics, the underpinning structures or forces that would
allow a political analysis to generate arguments in favour of one measure
or another.

DMN relied on its rugged society concept. COVID-19 was not something from which society needed protecting, it was something that society needed to combat. This position expressed itself in various ways. In the first place – and in boldest contrast with Identitarian Socialism – DMN did not consider lockdown as the central policy in the public health response. Lockdown was, rather, the quintessence of a cosseting and protectionist response that was based on the premise that society was weak and vulnerable. DMN frequently questioned the degree to which this was the case, using evidence that showed how people below the age of 70 and without underlying health problems tended to get the virus and then return to health. It was especially cynical about 'long COVID', which was not defined by a clear set of diagnostic conditions. Beyond the lack of parsimonious symptoms to clearly identify the condition, Democratic Marxist Nationalists criticised what seemed to be a kind of victimology in which headaches, shortness of breath, anxiety, and other very generalised conditions were labelled as part of a viral infection. The notion that people might be afflicted by a disease for years was considered a pernicious way to treat populations as permanently vulnerable and sickly, in need of safety measures.

The hostility towards a vision of a vulnerable population in need of protection was also expressed in relation to masks and school shutdowns, both of which, again, were questioned on empirical grounds as well as biopolitical ones. The same hostility was not expressed in relation to the vaccination campaign.

There was within the DMN analysis of COVID-19 an acceptance that people would die. Certain groups of the population would need focused protection, but mass society should have been allowed to carry on. Herd immunity or 'living with' was preferred to zero COVID-19. Indeed, the latter was understood as a political goal that was in substance about medicalising a population.

Identitarian Socialism established a different conceptual articulation to understand the social dynamics of public health emergency. At the heart of this was an association of socialist ethics with social care. In short, COVID-19 was a kind of test or even opportunity to realise a socialist culture out of two things: caring for others and having a common cause.

This meant that, rather than mask wearing being a sign of a society cowed into conformity with the biomedical state, mask wearing was a manifestation of collective social conscience. Obeying rules concerning lockdown or permitted spaces to meet, or keeping children out of school, was seen as communally minded.

'We are all vulnerable' was articulated as 'we are all equal'. COVID-19 presented to the general public a challenge which was collectively to obey all protectionist measures in order to defeat the virus.

If the pandemic has taught us anything so far, it is that we are in urgent need of a politics that puts care front and centre of life. A caring state begins from building and maintaining an infrastructure based upon a recognition of our profound interdependencies and vulnerabilities, while ensuring that the necessary material, social, and cultural conditions exist for the mutual thriving of all.[42]

Knowledge

Throughout the pandemic, there was constant debate concerning scientific analysis, evidence, and their relation to public policy. Of course, both proto-ideologies wished to claim that they had the best purchase on the best evidence. But, despite this common aim, their accounts of the evidence differed significantly. Identitarian Socialism assessed the validity of evidence through a rough metric of consensus. In other words, major UN organisations and government-assembled scientific working groups that disseminated high public profile reports with clear policy recommendations were the best empirical points of reference. Identitarian Socialist analysis of the pandemic relied on SAGE reports and did not consider them critically.

In politics, there is no such thing as innocent evidence. The gist of Identitarian Socialism was that evidence served to intensify the gravity of the pandemic. This fit with the cautionary sentiment noted in the previous section. There was a deeper epistemic aspect to this which was that full and valid knowledge of the pandemic was measured by how seriously one took the health crisis. This connected to the concept of crisis and its embedding in this proto-ideology more generally: the greater the expression of crisis, the more radical the argument. Ignorance, then, was largely associated with those points of view that did not treat the pandemic as seriously as they should.

Identitarian Socialism established a strong association between valid truth claim and gravitas. Evidence, then, took on a distinct aesthetic quality in which the more globally serious the virology, the more shocking the prognoses, the more powerful and 'truthy' the evidence became.[43] Upper-limit estimates had more impetus as vectors of meaning. Furthermore, the more gravitas in the narrative, the more it served to degrade proposals that things might not be so bad. To question the virus's effect on people was seen as flippant or socially derelict.

Knowledge was, then, defined by consensus and prudence. Forms of knowledge that expressed heterodoxy and which reduced the import of the pandemic were understood as wrong-minded and reckless. The facts of the disease trumped more wholeheartedly political analyses of the pandemic. To raise questions about power, liberty, surveillance, and so on was not so much illegitimate as it was a confession of ignorance as to how the scientific evidence showed how serious the virus was.

DMN did not deny the pandemic as a major-order public health emergency, but it did not treat the evidence consensus that was constructed around official sources as definitive and it did not endow them with a supra-political status. By the latter, I mean that Democratic Marxist Nationalists did not take orthodox scientific statements as the external facts around which one should assemble a political analysis. The term 'follow the science' was treated ironically or acerbically by Democratic Marxist Nationalists.[44]

If DMN downgraded the status of received scientific orthodoxy, how did it maintain a claim to be basing its analysis on evidence? Knowledge was created within DMN through a juxtaposition of something Foucauldian and something testing. In relation to the former, DMN treated orthodox presentations of scientific evidence as knowledge/power: a form of evidence that was inextricably also an expression of the devices and desires of a governing elite. Exaggeration, selectivity, and framing of evidence were all devices which collectively expressed a maximal position of biopolitics, a means to disseminate a dominating power over a general population. This was most clearly revealed in relation to arguments that populations should be subjected to track and trace, vaccination IDs, mobility restrictions, and so on. Scientific arguments were made for all of these – consider the colour-coded and evidentiary three-tier system – but for DMN this evidence was principally an exercise in state power, not a value-neutral epidemiology.

In relation to the latter, testing refers to a well-established procedure in scientific inquiry which is to seek to refute evidence presented, to stress test its validity. All scientific knowledge is considered as close to truth as possible until something better comes along; evidence generated is subjected to various forms of challenge: reconsidering procedures, reviewing raw data, performing replicability. So, DMN did not fully embrace a Foucauldian epistemology in which knowledge is entirely internalised into power networks (truth claims) but rather insisted that the best evidence is that which is resistant to – or cynical towards – established orthodoxy.

As a result, DMN reportage constantly questioned the mainstream evidence on masking, lockdown, and the morbidity of the virus. Masks did not work nearly as effectively as was claimed to stop the virus; lockdowns did not have a clear positive effect on transmission; death rates from the virus did not properly account for co-morbidity or the specific effects of age. In short, DMN defended an evidence-based approach to the pandemic but understood the best knowledge not as that that came from orthodoxy but rather an exacting heterodoxy.

The direction of travel presented by Democratic Marxist Nationalist treatments of evidence was that the disease was not as serious as was claimed. This keyed in with its more foregrounded political messaging that people should be allowed to carry on with life as normal. It also connected with attitudes towards the state.

Governing pandemic

Naturally, both proto-ideologies needed to speak about measures to be taken to deal with COVID-19, and this required a model of governance. In each case, judgements and expectations of the state derived from their conceptual assemblages. Indeed, it was within the constructions of state agency that much of the contention between the two traditions revealed its most salient analytical differences. Much like the issue of class and representation in the midst of Brexit, understandings of the state did not only differ but also open up incommensurability.

Performance metrics

Identitarian Socialism, we have argued, relies on a relativistic position in relation to the parliamentary system of government. The marker 'socialism' serves to anchor Identitarian Socialism constantly towards a more radical-Left position in relation to parties and policy. Unlike DMN, Identitarian Socialism is centrally interested in the politics of the possible in relation to party governance. It supports left-wing politicians, celebrates moves to the Left, entertains smaller parties (the Green Party) that seem to be moving leftwards, and express solidarity with social movements which are expected to pressure politics to the Left.

This orientation has two effects in relation to the state in times of pandemic. In the first place, there is an assumption that the government is potentially amenable to pressure and able to act effectively. The right kinds of pressure need to be exercised on it. It is possible to galvanise a cross-party consensus in relation to matters supra-political. It did not mean that Identitarian Socialism claimed that the Tory government was responding well to the pandemic. Rather, it was that parts of the Labour Party, institutions of government, public intellectuals, and experts could pressure government into taking the pandemic more seriously.

The corollary of this position was that much of the critical commentary of the government was a species of more general critical commentary that all manner of Left and liberal positions held during the pandemic: the language of 'the government is not doing enough', 'the government is ignoring', 'the government urgently needs to'. There is nothing intrinsically wrong with this, but it does set parameters on the Identitarian Socialist critique of the government.

The exceptional or emergency nature of COVID-19 meant that the government should be expected to perform the duty of executing a public health strategy which was above politics and therefore not necessarily beholden to party-ideological difference. This was how Parliament presented COVID-19, as a cross-party national emergency. Within these parameters, performance becomes the main metric of critique.

This leads to the second point, which is that Identitarian Socialism focused its attention on the Tories, with a view to attacking them and reducing their electability. Boris Johnson was portrayed as an exceptionally terrible Prime Minister.[45] The Tory leadership was criticised as exceptionally incompetent, riven with cronyism, dishonest, contemptuous of ordinary people's lives (which needed protecting). Self-evidently true but analytically set in a discussion about how a different party or different groups of politicians – ones that have listened to the best scientific advice – might perform better. This was not a critique of the state; it was a critique of the right wing of the Tory party, or the balance of forces within and between political parties. The state itself was not subjected to a deeper critique.

Lockdown authoritarianism

DMN started with a critical analysis of the state. COVID-19 governance was an expression of a joint global project of social engineering that involved groups of scientists, the police, and Parliament. As such, the bone of contention was not so much the degree to which a political tendency could be nudged towards common sense but rather the degree to which the parameters of state power were being systemically transformed. DMN used the notion of technopolitics to express this: the gathering of mass data and its processing into systems of qualified citizenship and surveillance. Rather than citizenship being the inalienable starting value of politics, citizenship as *given* or qualified by state assessment. This connects with DMN's advocacy of liberty. It oriented DMN towards a deep cynicism of the state which seemed to be prosecuting a politically motivated project of desocialisation (through lockdown, school closures, and the rise of virtual work) and social control (through passes, IDs, tracing, criminalisation of public sociability).

Accordingly, DMN did not focus its ire centrally on the Tories but rather the political elite as a whole. Indeed, in the moments when Johnson expressed a kind of cod libertarianism, Democratic Marxist Nationalists were relatively favourable towards him. Labour and the SNP's desire for more extensive restrictions on people's liberty were heavily criticised as examples of that form of patronising Left-leaning elite governance that we identified in Chapter 5.

Identitarian Socialism focused its critical attention on the Tories; DMN focused on the state. This did not only cause Democratic Marxist Nationalists to focus on the repression of liberties rather than the policies of social protection, it also led to a different line of attack in relation to the more prosaic political decision making during pandemic. Democratic Marxist Nationalists referred to the failure of the political elite as a whole. This failure was not framed in terms of insufficient social protection but rather insufficient boldness and imagination. Chiming with conceptual aesthetics around resilience of ruggedness and work,[46] Democratic Marxist Nationalists attacked elites for their timidity and ineffectiveness.

The lack of 'politics in command', even during periods of crisis which desperately needed political leadership, fed into a key argument about the changing form of statehood since at least 2008. This was that, after decades of neoliberal erosion of authoritative state action and political capitulation to the market, states were weak and governing elites had little sense of the specific value of the political. In the absence of a robust political class, governance has become a set of failures, inconsistencies, and rhetorical hyperbolae: a void. This characterisation was at the heart of connected academic work.[47] It was also the source of a turn of phrase often used in the Bungacast podcasts: neoliberal order breakdown syndrome.[48]

There is no categorical distinction between Labour and the Conservatives within this analysis. Both parties are manifestations of neoliberal order breakdown syndrome, a legacy of Thatcher and Blair, a form of politics that is systemic and trans-party. COVID-19: a public health crisis which – like other crises – was a part of this breakdown, a manifestation of a structural or epochal change in which the virus itself was not the primary historical agent but rather something more like a catalyst.

This distinction between Identitarian Socialism and DMN is revealing. On the one hand, Democratic Marxist Nationalists can critique Identitarian Socialists' open support for Momentum, Corbyn, or some actually existing 'Left' politics. These can be coloured as reformist, elitist, or strategically naïve. Momentum might be full of millennials; Corbyn might be 'magic grandpa', and the few politicians who express radical-Left views[49] might be treated as self-serving or easily nudged towards more moderate positions. Conversely, DMN itself rarely displays any positive attention towards existing political parties.[50] It is impossible to discern what Democratic Marxist Nationalists do in the polling booth. As such, its political horizons as a proto–ideology are relatively constrained. How might DMN contribute to a political project of socialist transformation?

There is a constructive tension within ideology building. The tension resides in the equivocations of being right and being relevant. As discussed in Chapter 3, the historic sensibility of socialism is often 'obstetric': having a belief in a certain kind of political economy as a solution to capitalism's various oppressions and dysfunctions and also having an awareness that the conditions of realisation for this political economy are barely present. For Marxists who are principally political theorists, this condition is fine. It provides a context in which critique and analysis of capitalism can continue for as long as capitalism does. For those principally interested in the work of political-ideological construction, obstetric time puts people in a frustrating position. There is ideological work to be done within and against any party or movement that captures broad public attention, but the arguments generated can become equivocal, moderated, and fallible. These are the attendant characteristics of political engagement. Contrastingly, there are clearer lines of analysis in ideological work that is less engaged but the prospects for broader public recognition are lower.

That the Momentum social movement that supported Corbyn has fizzled out might be seen as a defeat for Identitarian Socialism's attempts to push Labour towards the Left in the name of a socialist position. Or it might be seen as another example of how the Labour Left is politically exhausted and divorced from working-class constituencies. With some licence, one or both can be true: a failure of effort or strategy, a failure to adhere to a proper historical–materialist theory of political change. There is no reconciliation or solution to the dynamics of tension between analytical purity and political 'dirtiness'.

The implication thus far is that Democratic Marxist Nationalists do not have the sense of political engagement and active struggle that Identitarian Socialism has and, as a result, it is weaker in its mobilisational properties. But, some qualification is needed here. DMN does advocate. It has focused on mass popular democratic protest movements, most prominently the *gilets jaunes*, but also anti-authoritarian protest movements in Hong Kong and elsewhere. One might read into the supportive discussion of these movements two salient features.

Firstly, a passive sense of advocacy. Expressing support for student protests or *gilets jaunes* or workers striking in the name of liberty is articulated without a sense of active solidarity. There is no autobiographical activism or detailed account of mobilisation as there is within Identitarian Socialism's livelihood-Left morphology. This 'removed support' is consistent with a deeper political position that any political movement worth supporting should not be commandeered by elite-intellectual oversight.

This is not stated by Democratic Marxist Nationalists; it is implied by this tradition's relative removal from active engagement with political movements and parties. This implication is bolstered by this tradition's conceptual arrangements in another way. We noted in Chapter 5 that democracy was the most important anchorage of this proto-ideological tradition. As such, forms of political mobilisation in the present day have as their primary value defending or advocating deeper democracy. Socialism is largely absent from the present day. It is not that movements of the Left or socialism are not discussed; they often are in Bungacasts. Rather, it is that they are not specified or discussed as active and practical socialist possibility. Instead, they are framed as the potential vanguard of a democratic revival. Fights for liberty and citizenship against the state are discussed and analysed *in specifica*, as active and feasible political struggle. Democracy is the active and present matter; socialism is the greater goal that a healthy democracy might realise.

Conclusion

We have focused on Brexit and COVID-19 as the two most prominent bones of contention within British politics in the crisis years. We could have discussed other topics which also reveal the differences between the two, albeit with less detailed content: climate change, trans politics, antisemitism, and cancelling being the main ones. Each of these tends to refract through the contrasting morphologies in ways that reveal similar differences and contentions as we have seen in relation to Brexit and lockdown.

In relation to Brexit, we suggested that, amid the various differences of viewpoint, it was the mode of representation of class that was fundamental and revealed a constitutive irreconcilability. DMN reads class differently and it conceptualises its agency differently to Identitarian Socialism. The former sees a popular mass class which is gaining consciousness as a class in an age when neoliberal order is breaking down; the latter sees class as a multifarious set of social identities, some of which have suffered from a failure of political cognition. In relation to COVID-19, we identified the conceptualisation of the state as the difference that makes a difference. Identitarian Socialists, focused on active political engagement, sought out a cross-party public health response that was based in an understanding of supra-political emergency and a desire to protect society; Democratic Marxist Nationalists saw a kind of liberal authoritarian that expressed the exhaustion of a political elite's ability to govern effectively.

As proto-ideologies, distinctive conceptual arrangements are not the whole story. The affective and aesthetic aspects of discourse also matter. In this regard, conceptual difference is intensified, not mollified. DMN communicates a kind of realism and ruggedness; Identitarian Socialism communicates a sense of outrage at multiple forms of social injustice. The former's medium/message is the blog and podcast; the latter's is more likely the tweet, YouTube discussion, or an Insta account.

8

Conclusion

Summary

Succeeding a (supposed) period of stability, the political mood of our times is dour. Previously accepted expectations of stability, growth, improvement, good governance, and global integration have been undermined. Since at least 2008, we have lived in an age of crisis. Public and intellectual attention has been turned towards a set of declinist or eschatological political possibilities. Within the midst of this, discussions of social media have served as a key reference point for anxieties and pessimisms. The volatile, sporadic, unmediated, and emotional discourses of social media have ostensibly undermined public cultures of deliberation, tolerance, respect for evidence, and civic identity. Echo chambers, hate speech, and conspiracy abound. It is difficult to imagine a more inauspicious context within which to discuss the construction of socialist ideologies, at least within a formally democratic country. Indeed, even the descriptor 'democratic' seems increasingly aspirational rather than a working premise.

But, social media is not only a lurid and noisy fairground of dissonance and dissensus. There is, within its tweets, blogs, podcasts, discussion groups, and YouTube channels, a province that we dubbed PSM. PSM is defined through a twofold protocol. Firstly, an adherence to broadly deliberative rules of discussion: evidential backing, tolerance, a degree of measure. Secondly, the deployment of social media signifiers to move political discourse into a social realm where it might be noticed and even engaged with by a broader public: the use of imagery and logos, memes, hot takes, and more 'sassy' language.

It is a fact that PSM has emerged into a thriving virtual arena over the same period as politics more generally has been understood as a series of disasters. This, we argue, is a moderate corrective to the images of democratic breakdown, post-truth, political disorder, and a range of post-liberal positions that seem transfixed by reactionary populisms. Within the province of PSM, there exists a vibrant socialist intellectual activism.

Socialism has bequeathed to us a historiography of impatient optimism, based in the conviction that, although capitalism has pushed societies out of absolutist, feudalist, and stagnant states, it is constrained by its own contradictions and exploitations. Socialism emerged as the ideological tradition that wanted more out of political modernity. Of course, socialism has been much predicted and rarely, if ever, realised. Once one accepts this, its persistence seems remarkable. As the rise of socialist PSM instantiates, socialist thinking has not dissolved with the collapse of the Berlin Wall, the rise of depoliticised economic liberalism, or the ongoing consolidation of capital in the Global South. In fact, it is written into the heart of socialism's historiography that it should necessarily sustain a kind of tenacious denial of lived-in times. It insists, across generations, we can do better.

As an ideological tradition, socialism is replete with definitional confusions. We make some distinctions to enable us to analyse the ideological properties of social media socialism. We define socialism as an ecumenical terrain, encompassing Marxism and a broad range of socialist traditions. Marxism, we argue, has its own more exacting theoretical and traditional coordinates that derive most strongly from *Capital I*. Marxism identifies the social relations of wage labour as its foundation and it constructs a theory of history, class, and market therefrom.

Socialism is a much broader political tradition that equally bases itself in a profound critique of capitalism, but this critique is articulated through a range of normative positions concerning the community, fulfilling work, equality, and citizenship.

We make a distinction between 'socialism' as a general term for a tradition that encompasses socialisms and Marxism, and 'Socialism' to identify non-Marxist ideas. These distinctions become important when we come to consider some case studies. DMN's Marxism connects to socialism, but it is not of it; it opposes leftward reformism social democracy and non-Marxist categorisations, whereas Identitarian Socialism's socialism encompasses some Marxism and some (post-colonial and intersectional) Socialism.

These ideational distinctions within socialist thought give us the coordinates through which to make sense of socialism within PSM. But if we are to make our argument, we need to do more than simply describe the socialist content in PSM and claim that socialist thinking is not on its way out. Our argument is that this content connects to political projects political activisms that have a broader significance.

It is the focus on political projects that informs our discussion of political ideology: ideas thought and fought. In order to treat the volatility of socialist discourse in PSM appropriately, we accept that there are projects of concept building being pursued but acknowledge that these are in construction: proto-ideologies.

Relying on Freeden's morphological approach, we can trace the contours of conceptual arrangements. We modify Freeden's model by highlighting the combative, aspirational, and aesthetic aspects of ideology. This helps us recognise that these ideologies are in construction. There is a sense of the arriviste: wanting to ascend, to take on other positions. We noted that this aspirationalism is focused not only on the enemies of socialism but also other traditions of socialist thought. There is a battle to win hearts and minds and a battle to put an imprimatur of the meaning of socialism.

With our anti-pessimistic orientation based in an identification of PSM, our awareness of the internal complexities of socialist political ideology, we explored two major socialist traditions of political thought that have flourished in the last decade or so. We started with DMN, noting that it has a core conceptual arrangement that connects democracy, a Marxist understanding of class, and a conviction that politics is best realised through contestations that revolve around an accountable sovereign state. Adjacent concepts connect closely to core concepts: we saw a strong figuring of class and an equally strong valuing of mass democracy. Peripheral concepts have more flexibility and are also more easily deployed as ways to argue and intervene in matters of general political interest: education, the nature of society, hypocrisy, and the future of humankind.

Identitarian Socialism has a socialist core. The composition of socialism here is less delineated: it encompasses facets of Marxism, as well as broader Socialist ideas which enable Identitarian Socialism to ground a general 'Left' centre of gravity vis-à-vis social movements, political parties, and other political agencies. Socialism in this political tradition serves better as a way to be engaged and eye-catching. The second core is intersectionality which generates a different orientation in relation to class. The working class is understood as a composition of social identities that share a general condition of subordination or oppression but are realised through race, ethnicity, gender, sexuality, nationality, 'ability', and so on. A 'horizontal' concept of class is, then, cut through with 'vertical' social classifications that also encompass some who would not ordinarily be seen as working class. This understanding of class is connected to a general epistemology of pluralism. Identitarian Socialism celebrates the multiplex, the diverse, and the local. In this sense, it reflects an established social justice movement understanding of political struggle.

Identitarian Socialism's adjacent concepts are less tightly connected to its core concepts and seem more oriented towards its desire to speak to the political issues of the day and to establish a radical-Left position that urges political movement or mobilisation. Crisis is key here, intensifying political stakes. An openness to diverse political movements is enabled by its faith that any movement on the Left can be moved further leftwards. The ways in which change takes place is through bottom-up activism, livelihoods, and lifestyle combined to produce aesthetically attractive political identities.

These two political traditions are set out and analysed in order to demonstrate how, between them, a considerable amount of intellectual labour is being expended to construct socialist ideological phenomena through virtual media. Of course, none of the ideas are entirely novel, but they are innovative: they adapt, recombine, and re-articulate to current matters of political contestation. Socialism is not dying; these two case studies make a case that it is in fact vibrantly alive and attuned to the political present and near future.

But, it was clear from the case study chapters that the two traditions have distinct conceptual morphologies. This has significant repercussions for the ways in which each engages in major political contentions during the crisis period. We explored how DMN and Identitarian Socialism portrayed profoundly different analyses in relation to Brexit and COVID-19. Drawing on their respective conceptual morphologies, Brexit was framed in disparate fashion: a working-class rebellion against a stale political system or a Right-shifting xenophobic reaction. Giving these contrasts some deeper analysis, we identified how these conceptualisations were not simply different but also antagonistic and incommensurate. They do not work together; they do not open up any clear zone of synthesis in relation to each other. At the heart of this, we argued, was a distinctly different understanding of class. Each proto-ideology represented class in ways that to some degree negated the other. The same qualitative difference ran through each proto-ideology's understanding of COVID-19. COVID-19 was a major public health emergency that required social protection, a determined and powerful government, and a socially responsible and compliant public; COVID-19 was a governmental strategy to enhance its authoritarian tendencies over a society that had the wherewithal to weather the virus with minimal social regulation. The incommensurability in relation to COVID-19 hung on the ways in which state authority was understood.

The meaning of incommensurability

That different ideologies generate different takes on the matter at hand is hardly surprising. That two proto-ideologies that derive from the same ideological tradition do the same thing is also not in itself that remarkable. Indeed, the intellectual history of socialist thought is often told as exceptionally factious in its disagreements. But, this book is not simply a demonstration that new currents in socialist thought continue to expend as much energy proving their fellow travellers wrong as they do challenging the regnant ideas of the ruling class. What we have shown is that each tradition has drawn on socialist thought to compose almost entirely different conceptual morphologies. This has led each not only to disagree on matters of political decision and value, it has also led each to see politics differently.

The repercussions of this constitutive difference are significant in how we might map the futures of each proto-ideology. In the first place, their conceptual morphologies establish distinct modes of practice, aspects of which have been touched on in earlier chapters. Identitarian Socialism's ontology of the intersectional, pluralist, the individual, and the lifestyle livelihood does not only set analytical coordinates for how it analyses, narrates, and critiques a political issue. It also establishes a protocol for its virtual media presence. It is way more visible than DMN. In autumn 2023, Novara Media's YouTube account had 360,000 subscribers, and one of its live podcasts attracted 310,000 views. It set up an Instagram stream in 2022. It has merch. In its podcasts, it seeks not only interesting guests but also relatively famous ones: people who have some left-wing political convictions but who have established success and profile in some niche of popular culture. The list includes: Chris Packham, China Miéville, and Frankie Boyle.

DMN is largely indifferent to the play of aesthetics, with the exception of the frequent ironic repositioning of Silvio Berlusconi in Bungacast tweets. It is a great deal more text-heavy. It relies on academics in the production of its content to a greater degree. Bungacast has a reading group, not a YouTube account. The aesthetic minimalism of DMN is not arbitrary. It connects to its understanding of agency and political change. In Chapters 5 and 6, we noted how DMN does not expect class-based popular revolutionary political insurgency any time soon. It is, so to speak, hemmed in by a very immediate conviction to defend national democracy and a more distant faith that working-class historic agency will overthrow capitalism at some point in the future. For Democratic Marxist Nationalists, when the revolution comes, it will not be an affair led by a middle-class intelligentsia who command the means of signification in any case. It is the overbearing cultural self-confidence of the PMC, the journalists, academics, and politicians that, as we saw, attracts more ire from Democratic Marxist Nationalists than the bourgeoisie does.

Both proto-ideologies conceptualise an ontology and episteme that also significantly colour their social media practices. This means that the medium of social media – designed as it is to set out flat, broad, and inclusive landscapes of communication – does not in fact enable a high degree of intellectual synthesis between the two traditions. They are autonomous not because they have not encountered each other but because they see things differently.

This has interesting repercussions for PSM more broadly. This is because each proto-ideology has more in common with non-socialist ideological traditions than with each other. Identitarian Socialism is sometimes called liberal Left in social media traffic. The liberal Left, however we define this, is clearly a substantial and culturally confident assemblage. It encompasses some Green politics, some *Guardian* journalism, much of the social justice movement, much of contemporary 'critical' social science in universities.

Although there is a Socialist position within this proto-ideology, it is deployed relationally and through idioms of intersectionality and this endows its discourse with an ease of fit to a broad range of Left-liberal positions that might see social justice, environmentalism, political identity, or inequality in ways that broadly conform to an equal opportunities and social-market optic.

If Identitarian Socialism seems more amenable to conversations with the liberal Left, DMN has more affinity with a political tradition that prioritises a heterodox, controversialist, quasi-libertarian normativity that often hosts conservative or right-wing positions. This is most obvious in relation to Spiked, but also Unherd and Compact. All of these are not Marxist but have Marxists writing for them.[1] They share these sites' editorial conviction to freedom of expression as a means to provoke, rethink, revise, and be offensive in order to push against what is often perceived as comfortable orthodoxy. Perhaps the best, albeit rather banal example of this is the re-tweeting of Matthew Goodwin's tweets by some within the DMN camp.[2] A more substantive example is the Battle of Ideas. This annual workshop-based intellectual festival has as its credo 'free speech allowed'. It has hosted speakers from the Right and Left, many of whom have contributed to the DMN proto-ideology. This means that these key intellectuals are speaking to audiences more likely to have authors who write for the *Daily Mail* than the *The Guardian*.[3]

In short, not only do these two proto-ideologies not engage with each other, they engage with rival traditions, rendering the legibility of PSM's Left–Right spectrum unstable.

Proximity

That both proto-ideologies are flourishing precludes any simple conclusion as to which, by some measure or other, outperforms the other. But, they do show themselves better in some areas than others. We shall take four themes, each moving outwards in terms of how an ideology is constructed.

In relation to the articulation of concepts, it is clear that DMN is more tightly arranged. That is to say, its core concepts are more clearly defined and therefrom, adjacent concepts connect very closely. This might be a corollary of its more fulsomely Marxist orientation. As we noted in Chapter 3, Marxism has an exacting theoretical tradition as much as an ideological one. DMN is not a theory of capital, but it does establish in its core a theory of mass democratic agency in the working class that then feeds closely into its other concepts and, indeed, its entire discursive field. There are correspondences: this is a middle-class phenomenon and therefore it is problematic. There are necessities: if this does not involve the working class it is politically defunct. There are a priori: this political idea is valid if it reflects a popular working-class sensibility that can be expressed commonsensically.

Identitarian Socialism's conceptual morphology is looser. Socialism and communism are both evoked and intermixed with 'Left', and the corollaries of this orientation are not expressed through logical necessities but rather more complex networks of vertical and horizontal pluralism. Identitarian Socialism is articulated through associations whose diversity is evocative of political energy more than analytical specificity. The value system generated by its concepts is not foundationally about liberty; it is about individual recognition, social justice, equality, freedom from exploitation.

Within this comparison, it seems that DMN moves towards a theoretical tradition and Identitarian Socialism moves towards a political movement. In regards to the former, we have recognised that 'schools' of Marxism have come and gone. It is possible that a certain kind of 'school' status will accrue to this proto-ideology and that, as a result, it will enjoy a kind of scholastic but also activist practice. Concerning the latter, Identitarian Socialism gravitates towards discourse in the sense that its values, arguments, and imagery have resonated with a broader Left-leaning public. The content of Identitarian Socialism, then, sits within a Left discourse that is substantially shared with Momentum, Black Lives Matter, a good deal of Extinction Rebellion, the Green Party, the Labour Left, and a clutch of celebrities. Inasmuch as Identitarian Socialism wins accolades, DMN might well consider itself to be struggling against an increasingly publicly prominent or even hegemonic 'Left' project rather than a capitalist class.

No political ideology is stable and all ideologies have within them both tendencies to formalise into theoretical agendas and broader sensibilities in public culture. It is missing the point, then, to expect ideological purity or to assess a political ideology according to either the way its concepts stand up to analysis or resonate with a broader public. It seems, though, that our two case studies are moving in different directions.

Prospective

> Social media is both an expression of the crisis of the social that pre-exists the internet and a potent accelerator of that crisis. Solving this does not mean fixing online. It means changing, IRL, the society that makes life empty and atomized in the first place.[4]

We have emphasised through the book that proto-ideologies are ascendant; they aspire to consolidate a set of concepts and interventions that allow them recognition, followers, and influence. Coded into each proto-ideology is a view of how this might be achieved. We have noted this immanence before: that the conceptual work done by a proto-ideology is both a means to understand the political world and also to understand this proto-ideology's own place within it.

With such deep ontological and epistemological divergence, it is unsurprising that each tradition sets out a different sense of the future. The reader can probably imagine this without it being set out. DMN has a sense of revolutionary moderation in which struggles to defend or expand mass democracy are the issue of the day and there is little evidence of socialist possibility.[5] Identitarian Socialism is open to ongoing socialist activism and it maintains a 'movement' sense of the near future in which coalitions, organisational innovation, and the winning of ideas through social media give a sense that it is always *if not now, then when*.

The sense of the future that each proto-ideology offers is important for our analysis not only in itself but in relation to the general framing of our argument. The burden of the case studies has been to demonstrate that the polycrisis declinism of the present is commonly presented in too foreclosed a fashion and that innovative, progressive, and even optimistic socialist political thinking has flourished within PSM. How, then, do these prospectives correct the prevailing sense that everything is getting worse and will continue to do so?

Each tradition contains within it what one might call a temporal glitch. This glitch is a mismatch between a narrative content that is optimistic and one that is pessimistic. Each facet, in part, undermines the other. So, Identitarian Socialism certainly holds close to its normativity an immediate hope: the radical-Left positionality, the focus on new social movements, and a sense of a 'thousand flowers' give a vibrant sense of ongoing activism, victories won, or lessons learned. Its general aesthetics within social media are colourful, passionate, and upbeat. Any review of its podcasts shows that. But, how does this relate to its intensified and holistic expectation of crisis? There is a distinct 'disasterology' within Identitarian Socialism that is expressed through narratives concerning climate change, neoliberalism, and racism.

One might resolve this apparent contradiction with a reference to the optimism or the will and pessimism of the intellect, but this is barely adequate beyond its familiarity as a Gramscian cliché. One might claim that political mobilisation is aided by the sense of panicked urgency that disaster presents. But the cohabitation of active optimistic activism and a coming apocalypse is not sustainable. The construction of strong political movements tasked with nothing less than the overthrow of capitalism (this is, necessarily, the foundation of Identitarian Socialism's conceptualisation) cannot endure repeated evocations of a disaster incoming.

Mobilisation through iterated claims of climate chaos, financial ruin, and the coming fascism deplete with iteration and they lose their cognitive coherence. They suggest two different temporalities: one that concerns movement building over decades with clear, strong, and attractive goals, the other with immediate sudden protests set within a 'now or never' temporality: the historiography of the precipice. In short, the engaged immediacy of Identitarian Socialism's sense of the future, set as it is in intensifying impending crisis narrative, does not map clearly on to a vision of socialist movement building.

Contrarily, DMN refutes the impending disaster narrative. It has, as we saw, a Promethean thread running through it, a judgement that crises are exaggerated by political elites and that societies and technologies can overcome climate change and pandemics. As such, DMN's sense of the near future is not apocalyptic but dialectic. Processes in play will continue but not in a way that feels like acceleration towards a precipice.

This should offer a better terrain upon which to think about socialist movement building. Furthermore, as we have seen, DMN has a kind of optimism about the future that derives from its 'end of the end of history' thesis in which a stolid neoliberal managerialism is crumbling under the pressures of new socio-political insurgencies. In short, DMN sees a future not defined by apocalypse but rather an epochal reinvigoration of political contention.

But, here, the optimism of the intellect is accompanied by a pessimism of the will. There is no active discussion of socialism as a historic possibility. Mass proletarian possibilities within democratic, populist, and nationalist irruptions define the scope of ambition within Democratic Marxist Nationalist speculations of political change. There is, at times, a sense of restraint within Democratic Marxist Nationalist discourse. For example, the death of Queen Elizabeth II was met by Identitarian Socialists with a case for a republic, a characteristic temporality that now was the time to think about this profound constitutional change. Democratic Marxist Nationalist analysis of the passing of a monarch was focused on why the Queen was so popular and how she, as a political figure, represented a kind of recompense in popular culture of the moral failure of Parliamentary politics. Agreeing with this latter position does not make one a socialist; nor does it speak to what socialists might do in relation to the monarchy, an institution that is most assuredly – even in its current form – both undemocratic and a key component in sustaining inheritable wealth and land.

This reflects, as we have argued, a realist underpinning to much DMN which maintains a cool attitude towards 'ideological' (here, in the sense of asserting a political principle regardless of concrete reality) positions. Contrary to cursory glosses, realism is not intrinsically a right-wing theoretical orientation. There is a discernible realism in Marx and most certainly in Lenin; there are realist schools within the theoretical Marxisms from the 1960s onwards, perhaps most prominently the Marxist traditions of critical realism (although this looks rather different in many ways from political theory's realism). But, the realism within a Marxist tradition has commonly lent itself to movement building: strategy, organisation, propaganda, and combat. The realist setting within DMN does not engage with this but rather establishes a sense of restraint that precludes active discussion of these things. In relation to the possibilities, say, of building a new proletarian political party, a new form of unionism, of internationalism, of setting out a programme of aims … these are all absent.

Identitarian Socialism seeks to build movements but have little confidence in the future; DMN has confidence in the future but has little interest in building movements. As a result, despite their major differences, neither proto-ideology currently presents a fulsome socialist case against the pessimism of our age. In this sense, more than any other, they remain proto-ideologies.

Notes

Chapter 1

1   Macintyre, S. (1980) *A Proletarian Science: Marxism in Britain 1917–1933*, Cambridge: Cambridge University Press, p 3.
2   See, for example, the contributors to Bernholz, L., Landemore, H., and Reich, R. (eds) (2021) *Digital Democracy and Democratic Theory*, Chicago: Chicago University Press.
3   McDowell-Naylor, D., Cushion, S. and Thomas, R. (2021) 'A typology of alternative online political media in the United Kingdom: a longitudinal content analysis (2015–2018)', *Journalism* 24(1): 1–21.
4   Although this is rare and there is only one prominent example of someone I have called an Identitarian Socialist engaging positively with a venue commonly seen as more DMN. Tellingly, there was some teasing commentary about that person in which it was openly mooted how long they could remain in that camp.

Chapter 2

1   Fukuyama, F. (1992) *The End of History and the Last Man*, London: Penguin.
2   Fukuyama clarifies that The Mechanism he uses is 'essentially an economic interpretation of history' (*The End of History*, p 131).
3   Fukuyama, *The End of History*, Chapters 15 and 16.
4   These upper-caps terms reflect Fukuyama's Hegelian stylisations of the metaphysics of history.
5   Fukuyama sporadically leaves some open space for a kind of Islamism to pose as a rival, although he does not put much store in this.
6   Fukuyama, *The End of History*, p 339.
7   Hutton, W. (1995) *The State We're in: Why Britain Is in Crisis and How to Overcome It*, London: Jonathan Cape; Giddens, A. (1998) *The Third Way: The Renewal of Social Democracy*, Oxford: Polity Press.
8   Williamson, J. (1990) 'What Washington means by policy reform', in Williamson, J. (ed.), *Latin American Adjustment: How Much Has Happened?*, Washington, DC: Institute for International Economics, pp 7–20.
9   On the liberal properties of neoconservatism, see Williams, M. (2005) 'What is the national interest? The neoconservative challenge in IR theory', *European Journal of International Relations* 11(3): 307–37; Bell, D. (2014) 'What is liberalism?', *Political Theory* 42(6): 682–715.
10 Roy, O. (2017) *Jihadism and Death*, London: Hurst.
11 Malik, K. (2009) *From Fatwa to Jihad*, London: Atlantic Books.
12 Jarsulic, M. (2015) 'The origins of the US financial crisis of 2007', in Wolfson, M. and Epstein, G. (eds), *The Political Economy of Financial Crises*, Oxford: Oxford University Press, p 24.

[13] A point emphasised in Tooze, A. (2019) *Crashed: How a Decade of Financial Crises Changed the World*, London: Penguin.

[14] Schwartz, H. (2016) 'Wealth inequality and secular stagnation: the role of industrial organization and intellectual property rights', *Journal of the Social Sciences* 2(6): 226–49; Benanav, A. (2019) 'Automation and the future of work', *New Left Review* 119 and 120.

[15] Not in all sectors or in all countries to the same degree, of course.

[16] The notion that a government and national economy are akin to a head of household and a family fails even a cursory comparative reflection.

[17] Argentina, Brazil, Canada, China, France, India, Mexico, Russia, South Africa, Turkey, the UK, the US.

[18] Goodhart, D. (2017) *The Road to Somewhere: The New Tribes Shaping British Politics*, London: Penguin.

[19] Goodhart, *The Road to Somewhere*, p 3.

[20] Goodhart, *The Road to Somewhere*, p 3.

[21] Goodhart, *The Road to Somewhere*, p 131.

[22] Indeed, without this caricature, generations of Oxbridge graduates would not have had the material for their BBC comedy series.

[23] Goodhart, *The Road to Somewhere*, p 59.

[24] Goodhart, *The Road to Somewhere*, p 20.

[25] Goodhart, *The Road to Somewhere*, p 55.

[26] Most notably, Paul Embery's (2020) *Despised: Why the Modern Left Loathes the Working Class* (London: Polity Press), which, like Goodhart, generated considerable opprobrium on social media.

[27] Goodhart, *The Road to Somewhere*, p 215 and following.

[28] Runciman, D. (2019) *How Democracy Ends*, London: Profile Books.

[29] Runciman is mainly interested in liberal democracies that have established themselves over a few generations, and he writes mainly about the UK and America.

[30] 'Democracy persists in a kind of frozen crouch' (Runciman, *How Democracy Ends*, p 210).

[31] Throughout the book, Runciman is ambiguous as to the extent and urgency of democracy's end times. But this doesn't stop him from concluding: 'This is not, after all, the end of the democracy. But this is how democracy ends' (*How Democracy Ends*, p 215).

[32] Runciman, *How Democracy Ends*, p 165.

[33] Runciman, *How Democracy Ends*, pp 87, 91.

[34] Runciman, *How Democracy Ends*, pp 142–3.

[35] Oborne, P. (2021) *The Assault on Truth*, London: Simon & Schuster.

[36] Oborne, *The Assault on Truth*, pp 2–3.

[37] Oborne, *The Assault on Truth*, p 115.

[38] Oborne, *The Assault on Truth*, pp 113, 162–3.

[39] Oborne, *The Assault on Truth*, p 78.

[40] Oborne, *The Assault on Truth*, pp 3, 33.

[41] Oborne, *The Assault on Truth*, pp 113, 99, 6.

[42] Most obviously, Peter Geoghegan's (2020) *Democracy for Sale: Dark Money and Dirty Politics* (London: Apollo Books) and Calvert, J. and Arbuthnot, G. (2021) *Failures of State: The Inside Story of Britain's Battle with Coronavirus* (London: Harper Collins) both play on the same themes: democratic crisis, post-truth, sleaze, and state failure. One treats these themes in relation to Brexit, the other COVID-19. Both – by the standards of politics books – enjoyed a broad audience.

[43] Oborne, *The Assault on Truth*, p 34.

[44] Goodhart, *The Road to Somewhere*, p 79.

[45] Runciman, *How Democracy Ends*, p 143.

[46] Fisher, M. (2013) 'Exiting the vampire castle', Open Democracy, www.opende mocracy.net/en/opendemocracyuk/exiting-vampire-castle; Nagle, A. (2017) *Kill All Normies: Online Culture Wars from 4Chan and Tumblr to Trump and the Alt-Right*, London: Zero Books; Seymour, R. (2019) *The Twittering Machine*, London: Indigo Press; Geoghegan, *Democracy for Sale*; Gilroy-Ware, M. (2022) 'What is wrong with social media? An anti-capitalist critique', *Socialist Register*.

[47] Shaik, A. (2016) *Capitalism: Competition, Conflict, Crises*, Oxford: Oxford University Press, p 72.

[48] A phrase used with some irony by Kees van der Pijl (1998) *The Lockean Heartland in the International Political Economy*, London: Routledge. A nuanced rethinking of embedded liberalism as both more contested and more malleable in its content than is often recognised is offered by Eric Helleiner (2019) 'The life and times of embedded liberalism: legacies and innovations since Bretton Woods', *Review of International Political Economy* 26(6): 1112–35.

[49] Newsinger, P. (2006) *The Blood Never Dried: A People's History of the British Empire*, London: Bookmarks.

[50] Vernon, J. (2017) *Modern Britain: 1750 to the Present*, Cambridge: Cambridge University Press, p 424 and following.

[51] Thompson, H. (2022) *Disorder: Hard Times in the 21st Century*, Oxford: Oxford University Press.

[52] Thane, P. (2018) *Divided Kingdom: A History of Britain, 1900 to the Present*, Cambridge: Cambridge University Press. On the protracted crisis of the British military in Northern Ireland, see O'Leary, B. (2019) *A Treatise on Northern Ireland, Volume 3: Consociation and Confederation*, Oxford: Oxford University Press, Section 3.2.

[53] Shaik, *Capitalism*, p 72.

[54] McQueen, A. (2018) *Political Realism in Apocalyptic Times*, Cambridge: Cambridge University Press. See also Sleat, M. (ed.) (2018) *Politics Recovered: Essays on Realist Political Thought*, Columbia: Columbia University Press.

[55] Fisher, 'Exiting the vampire castle'.

[56] Moore, M. (2018) *Democracy Hacked: Political Turmoil and Information Warfare in the Digital Age*, London: Oneworld.

[57] Nagle, *Kill All Normies*.

[58] Taibbi, M. (2019) *Hate, Inc.: Why Today's Media Makes Us Despise One Another*, London: OR Books; Gilroy-Ware, 'What is wrong with social media?', p 93.

[59] Singer, P.W. and Brooking, E.T. (2018) *Likewar: The Weaponization of Social Media*, New York: Mariner Books; Seymour, *The Twittering Machine*.

[60] Mills, S. (2019) '#DeleteFacebook: from popular protest to a new model of platform capitalism?', *New Political Economy* 26(5): 851–68.

[61] Seymour, *The Twittering Machine*; Wahlström, M., Törnberg, A., and Ekbrand, H. (2021) 'Dynamics of violent and dehumanizing rhetoric in far-Right social media', *New Media & Society* 23(11): 3290–311.

[62] Geoghegan, *Democracy for Sale*.

[63] Zuboff, S. (2019) *The Age of Surveillance Capitalism: The Fight for a Human Future at the New Frontier of Power*, London: Profile Books; Kotkin, J. (2020) *The Coming Neofeudalism*, London: Encounter Books, especially Chapter 5.

[64] Moore, *Democracy Hacked*; Hari, J. (2022) *Stolen Focus: Why You Can't Pay Attention*, London: Bloomsbury.

[65] Davies, W. (2021) 'The politics of recognition in the age of social media', *New Left Review* 128: 83–99.

[66] Major examples of this are: Spiked, Dissent, Unherd, Counterfire, Tribune, Open Democracy, Compact, the Intercept, and Jacobin.

Chapter 3

[1] See the well-cited distinction between problem solving and critical approaches in Cox, R. (1981) 'Social forces, states and world orders: beyond international relations theory', *Millennium: Journal of International Studies* 10(2): 126–55.

[2] On some occasions, I have been told by those who work within a Marxist tradition how they had to occlude their Marxism in the research bid applications.

[3] We will unpack this later but simply use 'socialism' for the time being.

[4] Therborn, G. (2007) 'After dialectics: radical social theory in a post-communist world', *New Left Review* 43: 63–114.

[5] Berman, M. (2010) *All That Is Solid Melts into Air*, London: Verso, p 33. I should emphasise here that Berman is speaking of late-19th-century political modernity generally in this quotation. He includes Marxism in that modernity (as the book's title suggests) but not only Marxism.

[6] Harrison, G. (2020) *Developmentalism: The Normative and Transformative within Capitalism*, Oxford: Oxford University Press.

[7] Erich Fromm makes this case especially in relation to *The Philosophic and Economic Manuscripts* (Fromm, E. and Marx, K. (2003) *Marx's Concept of Man*, London: Bloomsbury).

[8] Utopian socialisms may offer up models of society that are less connected to modernity, drawing on communitarian and anarchist political thought.

[9] There is too much to mention here. Illustratively, one might consider the major works of David Harvey, Doreen Massey, Manuel Castells, Tony Smith, the work of the Conference of Socialist Economists, the Gramscian ideas that emerged from Living Marxism, especially the thought to Stuart Hall, the re-launching of *New Left Review*, the Haymarket book series, and the inauguration of the journals *Historical Materialism* and *Salvage*.

[10] There is considerable debate about global social justice and its ideational components which are far from straightforwardly socialist or Marxist. But, there was clearly a lexical appropriation of socialism/Marxism in the ways global social justice movements understood the world and constructed notions of right and wrong.

[11] Miéville, C. (2022) *A Spectre, Haunting*, London: Bloomsbury.

[12] This observation through a reading of Marx, K. (2019) *The Political Writings*, London: Verso. On the usages of Marx's letters and articles as a source, see the lucid and nuanced Benner, E. (2018) *Really Existing Nationalisms: A Post-Communist View from Marx and Engels*, London: Verso. Even in his most polished work, Marx cannot resist the barbs. Towards the end of *Capital*, he calls Bentham an 'insipid, pedantic, leather-tongued oracle' (1995, Oxford: Oxford University Press, p 335). Ouch.

[13] As a stronger post-liberal current enters politics and academe, liberalism has shifted tone away from incumbency to defensiveness.

[14] Lukács, G. (1971) *History and Class Consciousness*, London: Merlin Press, p 1.

[15] Thompson, E.P. (1979) 'The great fear of Marxism', *The Observer*, 4 February.

[16] In the Preface to the second edition, Lukács identifies 'around 1918' as the start of his writing of this book.

[17] Anderson, P. (1976) *Considerations on Western Marxism*, London: Verso, Chapter 1.

[18] A concise flavour of this time is given by Cunliffe, P. (2017) *Lenin Lives! Reimagining the Russian Revolution 1917–2017*, London: Zero Books.

[19] Perhaps Marx's strongest statement of this is 'Freedom of the will is inherent in human nature', in Hudis, P. (2012) *Marx's Concept of the Alternative to Capitalism*, Chicago: Haymarket Books, p 44.

[20] On this, see especially Hudis, *Marx's Concept of the Alternative to Capitalism*.

[21] Or, more substantively, see Frederic Jameson's (2009) argument that 'it was not Marx but Engels that invented Marxism' (*Valences of the Dialectic*, London: Verso, p 8).

[22] Kolakowski (2005) offers an extremely detailed account of Marxism's development in the midst of socialist political thought, but the kernel of Marx's distinction and opposition to the main currents of socialist thought are summarised on pages 189–91 (*Main Currents of Marxism*, London: W.W. Norton). See also G.D.H. Cole's seven-volume *A History of Socialist Thought*, London: Macmillan.

[23] Indeed, Marx's own thoughts on ideology strongly indicate that Marxism or socialism are not ideologies at all. Marx's understanding of ideology is more akin to what Lukács calls a 'conceptual mythology': in which the totality of human existence is obscured. See especially Lukács, *History and Class Consciousness*, pp 17–18. See also Larrain, J. (1983) *Marxism and Ideology*, London: Macmillan.

[24] See Macintyre, *A Proletarian Science*, Chapter 2 on 'labour socialism'.

[25] Kolakowski, *Main Currents of Marxism*, pp 150–1.

[26] A term we take from Freeden, M. (1998) *Ideologies and Political Theory*, Oxford: Oxford University Press, p 420. The 'proto' aspect of ideological construction will be assessed in the next chapter.

[27] McPhee, P. (2002) *The French Revolution, 1789–1799*, Oxford: Oxford University Press, pp 129–30.

[28] Honneth, A. (2017) *The Idea of Socialism*, London: Polity, p 10.

[29] Most obviously Britain but also Belgium, France, and America. Germany and Russia did not yet undergo analogous transformations at that time, a fact that led intellectuals in both countries to concern themselves with the question of a perceived lag in their modernity.

[30] The peerless history of this is Sassoon, D. (2013) *One Hundred Years of Socialism: The West European Left in the Twentieth Century*, London: I.B. Tauris.

[31] Anderson, *Considerations on Western Marxism*, pp 49–50.

[32] Renaud, T. (2021) *New Lefts: The Making of a Radical Tradition*, London: Princeton University Press.

[33] LeFebvre, H. (2013) *Critique of Everyday Life*, London: Verso.

[34] Williams, R. (1977) *Marxism and Literature*, Oxford: Oxford University Press.

[35] Kay, G. (1975) *Development and Underdevelopment: A Marxist Analysis*, London: Macmillan; Warren, B. (1980) *Imperialism: Pioneer of Capitalism*, London: Verso.

[36] O'Connor, J. (1973) *The Fiscal Crisis of the State*, London: Routledge.

[37] Brenner, R. (1976) 'Agrarian class structure and economic development in pre-industrial Europe', *Past & Present* 70: 30–75; Hilton, R. (ed.) (1976) *The Transition from Feudalism to Capitalism*, London: Verso.

[38] Freeman, A. (2010) 'Marxism without Marx: a note towards a critique', *Capital and Class* 34(1): 87–8.

[39] There is a fragment of Marx's aesthetics of alienation and fetishism in Adorno and Horkheimer's (1997) 'mass deception', but this is clothed in a nihilism and misanthropy which is not shared by Marx. See *Dialectics of Enlightenment*, London: Verso, pp 12–167.

[40] It is noteworthy that a good many of these leaders went through European universities where Marxism was a strong presence. This was especially the case in relation to France and its former colonies.

[41] Jean-François Lyotard's well-used phrasing.

[42] Gorz, A. (1987) *Farewell to the Working Class: An Essay on Post-Industrial Socialism*, London: Verso. See also Hall, S. (1986) 'The problem of ideology: Marxism without guarantees', *Journal of Communication Inquiry* 10(2): 28–44.

[43] Bonefeld, W., Gunn, R., and Psychopdeis, K. (1992) 'Introduction', in Bonefeld, W., Gunn, R., and Psychopdeis, K. (eds), *Open Marxism: Dialectics and History*, London: Pluto Press, p ix.

[44] Marxism does not centrally derive its critique of capitalism from the notion of justice, although his work is full of opprobrium for capitalism. On this, see Elster, J. (1986) *An*

Introduction of Karl Marx, Cambridge: Cambridge University Press, pp 92–101. Inefficiency, exploitation, and alienation are the most well-realised terms Marx relies on to condemn capitalism (p 41).

[45] Hall, S. (1992) 'Cultural studies and its theoretical legacies', in Grossberg, L., Nelson, C., and Treichler, P. (eds), *Cultural Studies*, London: Routledge, p 279.

[46] From here on, *Capital* is Volume 1. Other volumes will be numbered. Although Elster (*An Introduction of Karl Marx*, pp 9–10) is overdoing it to say that *Capital II* is 'utterly boring' and *III* is 'irreparably flawed', they do yield far less than the first volume.

[47] In case it still needs saying after so much misrepresentation, 'materialism' does not necessarily mean economic determinism. Although 'mechanical forms of class reproduction' plagued early Marxist accounts, Marxism has been through a huge amount of negative caricature over the decades (Worth, O. (2014) 'Stuart Hall, Marxism without guarantees, and "the hard road to renewal"', *Capital and Class* 38(3): 481). Also on this, see Geras, N. (1990) 'Seven types of obloquy: travesties of Marxism', *Socialist Register*, pp 1-34.

[48] McLellan, D. (1971) *Marx's Grundrisse*, London: Macmillan. See also Burnham, P. (1994) 'Open Marxism and vulgar international political economy', *Review of International Political Economy* 1(2): 221–31. Marx offers an attack on political economy in *Economic and Philosophical Manuscripts* which concludes 'the morality of political economy is gain, work, thrift, and sobriety' (Fromm and Marx, *Marx's Concept of Man*, pp 121–3).

[49] Personal confession: I have tried to read *Capital II* a few times and never succeeded in finishing it.

[50] Weeks, J. (2010) *Capital, Exploitation and Economic Crisis*, London: Routledge. See also (from a different perspective, and one that is critical of Weeks) Mau, S. (2021) *Mute Compulsion: A Marxist Theory of the Economic Power of Capital*, London: Verso.

[51] 'Phenomenal forms of essential relations' (Marx, *Capital*, p 310).

[52] Marx called this the 'innermost secret, the hidden basis' of capitalism (Marx, K. (1992) *Capital III*, London: Penguin, Chapter 15). A concise outline of Marx's method in this regard is McLennan, G. (1981) *Marxism and the Methodologies of History*, London: Verso, Chapter 2.

[53] I did not select the smartphone by chance. A great illustration of how Marx's theory of value is realised through this particular commodity is No author (2019) *The Rate of Exploitation: The Case of the iPhone*, Tricontinental: Institute for Social Research Notebook No. 2 (www.thetricontinental.org/wp-content/uploads/2019/09/190922_Notebook-2_EN.pdf).

[54] A detailed treatment of the centrality of price in the form of money is Moseley, F. (2016) *Money and Totality*, London: Haymarket Books.

[55] Meiksins Wood, E. (1995) *Democracy against Capitalism*, Cambridge: Cambridge University Press.

[56] Weeks, *Capital, Exploitation and Economic Crisis*, pp 38–40.

[57] Weeks, *Capital, Exploitation and Economic Crisis*, p 22.

[58] Saville, J. (1969) 'Primitive accumulation and early industrialization in Britain', *Socialist Register*: 248–71; De Angelis, M. (2004) 'Separating the doing and the deed: capital and the continuous character of enclosures', *Historical Materialism* 12(2): 57–87.

[59] 'The labour, however, that forms the substance of value, is homogenous human labour, expenditure of one uniform labour-power' (Marx, *Capital*, p 16).

[60] Marx, *Capital*, p 321.

[61] Weeks, *Capital, Exploitation and Economic Crisis*, p 15.

[62] Marx, *Capital III*, Chapter 15.

[63] Each of these strategies is seen differently by Marxists. Repressing wages is 'absolute surplus extraction' which is the same as keeping wages the same and enforcing longer

hours of sped-up work. Relative surplus extraction derives from an increase in labour productivity which depends both on skills at work and the recombination of workers with technology.

[64] Marx characterised this as the pressure to reduce wages to 'socially necessary labour time': the time needed for a worker to produce enough value to compensate her for the accustomed material needs and pleasures of their household. Contrary to those who critique this notion as a claim to an immutable 'law', Marx's discussion of socially necessary labour time and the labour theory of value is clearly trying to identify tendencies. There is nothing in Marx that suggests literally an expectation that all workers will end up with bare subsistence.

[65] Altvater, E. (2009) 'The growth obsession', *Socialist Register*, Panitch, L. and Leys, C. (eds), pp 73–92; 'Accumulate, accumulate! That is Moses and the prophets!' (Marx, *Capital*, p 334). See also Harvey, D. (2010) *A Companion to Marx's Capital*, London: Verso, p 259.

[66] Marx, *Capital*, p 362. An earlier and more colourful statement of the same can be found in the *Economic and Philosophical Manuscripts*: marvels and privation, palaces and hovels, beauty and deformity (in Fischer, E. (1978) *Marx in His Own Words*, London: Pelican, p 20). Jameson concisely describes this as 'happiness and unhappiness all at once' (*Valences of the Dialectic*, p 551).

[67] Simon Clarke's (1994) peerless study of Marxist theories of crisis describes these two processes as underconsumption and disproportionality (*Marx's Theory of Crisis*, London: Macmillan Press).

[68] On the nature of manifesto discourse, see Miéville, *A Spectre*.

[69] Therein, J.P. (2002) 'Debating foreign aid: Left versus Right', *Third World Quarterly* 23(3): 449–67.

[70] This is routine in political journalism. For example, Sebastian Payne (2022) talks of 'left-leaning Tory MPs' in his analysis of factions within the Conservative Party after Liz Truss's leadership victory ('Can Liz Truss govern her own party?', *Financial Times*, 6 September).

[71] Cohen, N. (2007) *What's Left? How Liberals Lost their Way*, London: Fourth Estate.

[72] Hindmoor, A. (2018) *What's Left Now?*, Oxford: Oxford University Press.

[73] Ostrowski, M. (2020) *Left Unity: Manifesto for a Progressive Alliance*, London: Policy Network, p 11. Internal quotation marks removed.

[74] Jones, O. (2020) *This Land: The Struggle for the Left*, London: Penguin.

[75] Mouffe, C. (2019) *For a Left Populism*, London: Verso, especially p 22.

[76] 'This abstraction of labour is only the result of a concrete aggregate of different kinds of labour' (Marx in McLellan, *Marx's Grundrisse*, p 38).

[77] A lucid statement of this orientation is Bonefeld, W., Gunn, R., Holloway, J., and Psychopedis, K. (1995) 'Emancipating Marx', in Bonefeld, W., Gunn, R., Holloway, J., and Psychopedis, K. (eds), *Emancipating Marx*, London: Pluto Press.

[78] Marx, K. (1978) 'Theses on Feuerbach', in Tucker, R. (ed.), *The Marx-Engels Reader*, London: W.W. Norton.

[79] See, for example, the discussion about the extent to which John Rawls' justice theory can be seen as having 'socialist' repercussions. See also Stafford, W. (1998) 'How can a paradigmatic liberal call himself a socialist? The case of John Stuart Mill', *Journal of Political Ideologies* 3(3): 325–45; McCabe, H. (2018) *John Stuart Mill, Socialist*, London: McGill-Queen's University Press.

[80] Lenin, V. (1914) 'Karl Marx: a brief biographical sketch with an exposition of Marxism', in *Lenin's Collected Works*, Volume 21, Moscow: Progress Publishers, pp 43–91. See also Fromm and Marx, *Marx's Concept of Man*, p 125.

[81] Marx, *Capital*, p 349.

[82] Marx in McLellan, *Marx's Grundrisse*, p 94.

[83] This is often misrepresented as thesis–antithesis–synthesis. Hegel's understanding of dialectic was not this, nor was Marx's (Harvey, *A Companion to Marx's Capital*, pp 11–13).

Stalin's 'dialectical materialism' and the formulaic historical methodology it established neither relates to Marx's own work nor was taken seriously by Marxist scholars. Marx's own use of the term is also debated, although it is scattered throughout his work. See Bonefeld et al, *Open Marxism*; Reichelt, H. (1995) 'Why did Marx conceal his dialectical method?', in Bonefeld et al, *Emancipating Marx*.

84 In Walter Benjamin's (2015) powerful phrasing, 'there is no document of civilisation which nis not at the same time a document of barbarism … one single catastrophe which keeps piling wreckage upon wreckage' (*Illuminations*, London: Bodley Head, pp 248–9).

85 Kevin Anderson's (2010) summary of Marx's attitude towards progress of the colonies (*Marx at the Margins*, Chicago: Chicago University Press, p 35).

86 Greek tragedy was disaster followed by decline or chaos rather than progress.

87 See Harrison, G. (2024) 'A cultural history of poverty in the age of empire (1800–1920)', in Brunswick, B. (ed.), *A Cultural History of Poverty in the Age of Empire*, London: Bloomsbury Press. In later times, employment and economic stability have served as the foundations of national economic management. See Bartel, F. (2022) *The Triumph of Broken Promises*, London: Harvard University Press.

88 Sayers, S. (2015) 'Marxism and the doctrine of internal relations', *Capital and Class* 39(1): 25–31.

89 There are those who write in a 'platonic' fashion in relation to revolution, which is to say they offer very little on 'the social forces that will motivate the transition to socialism' (Meiksins Wood, E. (1986) *The Retreat from Class: A New 'True' Socialism*, London: Verso, p 116). There are those who write within an injustice framing and those who are less comfortable with the notion of injustice as it bleeds too easily into both liberal and 'social justice' framings. See Swift, D. (2019) *A Left for Itself*, London: Zero Books. Cohen argues that Marxism does have a theory of justice, based in an unjust distribution of resources that precedes liberal or libertarian accounts of injustice that focus on market and fiscal transactions (Cohen, G.A. (1995) *Self-Ownership, Freedom, and Equality*, Cambridge: Cambridge University Press).

90 Cohen, G.A. (2001) *If You're an Egalitarian, How Come You're So Rich?*, London: Harvard University Press.

91 This setting often relies on Gramsci.

92 Traverso, E. (2021) *Left-Wing Melancholia: Marxism, History and Memory*, Columbia: Columbia University Press.

Chapter 4

1 Freeden, M. (2005) 'Confronting the chimera of a "post-ideological" age', *Critical Review of International Social and Political Philosophy* 8(2): 247.

2 This is the core insight of the depoliticisation literature. See especially Burnham, P. (2002) 'New Labour and the politics of depoliticisation', *British Journal of Politics and International Relations* 3: 2; Harriss, J. (2002) *Depoliticizing Development: The World Bank and Social Capital*, London: Anthem.

3 Rationality can be bounded, efficiency polysemous, neutrality situational, and utility beset with discretionary decisions about calculation. On the inescapable political ambiguity in the scientific language offered by economics to the social sciences, see Fine, B. (2000) *Social Capital versus Social Theory: Political Economy and Social Science at the Turn of the Millennium*, London: Routledge.

4 See, for example, Stedman-Jones, G. (2012) *Masters of the Universe*, London: Princeton University Press; Slobodian, Q. (2020) *Globalists: The End of Empire and the Birth of Neoliberalism*, London: Harvard University Press. This is, of course, a gloss. Detailed studies of neoliberalism also argue that its core ideas emerged earlier and that aspects of the British Keynesian period were, in fact, better understood as both demand-stimulation

macroeconomics and supply/price-based microeconomics. Origin stories for all ideologies are endlessly debated. See, for example, Siedentop, L. (2014) *Inventing the Individual*, London: Allen Lane.

5   Eagleton, T. (1991) *Ideology*, London: Verso, pp 45–61.

6   Humphrey, M. (2005) '(De)contesting ideology: the struggle over the meaning of the struggle over meaning', *Critical Review of International Social and Political Philosophy* 8(2): 233.

7   Vincent, A. (1995) *Modern Political Ideologies*, Oxford: Blackwell, p 16.

8   Benford, R. and Snow, D. (2000) 'Framing processes and social movements: an overview and assessment', *Annual Review of Sociology* 26: 611–39.

9   Although the use of the term morphology in this sense can be found in Dunn, J. (1968) 'The identity of the history of ideas', *Journal of the Royal Institute of Philosophy* XLIII, 164: 87.

10 Freeden, M. (1996) *Ideologies and Political Theory: A Morphological Approach*, Oxford: Oxford University Press, p 54.

11 Freeden takes a good deal of space to explain the nature of concepts as well (*Political Ideology*, Chapter 2). For our purposes, we shall take the term as roughly self-evident: terms which aim to make descriptive abstractions.

12 Freeden, A. (2015) 'The morphological analysis of ideology', in Freeden, M., Sargent, L., and Stears, M. (eds), *The Oxford Handbook of Political Ideologies*, Oxford: Oxford University Press, p 125.

13 Freeden, *Political Ideology*, p 62.

14 Freeden, 'The morphological analysis', p 125.

15 Freeden, *Political Ideology*, p 68.

16 Freeden, *Political Ideology*, p 69.

17 Freeden, *Political Ideology*, p 72.

18 Freeden, 'The morphological analysis', p 125.

19 Freeden, *Political Ideology*, p 78.

20 Freeden, *Political Ideology*, p 80.

21 See especially Freeden, *Political Ideology*, Chapter 3.

22 Dunn, J. (2005) *Setting the People Free*, London: Atlantic Books, p 15.

23 Freeden, *Ideologies and Political Theory*, p. 142.

24 Finlayson, A. (2015) 'Ideology and political rhetoric', in Freeden, M., Sargent, L., and Stears, M. (eds) *The Oxford Handbook of Political Ideologies*, Oxford: Oxford University Press, p 207.

25 Eagleton, T. (2012) 'Ideology and its vicissitudes', in Žižek, S. (ed.), *Mapping Ideology*, London: Verso, p 207.

26 Therborn, G. (1980) *The Ideology of Power and the Power of Ideology*, London: Verso, p 2.

27 Vincent, *Modern Political Ideologies*, p 19. Relatedly, see Hobsbawm, E. and Ranger, T. (eds) (1992) *The Invention of Tradition*, Cambridge: Cambridge University Press.

28 Lefort, C. (1988) *Democracy and Political Theory*, Cambridge: Polity Press.

29 See especially Freeden, *Ideologies*, p 48.

30 Dunn, 'The identity of the history of ideas': 164.

Chapter 5

1   *Spiked*'s origins are in *Living Marxism* magazine and shared membership of the Revolutionary Communist Party. It is now not a Marxist source but has some Marxists writing for it who also write in other venues listed.

2   As with Spiked, Compact hosts some DMN content among a broadly anti-neoliberal but not entirely left-leaning spectrum.

3   https://damagemag.com/2023/05/10/deepening-the-void

4   'Embedded in the idea of the national interest is the principle that there is a greater good that can be institutionalised through state structures and policy, and that political power

can be meaningfully exercised to protect a people's collective interests' (https://thenorth ernstar.online/2022/11/04/whatever-happened-to-the-national-interest).

5   'The elites' abandonment of the ideal of national sovereignty and its embrace of the deathly, anti-democratic ideology of "post-borders"' (www.spiked-online.com/2021/11/25/now-can-we-talk-about-the-crisis-in-the-channel).

6   'The vestigial political structures of the nation remained one of the few means by which workers could hold their cosmopolitan-minded rulers to account' (www.thefullbrexit.com/workers-revolt-against-labour).

7   The EU 'exists precisely to insulate national elites from public pressure, to create a space in which laws, regulations and priorities can be made far from the madding crowds of voters and citizens' (www.spiked-online.com/2021/01/01/the-war-for-democracy-is-only-beginning).

8   Freeden, *Political Ideology*, pp 69–70, 78.

9   'Identity politics is a menace to solidarity. It is an implacable foe of class politics' (www.spiked-online.com/2021/09/29/there-is-no-such-thing-as-white-privilege). 'This identitarian reading of Leave voters had disastrous implications for the possibility of uniting people across the Brexit divide around a shared vision of the future' (www.thefullbrexit.com/why-labour-lost).

10   Hoare, G. (2022) 'Rise of the professionals', https://compactmag.com/article/rise-of-the-professionals.

11   Hochuli, A., Hoare, G., and Cunliffe, P. (2021) *The End of the End of History; Politics in the Twenty-First Century*, London: Zero Books, pp 126–30.

12   A 'a sense of disdain and even fear towards ordinary people' (www.spiked-online.com/2021/08/27/if-this-is-anti-fascism-count-me-out).

13   An 'impressionable throng' (www.spiked-online.com/2021/08/27/if-this-is-anti-fasc ism-count-me-out). '[P]eople lashing out against "stupid" working-class voters being "duped" by the "billionaire media"' (www.thefullbrexit.com/why-labour-lost). The commentariat seeing ordinary voters as 'Those dumb, dog-like voters, responding with tongue-wagging obedience to the shrill-pitched prejudices' (www.spiked-online.com/2021/11/07/winsome-sears-and-the-rise-of-woke-racism).

14   A middle-class 'contemptuous view of the population as a racist mob in waiting, as gammon, as always being just one Sun editorial away from turning into an animalistic force' (www.spiked-online.com/2021/08/05/there-was-no-outburst-of-racism-after-the-euro-final). 'The snotty suggestion that loads of Brits are racist' (www.spiked-online.com/2021/05/07/the-working-class-revolt-against-labour).

15   Middle-class 'minds were agitated more by the thought of stupid white people saying something rude' (O'Neill, B. (2018) *Anti-woke*, London: Connor Court Publishing, p 73).

16   A middle-class 'moralistic handwringing' concerning the deportment of the masses (www.spiked-online.com/2021/07/12/their-football-and-ours).

17   'Most the Left today is liberal' (https://twitter.com/Alex__1789/status/138448642466 2138880). In less Twitterish language, authoritarian liberalism (Cunliffe, P., Hoare, G., Jones, L., and Ramsay, P. (2022) *Taking Control: Sovereignty and Democracy after Brexit*, London: Polity).

18   Tongue in cheek, Hochuli et al reassure us that liberal middle-class ideas 'are unlikely to be infectious ... at least not without sustained contact with *The Guardian*' (*The End of the End of History*, p 63).

19   Paine, T. (2008) *Rights of Man, Common Sense and Other Political Writings*, Oxford: Oxford University Press, p 19.

20   In the texts of DMN generally, there is a warmth towards the republican revolutions of France and America. Alex Hochuli references 1789 in his Twitter handle.

21 See also Paine, *Rights of Man*, pp 214–19.

22 'Euphemism abounds. Linguistic duplicity is deployed to shroud the problem, to distract attention from it' (www.spiked-online.com/2021/11/25/now-can-we-talk-about-the-crisis-in-the-channel).

23 A characterisation of Identitarian Socialism given by Spiked when Novara Media's YouTube channel was suspended (www.spiked-online.com/2021/10/26/the-deletion-of-novara-media-is-an-outrage).

24 Fawcett, E. (2018) *Liberalism: The Life of an Idea*, Princeton: Princeton University Press, p 14.

25 Pettit, P. (2012) *On the People's Terms*, Cambridge: Cambridge University Press, p 17.

26 Brennan, J. (2012) *Libertarianism*, Oxford: Oxford University Press, Chapter 2.

27 'Free speech is for cringey pseuds, too' (www.spiked-online.com/2021/10/26/the-deletion-of-novara-media-is-an-outrage).

28 'Anyone who believes in freedom ought to be alarmed by the willingness of the police to suppress political dissent' (www.spiked-online.com/2021/02/04/we-must-defend-piers-corbyns-freedom-of-speech).

29 In Bhambra, G., Gebrial, D., and Nisancioglu K. (2018), decoloniality is defined as 'a way of thinking about the world which takes colonialism, empire, and racism ... as key shaping forces in the contemporary world' (*Decolonising the University*, London: Pluto, p 2).

30 'Too often today, all sorts of perfectly normal experiences are being redefined as mental-health problems' (www.spiked-online.com/2021/09/12/thank-god-emma-didnt-listen-to-the-mental-health-bores). '[T]his perverse cultural preference for mentally discombobulated victims over autonomous, free-willed individuals' (www.spiked-online.com/2021/11/19/why-britneys-freedom-matters).

31 'Being a victim – esp when unanchored from anything material – is available to everyone. When you see the rich & powerful playing victim, you see the truth behind the whole victimhood industry' (https://twitter.com/Alex__1789/status/1422514732494372865).

32 'The comfort blanket of a diagnosis of frailty, for the warm feeling of medically decreed incapacitation' (www.spiked-online.com/2021/11/19/why-britneys-freedom-matters).

33 This critique has focused especially on lockdown, which 'has allowed the middle classes supposedly to "work" remotely from home, while the working classes are compelled to continue working even longer hours in cramped kitchens, sewers, urban transport systems, supermarkets, hospitals and warehouses to support the stay-at-home middle classes' (www.thefullbrexit.com/not-in-control).

34 'It is amazing how swiftly woke corporations ditch their blather about lives mattering and justice being important the minute it comes to China' (www.spiked-online.com/2021/11/29/hey-disney-dont-chinese-lives-matter-too).

35 'Bad news for those who naively hoped the words Leaver and Remainer would disappear from daily chatter once we officially left the EU and instead everyone would sit down and sing "Kumbaya"' (www.spiked-online.com/2021/10/21/we-really-dont-regret-voting-for-brexit). 'We told you the European Union was not some hippyish, internationalist outfit' (www.spiked-online.com/2021/01/30/the-people-were-right).

36 Relatedly, see Aytac, U. and Rossi, E. (forthcoming) 'Ideology critique without morality: a radical realist approach', *American Political Science Review*.

37 The 'chattering classes' 'seem to think that lockdown measures don't apply to them. That the authoritarianism of the past 12 months that many of them demanded and celebrated is for other people, little people, those people whose views and beliefs and right to assemble are not nearly as important as ours' (www.spiked-online.com/2021/03/14/assembly-for-me-but-not-for-thee).

38 'Compare the sympathetic response middle-class political operators receive when they say someone once touched their bottom or their knee with the stony silence that too often greets the working-class girls who've been abused and raped by grooming gangs' (www.spiked-online.com/2021/11/17/the-women-we-listen-to-and-the-women-we-ignore).

39 'We need a human-centred view of the future, a human-centred morality, not the pre-modern, nature-worshipping fears and hysteria of contemporary environmentalism' (www.spiked-online.com/2021/11/12/keep-burning-those-fossil-fuels).

40 'The misanthropic prejudices of the depressed middle classes' (www.spectator.co.uk/article/the-perverse-fantasies-of-xr-s-founder).

41 O'Neill, 'Defying nature'.

Chapter 6

1 https://novaramedia.com/about

2 Moya Lothian-McLean approvingly quotes that the 'anti-racism from below and socialism from below movements are one and the same' in 'Direct action is just what the doctor ordered. Resistance isn't futile – and more people are realising it'. In the article, strikes, anti-deportation, and environmental protest are presented as different manifestations of direct action (https://novaramedia.com/2022/06/16/direct-action-is-just-what-the-doctor-ordered).

3 Additionally, Sarkar was interviewed by *Teen Vogue* magazine on the meaning of communism.

4 Ever-aware of its media presence, Novara has in some degree endeavoured to render this phrase mimetic. See, for example, James Meadway (2021) saying that Starmer 'doesn't need to be literally a communist' in 'The National Insurance hike is class warfare. Why won't labour say so?' Novara Media, 8 September (https://novaramedia.com/2021/09/08/the-national-insurance-hike-is-class-warfare-why-wont-labour-say-so).

5 See 'Aaron Bastani – why I am literally a communist' (www.youtube.com/watch?v=6Z-85q3eE0U).

6 This is manifested in the exceptionally partisan but critical support of Labour in comparison with other Left-leaning socialist social media. In one detailed content analysis, Novara Media's positive commentary on party elections went 100 per cent to Labour in 2017 at the peak of the 'Corbyn surge' (McDowell-Naylor et al, 'A typology of alternative online political media in the United Kingdom', p 12).

7 Jones, *This Land*.

8 Nash, J. (2008) 'Re-thinking intersectionality', *Feminist Review* 89: 2.

9 Dhamoon, R. (2011) 'Considerations on mainstreaming intersectionality', *Political Research Quarterly* 64(1): 230.

10 Hill Collins, P. (2019) *Intersectionality as Critical Social Theory*, Durham, NC: Duke University Press, p 21.

11 'We live in an international system of nation states, which has emerged in relationship with capitalism, white supremacy and patriarchy. Ramsay, A. (2021) 'Dismantling Britain is one thing. Dismantling Britishness is another', Novara Media, 6 October (https://novaramedia.com/2021/10/06/dismantling-britain-is-one-thing-dismantling-britishness-is-another).

12 'Movements, along with the Black sections of the Labour party and trade unions were borne out of the power of grassroots organising, with activists from different racialised communities coming together to recognise and fight interlocking systems of oppression (race, class, gender, etc)' (https://novaramedia.com/2021/07/08/englands-football-team-is-changing-because-england-is-changing)

13 'Full autonomy over our bodies, free and universal healthcare, affordable housing for all, power in the hands of those who work rather than those privileged few who extract

profit from our vastly inequitable system, sexual freedom (including freedom from sexual violence) and the end to the mass incarceration of human beings are all crucial ingredients in the construction of a society in which trans people are no longer abused, mistreated or subjected to violence' (Faye, S. [2021] 'Liberating trans people means liberating everyone' https://novaramedia.com/2021/09/01/liberating-trans-people-means-liberating-every one/).

[14] Kimmi Chaddah argues that BLM suffers from its erroneous association with Marxism in 'The Tories are on a mission to destroy Black Lives Matter' (https://novaramedia.com/2021/07/26/the-tories-are-on-a-mission-to-destroy-black-lives-matter).

[15] On this, see Embery, *Despised*, Chapter 3. There was also a deployment of the pejorative term 'gammon' by some Identitarian Socialists, for example, Owen Jones.

[16] https://novaramedia.com/2021/07/08/englands-football-team-is-changing-because-engl and-is-changing

[17] https://novaramedia.com/2021/07/08/englands-football-team-is-changing-because-engl and-is-changing

[18] https://novaramedia.com/2021/06/15/dont-believe-the-bigots-trans-rights-arent-a-thr eat-to-women

[19] 'We must move beyond the parliamentary Leninism ... we must achieve a high level of organisation among progressive forces' (https://novaramedia.com/2021/03/17/how-we-win-the-state).

[20] 'Migrant rights, climate justice, workplace organising, criminal justice and surveillance, war, occupation, empire and its legacy' (https://novaramedia.com/2021/08/09/we-cant-dismantle-capitalism-without-antiracist-solidarity).

[21] https://novaramedia.com/2021/03/15/how-we-win-the-movements

[22] Ash Sarkar reports that 'I think they are doing the right thing ... critical but unconditional support for XR' (https://novaramedia.com/2019/10/08/ash-sarkar-x-extinction-rebellion-lovebomb-the-cops). 'Undoubtedly, Extinction Rebellion have, in many ways, been incredibly successful. They have created a mass movement, raised awareness of the climate emergency, and alongside youth strikers and other political campaigners they have created a political environment in which groups like Labour for a Green New Deal have been able to push a radical policy platform' (https://nova ramedia.com/2019/12/07/beyond-politics-the-limits-of-extinction-rebellions-strat egy-are-beginning-to-show).

[23] 'I've been convinced that the left should have some relationship to XR. It need not be one of uncritical adulation or participation, but nor should it be one of derision or disengagement ... To win, we need broad alliances spanning the labour movement to liberal direct-action groups like XR. Through trade unions and socialist organisations like Momentum and Labour for a Green New Deal, socialists should build power and provide political and strategic leadership where its lacking (https://novaramedia.com/2021/11/22/why-i-was-wrong-to-write-off-extinction-rebellion-in-2018). 'A street movement that has been largely divorced from all other struggles will never hold within it the strategy, tactics or resolve to truly win. What's clear is that salvation lies in working together – in throwing our weight not behind organisations, but behind each other. It's in taking and exploiting every opportunity to leverage the power needed to effect change' (https://novaramedia.com/2020/12/10/why-are-ngos-so-bad-at-saving-the-planet).

[24] 'Capitalism–colonialism–patriarchy is the nexus organising our global economy and underwriting climate breakdown' (https://novaramedia.com/2018/11/18/5-reasons-im-not-joining-the-extinction-rebellion).

[25] Folan, E. (2021) 'As Labour sleeps, the Greens are awakening. Corbyn held back the Green tide. Starmer has opened the floodgates', https://novaramedia.com/2021/08/02/as-labour-sleeps-the-greens-are-awakening/.

26 Bastani, A. (2022) 'Could this be the Green Party's second MP? The new co-leader wants to be ready for when "something snaps"' (https://novaramedia.com/2022/01/25/could-this-be-the-green-partys-second-mp).

27 https://novaramedia.com/2020/04/06/the-corona-crisis-reveals-there-is-no-such-thing-as-low-skill-labour

28 '12 years to deal with climate change sounds dramatic enough, but the reality is worse' (https://novaramedia.com/2018/12/09/brexit-and-the-climate-crash-time-for-a-reality-check).

29 Malm, A. (2020) *Corona, Climate, Chronic Emergency*, London: Verso.

30 https://novaramedia.com/2021/11/09/climate-change-is-violent-thats-why-we-need-sabotage-aaron-bastani-meets-andreas-malm

31 https://novaramedia.com/2021/02/07/covid-19-has-shown-humanitys-vulnerability-its-time-to-take-existential-risks-seriously

32 https://novaramedia.com/2020/08/31/is-capitalism-to-blame-for-covid-19. Also: 'the pandemic, and the wider ecological crises of which it is an example' (https://novaramedia.com/2021/07/19/freedom-day-wont-set-us-free).

33 Bastani, A. (2020) *Fully Automated Luxury Communism: A Manifesto*, London: Verso.

34 Bastani, A. (2021) 'Meat without animals isn't some utopia. It's a future already on its way', Novara Media, 9 December (https://novaramedia.com/2020/12/09/meat-without-animals-isnt-some-utopia-its-a-future-already-on-its-way).

35 The peerless account of Marx's theories of crisis is Clarke, *Marx's Theory of Crisis*.

36 There was also a Novara podcast called *The Fix*.

37 Walker, M. and Gebrial, D. (2021) 'Keir Starmer's nightmare media stunt', Novara Media (TyskySour), YouTube, 15 October (www.youtube.com/watch?v=fC9oQRx_l6Q&t=1s).

38 Walker, M. and Bastani, A. (2022) 'Jordan Peterson's *bizarre* rant on racism & "low resolution thinking"', Novara Media (TyskySour), YouTube, 2022 (www.youtube.com/watch?v=JMuJ3R1dX0w).

39 Butler, J. (2021) (@piercepenniless), Twitter, 21 August, 'I am (unlike a lot of comrades) sympathetic to the idea that the pandemic has inhibited a lot of normal political processes' (https://twitter.com/piercepenniless/status/1429160282878877701).

40 Rosa, S.K. (2021) 'In defence of sex and parties', Novara Media, 5 February (https://novaramedia.com/2021/02/05/what-happened-to-the-lefts-love-of-partying). See also Berthet, M.A. (2020) 'Rave culture is culture: instead of starting a moral panic, the government should make them safe', Novara Media, 22 June. The ACFM podcast (Acid FM) mentioned earlier describes its remit as 'left-wing politics, culture, music and experiences of collective joy'.

41 On YouTube, Ash Sarkar (2021) begins a reflection on British nationalism thus: 'I always find it funny when people accuse me of hating this country, and its culture and its people. Because one: I'm fucking here ain't I? And two: there is no other country on this earth which could make somebody as obnoxious as me, only Britain could do it. And I love this country's culture and history. I did English literature for fuck's sake – you don't do that unless you really like something about it' ('This is England: Ash Sarkar's alternative race report', Double Down News (YouTube), 11 April, www.youtube.com/watch?v=NFNiTcFbNu0). On the democratic repercussions of Leave: 'And let's not forget: we still have a fucking monarchy' (https://novaramedia.com/2016/06/17/the-leave-campaign-couldnt-care-less-about-democracy).

42 Sarkar's original Twitter profile (now replaced) declared that she 'fucks like a champion'. Michael Walker introduces a podcast about influencing the Labour Party thus: 'like a butt without lube – apologies – this episode's going to be a little bit dry' (www.newstatesman.com/politics/media/2017/09/luxury-communism-now-rise-pro-corbyn-media).

[43] During the Tory leadership campaign of 2022, Sarkar tweets that 'Liz Truss always looks like she's just taken a hit off a NOS canister, and I love that for her [sic]' (https://twitter.com/AyoCaesar/status/1547527706232881154).

[44] https://novaramedia.com/2022/06/28/why-the-media-needs-more-labour-correspondents

[45] Sarkar, A. (2021) (@AyoCaesar), Twitter, 31 August, 'That Spectator piece by Lionel Shriver is one of the most intellectually dishonest pieces I've ever had the misfortune of reading' (https://twitter.com/AyoCaesar/status/1432708225833521168).

[46] Sarkar, A. (2021) (@AyoCaesar), Twitter, 24 August, 'This isn't a serious country' (https://twitter.com/AyoCaesar/status/1430073866928410641).

[47] https://novaramedia.com/2021/07/16/england-is-in-the-midst-of-an-african-cultural-renaissance-but-its-still-racist-as-hell

[48] 'This is England: Ash Sarkar's alternative race report' (www.youtube.com/watch?v=NFNiTcFbNu0).

[49] Paul Gilroy's (2004) phrase in *After Empire: Melancholia or Convivial Culture?* (London: Routledge), although his book is far richer and more nuanced than the common use of this one phrase suggests.

[50] This phrase used in relation to Western military abuses in Afghanistan and Iraq (https://novaramedia.com/2021/09/18/western-elites-arent-mourning-the-loss-of-afghan-life-but-of-their-own-power).

[51] (1992) Chambers, R. and Conway, C. 'Sustainable Rural Livelihoods: Practical Concepts for the 21st Century' IDS Discussion Paper 296, University of Sussex, p 6.

[52] For example: https://novaramedia.com/2019/02/09/another-lewisham-is-possible-overcoming-housing-crisis-and-the-democratic-deficit/; https://novaramedia.com/2015/06/12/7-tips-for-getting-organised-in-your-community.

Chapter 7

[1] Eagleton, T. (2022) *Humour*, New Haven: Yale University Press, p 55.

[2] See Friedman, S. (2014) *Comedy and Distinction*, London: Routledge.

[3] Much of this is derived from Cunliffe et al, *Taking Control*, which is based on *Northern Star* blogs.

[4] Bickerton, C. (2012) *European Integration: From Nation-States to Member States*, Oxford: Oxford University Press; Heartfield, J. (2013) *The European Union and the End of Politics*, London: Zero Books.

[5] 'This thrilling working-class revolt is a tremendous moment in British political history and opens up a new opportunity for the future of radical politics' (www.thefullbrexit.com/workers-revolt-against-labour).

[6] 'Much of the Leave vote expressed disgust and disenchantment with the mainstream political establishment in Westminster' (www.thefullbrexit.com/the-eu-s-democratic-deficit).

[7] https://bungacast.com/2021/03/30/the-age-of-technopopulism

[8] Novara content during the run-up to the referendum was fairly equivocal about Brexit, recognising that there was a Left case to leave and generally presenting the referendum as two poor choices. After the vote, reportage became more distinctly negative.

[9] https://novaramedia.com/2017/06/11/where-we-go-from-here

[10] See the podcast: https://novaramedia.com/2016/07/07/the-unbearable-whiteness-of-brexit. Also: 'In one sense, there's the view that having the word "great" in our country's name literally means that we are great, i.e. special, excellent, da best. Add to this the massive rise in racist and xenophobic hate crime, and the vehement nationalism which Brexit seems to have unlocked in our national psyche, I can't help but think it is time to take the "Great" out of "Great Britain"' (https://novaramedia.com/2016/09/13/is-it-time-to-take-the-great-out-of-great-britain).

11 'In that important sense, there is much continuity with the days of the British empire' (https://novaramedia.com/2021/05/14/post-brexit-global-britain-is-becoming-a-thr eat-to-international-security).

12 On this, see: https://medium.com/@eddiedempsey/a-reply-to-owen-jones-keep-it-comradely-32e034eeaa49; https://owenjones84.medium.com/the-british-working-class-is-a-rainbow-of-diversity-to-claim-otherwise-is-dangerous-and-wrong-138ca4159c6. Both Sarkar and Owen Jones declared that they had other engagements (the Remainer Stop the Coup Demonstration for Jones), but it is difficult to take this at face value.

13 'One of the major issues with referendums in the UK is public education about the debated issue. As mentioned, this is difficult when the topics and questions themselves are so inaccessible anyway. But enabling the public to find independent information they can trust in the run up to referendums would of course make a huge difference to the quality of debate and engagement during campaigns. You are likely (and rightly) thinking about the EU referendum right now' (https://novaramedia.com/2016/08/14/whats-the-point-of-referendums).

14 Aaron Bastani expressed a preference for Leave throughout the period 2016–2019, although he voted Remain.

15 'We cannot simply blame the people who Ukip and Vote Leave targeted and manipulated with their powerful ideological message' (https://novaramedia.com/2016/07/19/post-ind ustrial-towns-the-future-of-the-british-left-post-brexit).

16 Emphasis added (https://novaramedia.com/2019/07/14/corbynism-and-the-remain-movement-need-each-other-to-survive).

17 'The remain movement is a mass movement, and has put serious numbers of people onto the streets. It represents a demographic that is young, urban and socially progressive' (https://novaramedia.com/2019/08/26/why-is-the-remain-movement-so-full-of-centrists).

18 Not the UK. Englishness and English national history were the focus of negative associations that emanated from Brexit: the racism, xenophobia, imperial nostalgia, and narcissism. Scotland was portrayed as a progressive and pro-EU nation. See, for example, 'There is little embarrassment, for many English, in belting out Rule Britannia on public occasions … that a form of Englishness is being asserted which has nothing to offer the Scots or the Irish, who see no reason to leave themselves pegged to this incoherent, non-reflexive drift into destructive, farcical and exclusionary Empire 2.0' (https://novarame dia.com/2017/03/14/the-real-threat-to-the-union-is-english-nationalism). 'Brexit was essentially a xenophobic referendum on immigration' (https://twitter.com/mlothianmcl ean/status/1661289306571382784)

19 'A genuine belief that there is some hope in the left-wing movements emerging across Europe and that there could be a truly "social" Europe if we fight for it – across borders' (https://novaramedia.com/2016/02/12/the-left-enters-the-eu-debate-is-another-eur ope-possible). See also www.theguardian.com/commentisfree/2019/may/29/jeremy-cor byn-remain-labour-eu-elections.

20 'A lot of this referendum was built on lies' (www.youtube.com/watch?v=W0n3TpCL Acg&t=15s). 'I voted remain, but ignoring the outcome would be terrible for democracy'.

21 The presenters of Bungacast commonly used the term 'gammon' playfully and ironically in this fashion. See the following note.

22 Owen Jones: 'The Gammon Army is going to defeat us with their devastatingly *hilarious* memes' (https://twitter.com/owenjones84/status/986192714009120768). In response to accusations of racial slurring, see Jones, 'No, "gammon" is not a racial slur. Now let's change the conversation' (www.theguardian.com/commentisfree/2018/may/14/gam mon-not-racial-slur-change-conversation).

23 'British society is often reluctant to make changes to its fundamental assumptions about how the world works. The UK has reached the point where a kind of atavistic conservatism

rejects out-of-hand any suggestion that change must be made' (https://novaramedia.com/2021/11/26/to-solve-britains-mental-health-crisis-we-must-fundamentally-change-society).

24 https://novaramedia.com/2021/11/26/to-solve-britains-mental-health-crisis-we-must-fundamentally-change-society

25 But sometimes: 'An already fairly awful society is going to get brutally worse. And it is difficult to see how this won't feed into yet more violent racism and hatred of foreigners predicated on zero-sum ethnic competition' (https://novaramedia.com/2019/12/13/no-false-consolations).

26 'Is this England's referendum?' (www.youtube.com/watch?v=y8okivqS5-U).

27 www.thefullbrexit.com/why-did-britain-vote-to-leave-the-e

28 www.thefullbrexit.com/why-did-britain-vote-to-leave-the-e

29 'Lockdown is ending – every day this becomes a little clearer. But rather than being led and backed by science, the government's approach to easing the measures appears to be driven by ideology' (https://novaramedia.com/2020/06/09/all-work-no-sex-boris-johnsons-road-map-for-leaving-lockdown-is-driven-by-ideology-not-science).

30 'Because of how the virus is transmitted, it is necessary to prevent normal human contact occurring, or risk death on a massive scale and the disintegration of healthcare systems' (https://novaramedia.com/2020/04/22/this-weeks-oil-price-slump-signals-economic-dangers-ahead).

31 https://novaramedia.com/2020/07/09/coronavirus-has-had-a-devastating-impact-on-mental-health-but-it-didnt-have-to-be-this-way; https://novaramedia.com/2020/07/14/the-real-reason-lockdown-is-ending-our-broken-economic-system-has-no-alternative.

32 'Boris Johnson gives press conference saying absolutely nothing. Maddening. We could turn the tide in 12 weeks if we follow the advice. But it's not being followed, and barely being communicated. Pubs near me rammed. Close the damned things!' (https://twitter.com/piercepenniless/status/1240693767159468032).

33 In this podcast, a table comparing the UK to other countries that had social distancing, school closure, track and trace, and so on was presented as a sign of how poorly the UK was doing (https://novaramedia.com/2020/03/13/herd-immunity). See also: 'the spread of the coronavirus, and the patchy measures the government has taken in response, suggest a significant crisis – economic and social – is on the way. The government response, so far, has been inadequate: in its reluctance to enforce social distancing measures' (https://novaramedia.com/2020/03/20/coronavirus-a-letter-to-our-readers).

34 https://novaramedia.com/2020/05/10/independent-and-diy-venues-offer-us-steps-towards-a-lived-socialist-culture

35 Perhaps most discussed, the following from Owen Jones: 'Never thought I'd be relieved to be placed under house arrest along with millions of people under a police state by a right wing Tory government' (https://twitter.com/OwenJones84/status/1242219020625076226). Jones claimed this was a joke, but the humour seems to reside in the veracity of the core sentiment and the ostensible ridiculousness of its appearance.

36 A good example is the tone of this piece which, at times, resembles something one would expect in the *Daily Mail*! (https://novaramedia.com/2020/06/22/rave-culture-is-culture-instead-of-starting-a-moral-panic-the-government-should-make-raves-safe).

37 See discussion here: https://bungacast.podbean.com/e/321-covid-dissensus-ft-toby-green-thomas-fazi.

38 Aesthetically, there is something of Ibsen's *An Enemy of the People* in this.

39 'The British [liberal] left's ideological commitment to the virtue of vulnerability' (https://thenorthernstar.online/analysis/vulnerability-as-ideology-i).

40 'This decree has allowed the middle classes supposedly to "work" remotely from home, while the working classes are compelled to continue working even longer hours in

cramped kitchens, sewers, urban transport systems, supermarkets, hospitals and warehouses to support the stay-at-home middle classes' (www.thefullbrexit.com/not-in-control).

[41] 'Most of the professional middle classes worked from home, enjoying quarantines and swapping sourdough bread recipes' (www.thefullbrexit.com/lockdown).

[42] https://novaramedia.com/2020/04/01/coronavirus-has-shown-that-care-services-are-vital-now-lets-build-a-state-that-cares

[43] As many have observed, predictions of COVID-19's impact were highly uncertain and sometimes guesses in the first few months, as is the case with any novel outbreak that travels through diverse socio-economic terrains.

[44] https://compactmag.com/article/authoritarianism-without-authority

[45] Identitarian Socialism has a penchant for 'worst/most useless politician ever' in its discursive toolbox. Cameron, May, Johnson, and of course Truss have come in for this treatment. 'Worst ever' fits with the broader aesthetics of social media well, which might also explain the frequency of 'five reasons' phrasing as well, a framing also used in media like Upworthy and Reddit.

[46] www.spiked-online.com/2020/05/13/the-lockdown-left-is-no-friend-of-the-working-class

[47] Jones, L. and Hameiri, S. (2022) 'COVID-19 and the failure of the neoliberal regulatory state', *Review of International Political Economy* 29: 4.

[48] See also Cunliffe et al, *Taking Control*.

[49] The politicians who get it in the neck here are American, especially Ocasio-Cortez.

[50] The one telling exception was James Heartfield's standing as a UKIP MEP in the name of democracy (www.thefullbrexit.com/brexit-party-heartfield). Heartfield honestly and explicitly accounts for his decision with reference to the core concepts of democracy and nation.

Chapter 8

[1] More rarely and a more extreme stretch would be articles by Marxists in *The Spectator* or *Quilette*.

[2] During final revisions of this book, Goodwin was the guest for a Bungacast episode.

[3] In 2022, Aaron Bastani attended the Battle of Ideas, creating some humorous speculation on social media concerning the length of time before he would separate from his Novara colleagues.

[4] https://damagemag.com/2022/04/28/voluntary-twitter-extinction-society

[5] Cunliffe, P. (2022) 'We are far away from class war' (https://unherd.com/2022/06/this-is-not-a-class-war).

Bibliography

Adorno, T., and Horkheimer, A. (1997) *Dialectics of Enlightenment*, London: Verso.

Altvater, E. (2009) 'The growth obsession', *Socialist Register*: 73–92.

Anderson, K. (2016) *Marx at the Margins*, Chicago: Chicago University Press.

Anderson, P. (1976) *Considerations on Western Marxism*, London: Verso.

Aytac, U., and Rossi, E. (forthcoming) 'Ideology critique without morality: a radical realist approach', *American Political Science Review*.

Bartel, F. (2022) *The Triumph of Broken Promises*, London: Harvard University Press.

Bastani, A. (2020) *Fully Automated Luxury Communism: A Manifesto*, London: Verso.

Bell, D. (2014) 'What is liberalism?', *Political Theory* 42(6): 682–715.

Benanav, A. (2019) 'Automation and the future of work', *New Left Review* 119 and 120.

Benford, R., and Snow, D. (2000) 'Framing processes and social movements: an overview and assessment', *Annual Review of Sociology* 26: 611–39.

Benjamin, W. (2015) *Illuminations*, London: Bodley Head.

Benner, E. (2018) *Really Existing Nationalisms: A Post-Communist View from Marx and Engels*, London: Verso.

Berman, M. (2010) *All That Is Solid Melts into Air*, London: Verso.

Bernholz, L., Landemore, H., and Reich, R. (eds) (2021) *Digital Democracy and Democratic Theory*, Chicago: Chicago University Press.

Bhambra, G., and Nisancioglu, K. (2018) *Decolonising the University*, London: Pluto.

Bickerton, C. (2012) *European Integration: From Nation-States to Member States*, Oxford: Oxford University Press.

Bonefeld, W., Gunn, R., and Psychopedis, K. (1992) 'Introduction', in Bonefeld, W., Gunn, R., and Psychopedis, K. (eds), *Open Marxism: Dialectics and History*, London: Pluto Press.

Bonefeld, W., Gunn, R., and Psychopedis, K. (eds) (1992) *Open Marxism: Dialectics and History*, London: Pluto Press.

Bonefeld, W., Gunn, R., Holloway, J., and Psychopedis, K. (1995) 'Emancipating Marx', in Bonefeld, W., Gunn, R., Holloway, J., and Psychopedis, K. (eds), *Emancipating Marx*, London: Pluto Press.

Brennan, J. (2012) *Libertarianism*, Oxford: Oxford University Press.

Brenner, R. (1976) 'Agrarian class structure and economic development in pre-industrial Europe', *Past & Present* 70: 30–75.

Burnham, P. (1994) 'Open Marxism and vulgar international political economy', *Review of International Political Economy* 1(2): 221–31.

Burnham, P. (2002) 'New Labour and the politics of depoliticisation', *British Journal of Politics and International Relations* 3(2): 127–49.

Calvert, J., and Arbuthnot, G. (2021) *Failures of State: The Inside Story of Britain's Battle with Coronavirus*, London: Mudlark.

Clarke, S. (1994) *Marx's Theory of Crisis*, London: Macmillan Press.

Cohen G.A. (1995) *Self-Ownership, Freedom, and Equality*, Cambridge: Cambridge University Press.

Cohen, G.A. (2001) *If You're an Egalitarian, How Come You're So Rich?*, London: Harvard University Press.

Cohen, N. (2007) *What's Left? How Liberals Lost their Way*, London: Fourth Estate.

Cole, G.D.H. (various) *A History of Socialist Thought*, London: Macmillan.

Cox, R. (1981) 'Social forces, states and world orders: beyond international relations theory', *Millennium: Journal of International Studies* 10(2): 126–55.

Cunliffe, P. (2017) *Lenin Lives! Reimagining the Russian Revolution 1917–2017*, London: Zero Books.

Cunliffe, P., Hoare, G., Jones, L., and Ramsay, P. (2022) *Taking Control: Sovereignty and Democracy after Brexit*, London: Polity.

Davies, W. (2021) 'The politics of recognition in the age of social media', *New Left Review* 128: 83–99.

De Angelis, M. (2004) 'Separating the doing and the deed: capital and the continuous character of enclosures', *Historical Materialism* 12(2): 57–87.

Dhamoon, R. (2011) 'Considerations on mainstreaming intersectionality', *Political Research Quarterly* 64(1): 230–43.

Dunn, J. (1968) 'The identity of the history of ideas', *Journal of the Royal Institute of Philosophy* 43(164): 85–104.

Dunn, J. (2005) *Setting the People Free*, London: Atlantic Books.

Eagleton, T. (1991) *Ideology*, London: Verso.

Eagleton, T. (2012) 'Ideology and its vicissitudes', in Žižek, S. (ed.), *Mapping Ideology*, London: Verso.

Eagleton, T. (2022) *Humour*, Yale: Yale University Press.

Elster, J. (1986) *An Introduction of Karl Marx*, Cambridge: Cambridge University Press.

Embery, P. (2020) *Despised: Why the Modern Left Loathes the Working Class*, London: Polity Press.

Fawcett, E. (2018) *Liberalism: The Life of an Idea*, Princeton: Princeton University Press.

Fine, B. (2000) *Social Capital versus Social Theory: Political Economy and Social Science at the Turn of the Millennium*, London: Routledge.

Finlayson, A. (2015) 'Ideology and political rhetoric', in Freeden, M., Sargent, L., and Stears, M. (eds), *The Oxford Handbook of Political Ideologies*, Oxford: Oxford University Press.

Freeden, A. (2015) 'The morphological analysis of ideology', in Freeden, M., Sargent, L., and Stears, M. (eds), *The Oxford Handbook of Political Ideologies*, Oxford: Oxford University Press.

Freeden, M. (1996) *Ideologies and Political Theories: A Conceptual Approach*, Oxford: Oxford University Press.

Freeden, M. (2005) 'Confronting the chimera of a "post-ideological" age', *Critical Review of International Social and Political Philosophy* 8(2): 247–62.

Freeman, A. (2010) 'Marxism without Marx: a note towards a critique', *Capital and Class* 34(1): 87–8.

Friedman, S. (2014) *Comedy and Distinction*, London: Routledge.

Fromm, E., and Marx, K. (2003) *Marx's Concept of Man*, London: Bloomsbury.

Fukuyama, F. (1992) *The End of History and the Last Man*, London: Penguin.

Geoghegan, P. (2021) *Democracy for Sale: Dark Money and Dirty Politics*, London: Apollo.

Geras, N. (1990) 'Seven types of obloquy: travesties of Marxism', Socialist Register.

Giddens, A. (1998) *The Third Way: The Renewal of Social Democracy*, Oxford: Polity Press.

Gilroy-Ware, M. (2021) 'What is wrong with social media? An anti-capitalist critique', Socialist Register.

Gilroy, P. (2004) *After Empire: Melancholia or Convivial Culture?*, London: Verso.

Goodhart, D. (2017) *The Road to Somewhere: The New Tribes Shaping British Politics*, London: Penguin.

Gorz, A. (1987) *Farewell to the Working Class: An Essay on Post-Industrial Socialism*, London: Verso.

Hall, S. (1986) 'The problem of ideology: Marxism without guarantees', *Journal of Communication Inquiry* 10(2): 28–44.

Hall, S. (1992) 'Cultural studies and its theoretical legacies', in Grossberg, L., Nelson, C., and Treichler, P. (eds), *Cultural Studies*, London: Routledge.

Hari, J. (2022) *Stolen Focus: Why You Can't Pay Attention*, London: Bloomsbury.

Harrison, G. (2020) *Developmentalism: The Normative and Transformative within Capitalism*, Oxford: Oxford University Press.

Harrison, G. (2024) 'A cultural history of poverty in the age of empire (1800–1920)', in Brunswick, B. (ed.), *A Cultural History of Poverty in the Age of Empire*, London: Bloomsbury Press.

Harriss, J. (2002) *Depoliticizing Development: The World Bank and Social Capital*, London: Anthem.

Harvey, D. (2010) *A Companion to Marx's Capital*, London: Verso.

Harvey, D. (2010) *The Enigma of Capital: And the Crises of Capitalism*, London: Profile Books.

Heartfield, J. (2013) *The European Union and the End of Politics*, London: Zero Books.

Helleiner, E. (2019) 'The life and times of embedded liberalism: legacies and innovations since Bretton Woods', *Review of International Political Economy* 26(6): 1112–35.

Hill Collins, P. (2019) *Intersectionality as Critical Social Theory*, Durham, NC: Duke University Press.

Hilton, R. (ed.) (1976) *The Transition from Feudalism to Capitalism*, London: Verso.

Hindmoor, A. (2018) *What's Left Now?*, Oxford: Oxford University Press.

Hobsbawm, E., and Ranger, T. (eds) (1992) *The Invention of Tradition*, Cambridge: Cambridge University Press.

Honneth, A. (2017) *The Idea of Socialism*, London: Polity.

Hudis, P. (2012) *Marx's Concept of the Alternative to Capitalism*, Chicago: Haymarket Books.

Humphrey, M. (2005) '(De)contesting ideology: the struggle over the meaning of the struggle over meaning', *Critical Review of International Social and Political Philosophy* 8(2): 225–46.

Hutton, W. (1995) *The State We're in: Why Britain Is in Crisis and How to Overcome It*, London: Jonathan Cape.

Jameson, F. (2009) *Valences of the Dialectic*, London: Verso.

Jarsulic, M. (2015) 'The origins of the US financial crisis of 2007', in Wolfson, M., and Epstein, G. (eds), *The Political Economy of Financial Crises*, pp 20–37.

Jones, L., and Hameiri, S. (2022) 'COVID-19 and the failure of the neoliberal regulatory state', *Review of International Political Economy* 29(4): 1027–52.

Jones, O. (2020) *This Land: The Struggle for the Left*, London: Penguin.

Kay, G. (1975) *Development and Underdevelopment: A Marxist Analysis*, London: Macmillan.

Kolakowski, L. (2005) *Main Currents of Marxism*, London: W.W. Norton.

Kotkin, J. (2020) *The Coming Neofeudalism*, London: Encounter Books.

Larrain, J. (1983) *Marxism and Ideology*, London: Macmillan.

LeFebvre, H. (2013) *Critique of Everyday Life*, London: Verso.

Lefort, C. (1988) *Democracy and Political Theory*, Cambridge: Polity Press.

Lenin, V. (1914) 'Karl Marx: a brief biographical sketch with an exposition of Marxism', in *Lenin's Collected Works*, Volume 21, Moscow: Progress Publishers.

Lukács, G. (1971) *History and Class Consciousness*, London: Merlin Press.

Macintyre, S. (1980) *A Proletarian Science: Marxism in Britain 1917–1933*, Cambridge: Cambridge University Press.

Malik, K. (2009) *From Fatwa to Jihad*, London: Atlantic Books.

Malm, A. (2020) *Corona, Climate, Chronic Emergency*, London: Verso.

Marx, K. (1971) *Grundrisse: Foundations of the Critique of Political Economy*, London: Penguin.

Marx, K. (1992) *Capital II*, London: Penguin.

Marx, K. (1992) *Capital III*, London: Penguin.

Marx, K. (1995) *Capital I*, London: Penguin.

Marx, K. (2019) *The Political Writings*, London: Verso.

Marx, K. (1978) *Theses on Feuerbach*, in Tucker, R. (ed.), *The Marx-Engels Reader*, London: W.W. Norton.

Mau, S. (2021) *Mute Compulsion: A Marxist Theory of the Economic Power of Capital*, London: Verso.

McCabe, H. (2018) *John Stuart Mill, Socialist*, London: McGill-Queen's University Press.

McDowell-Naylor, D., Cushion, S., and Thomas, R. (2021) 'A typology of alternative online political media in the United Kingdom: a longitudinal content analysis (2015–2018)', *Journalism* 24(1): 41–61.

McLellan, D., (1971) *Marx's Grundrisse*, London: Macmillan.

McLennan, G. (1981) *Marxism and the Methodologies of History*, London: Verso.

McPhee, P. (2002) *The French Revolution, 1789–1799*, Oxford: Oxford University Press.

McQueen, A (2018) *Political Realism in Apocalyptic Times*, Cambridge: Cambridge University Press.

Meiksins-Wood, E. (1986) *The Retreat from Class: A New 'True' Socialism*, London: Verso.

Meiksins-Wood, E. (1995) *Democracy against Capitalism*, Cambridge: Cambridge University Press.

Miéville, C. (2022) *A Spectre, Haunting*, London: Bloomsbury.

Mills, S. (2019) '#DeleteFacebook: from popular protest to a new model of platform capitalism?', *New Political Economy* 26(5): 851–68.

Moore, M. (2018) *Democracy Hacked: Political Turmoil and Information Warfare in the Digital Age*, London: Oneworld.

Moseley, F. (2016) *Money and Totality*, London: Haymarket Books.

Mouffe, C. (2019) *For a Left Populism*, London: Verso.

Nagle, A. (2017) *Kill All Normies: Online Culture Wars from 4chan and Tumblr to Trump and the Alt-Right*, London: Zero Books.

Nash, J. (2008) 'Re-thinking intersectionality', *Feminist Review* 89(2): 1–15.

Newsinger, P. (2006) *The Blood Never Dried: A People's History of the British Empire*, London: Bookmarks.

O'Connor, J. (1973) *The Fiscal Crisis of the State*, London: Routledge.

O'Leary, B. (2019) *A Treatise on Northern Ireland, Volume 3: Consocation and Confederation*, Oxford: Oxford University Press.

Oborne, P. (2021) *The Assault on Truth*, London: Simon & Schuster.

Ostrowski, M. (2020) *Left Unity: Manifesto for a Progressive Alliance*, London: Policy Network.

Paine, T. (2008) *Rights of Man, Common Sense and Other Political Writings*, Oxford: Oxford University Press.

Pettit, P. (2012) *On the People's Terms*, Cambridge: Cambridge University Press.

Reichelt, H. (1995) 'Why did Marx conceal his dialectical method?', in Bonefeld, W., Gunn, R., Holloway, J., and Psychopedis, K. (eds), *Emancipating Marx*, London: Pluto Press.

Renaud, T. (2021) *New Lefts: The Making of a Radical Tradition*, London: Princeton University Press.

Roy, O. (2017) *Jihadism and Death*, London: Hurst.

Runciman, D. (2019) *How Democracy Ends*, London: Profile Books.

Sassoon, D. (2013) *One Hundred Years of Socialism: The West European Left in the Twentieth Century*, London: I.B. Tauris.

Saville, J. (1969) 'Primitive accumulation and early industrialization in Britain', *Socialist Register*, 247–271.

Sayers, S. (2015) 'Marxism and the doctrine of internal relations', *Capital and Class* 39(1): 25–31.

Schwartz, H. (2016) 'Wealth inequality and secular stagnation: the role of industrial organization and intellectual property rights', *Journal of the Social Sciences* 2(6): 226–49.

Seymour, R. (2019) *The Twittering Machine*, London: Indigo Press.

Shaik, A. (2016) *Capitalism: Competition, Conflict, Crises*, Oxford: Oxford University Press.

Siedentop, L. (2014) *Inventing the Individual*, London: Allen Lane.

Singer, P.W., and Brooking, E.T. (2018) *Likewar: The Weaponization of Social Media*, New York: Mariner Books.

Sleat, M. (ed.) (2018) *Politics Recovered: Essays on Realist Political Thought*, Columbia: Columbia University Press.

Slobodian, Q. (2020) *Globalists: The End of Empire and the Birth of Neoliberalism*, London: Harvard University Press.

Stafford, W. (1998) 'How can a paradigmatic liberal call himself a socialist? The case of John Stuart Mill', *Journal of Political Ideologies* 3(3): 325–45.

Stedman-Jones, G. (2012) *Masters of the Universe*, London: Princeton University Press.

Swift, D. (2019) *A Left for Itself*, London: Zero Books.

Thane, P. (2018) *Divided Kingdom: A History of Britain, 1900 to the Present*, Cambridge: Cambridge University Press.

Therborn, G. (1980) *The Ideology of Power and the Power of Ideology*, London: Verso.

Therborn, G. (2007) 'After dialectics: radical social theory in a post-communist world', *New Left Review* 43: 63–114.

Therein, J.P. (2002) 'Debating foreign aid: left versus right', *Third World Quarterly* 23(3): 449–67.

Thompson, H. (2022) *Disorder: Hard Times in the 21st Century*, Oxford: Oxford University Press.

Tooze, A. (2019) *Crashed: How a Decade of Financial Crises Changed the World*, London: Penguin.

Traverso, E. (2021) *Left-Wing Melancholia: Marxism, History and Memory*, Columbia: Columbia University Press.

van der Pijl, K. (1998) *The Lockean Heartland in the International Political Economy*, London: Routledge.

Vernon, J. (2017) *Modern Britain: 1750 to the Present*, Cambridge: Cambridge University Press.

Vincent, A. (1995) *Modern Political Ideologies*, Oxford: Blackwell.

Wahlström, M., Törnberg, A., and Ekbrand, H. (2021) 'Dynamics of violent and dehumanizing rhetoric in far-right social media', *New Media & Society* 23(11): 3290–311.

Warren, B. (1980) *Imperialism: Pioneer of Capitalism*, London: Verso.

Weeks, J. (2010) *Capital, Exploitation and Economic Crisis*, London: Routledge.

Williams, M. (2005) 'What is the national interest? The neoconservative challenge in IR theory', *European Journal of International Relations* 11(3): 307–37.

Williams, R. (1977) *Marxism and Literature*, Oxford: Oxford University Press.

Williamson, J. (1990) 'What Washington means by policy reform', in Williamson, J. (ed.), *Latin American Adjustment: How Much Has Happened?*, Washington, DC: Institute for International Economics.

Worth, O. (2014) 'Stuart Hall, Marxism without guarantees, and "the hard road to renewal"', *Capital and Class* 38(3): 480–87.

Zuboff, S. (2019) *The Age of Surveillance Capitalism: The Fight for a Human Future at the New Frontier of Power*, London: Profile Books.

Index

References to figures appear in *italic* type. References to endnotes show both the page number and the note number (159n40).

171